PLEIADIAN PERSPECTIVES

PLEIADIAN
PERSPECTIVES
ᴏɴ HUMAN
EVOLUTION

Amorah Quan Yin

Foreword by
Barbara Hand Clow

BEAR & COMPANY
PUBLISHING
SANTA FE, NEW MEXICO

LIBRARY OF CONGRESS CATALOGING-IN-PUBLICATION DATA

Yin, Amorah Quan.
Pleiadian perspectives on human evolution / Amorah Quan Yin.
    p. cm.
ISBN 1-879181-33-9
1. Parapsychology.   2. Pleiades—Miscellanea.   3. Evolution—
Miscellanea.   4. Spiritual life.   5. Mental healing   I. Title.
BF1031 Y458 1996
133.9—dc20   96-6205
                                                                CIP

Bear & Company, Inc,
PO Box 2860
Santa Fe, NM 87504-2860

Cover design: © 1996 by Lightbourne Images
Cover photo art: © 1996 by Bill Binger
Interior design and typography: Melinda Belter
Text illustrations: © 1996 by Bryna Waldman
Printed in the United States of America by BookCrafters, Inc.

10   9   8   7   6   5   4   3

With deepest gratitude and love, I dedicate this book to the Pleiadian Emissaries of Light and the success of their, and our, Divine Plan.

CONTENTS

FOREWORD

In her introduction for *Pleiadian Perspectives*, Amorah Quan Yin asks you to read the stories of the evolutionary histories of Venus, Mars, Maldek (the destroyed planet that has become the asteroid belt between Mars and Jupiter) and Earth, as if these ancient stories are your own stories. She asked me to write a foreword for this brilliant, time-sweeping, and fantastic journey, and, because it is such advanced Pleiadian material, I honestly could not think of anyone else who *could* assist in preparing you for this truly amazing journey.

For those of you who have read my latest book, *The Pleiadian Agenda: A New Cosmology for the Age of Light*, you will know that Quan Yin and I, as well as others, are Pleiadian Emissaries of Light. Actually, many of you are also emissaries of light from many parallel realities; the difference is that Amorah and I identified this part of our soul essence at a young age and then began creating out of it. Amorah and I admit that we have remembered coming into Earth to assist her through her birthing canal. What is the birthing canal of Earth? It is us! Humans have become a body of ancient patterns that restrict Earth. More than 104,000 years ago, as recorded in the Aztec Calendar of the Fifth Sun, we Pleiadians passed through the same transcendence that is now precipitating into your reality. All of you who remain in your bodies through 2012 A.D. will release control patterns that block Earth's natural ecstasy. Then you will live on her surface as fully grounded beings who participate in Earth evolvement with full access to the intelligence of the galaxy itself. You are not going out of your bodies, instead you are finally choosing to fully inhabit your bodies.

We are able to reach you now because Earth has released a great cry into the galaxy; Earth is "keening" over your limited sense of self. We Pleiadians are excited as we feel you waking up and manifesting the conscious expression of Earth's desires, because we know you will remember the great cosmic ecstasy that we enjoy all the time. Why? Because we discovered how to live without limitation. We ask you: Who said Earth was limited? We Pleiadian Emissaries are here now as guides to assist you in seeing the universe of light, a universe that defines matter as darkness, or Earth as conscious and manifested creativity and thought. You are ready now to play freely in her Garden.

As a person who is conscious of my own Pleiadian heritage, like Quan Yin, I have inner records on the evolution of Mars, Venus, Maldek, and Earth. I forgot about these grand dualities and great dramas when I was born. As I read Quan Yin's stories, I went through a process of identifying many sources of the inner conflicts that I've dealt with all my life. I could better see how these repetitive conflicts are merely old residues of mental junk littering human minds. I say "merely" with a dose of irony, because that is the litter that is manifesting in physical form as all the toxic waste piled up all over the planet. Perhaps because of my assiduously developed Pleiadian eye, I see easily how these stories are the basis for subconscious patterning in the human mind. It is my hope that you will have a similar experience, because we all live on this planet together. The toxic waste emanating from the mental junk in your brains is poisoning our Garden. I ask you to deeply contemplate these ancient records; they reveal the subconscious patterns that threaten your home. And, as you read about them, this simple action will cause them to break down. Space will open for the rising of the new and potent evolutionary spiral. It is time for you to see clearly that what you think about creates your world, and your inner brains look exactly like junkyards.

My personal expertise for putting this book in context comes from writing *The Mind Chronicles* trilogy. When I wrote these books from 1984 through 1992, I discovered a whole new method for reading materials that effectively accesses and sorts out data in ancient stories. As Quan Yin says about Ra—Pleiadian Archangel of Light who is the past, present, and future lens of this book—*how* you look through the "lens of Ra" will determine how much you can really see about your own profound subconscious patterning. Now that Earth is crying for you to attain this galactic lens as you live on her surface, each one of you who transcends these patterns actually makes space for Earth to breathe again. By creating *Eye of the Centaur* (volume 1 of the trilogy), I dumped out my own memory banks and entered into the present moment. By creating *Heart of the Christos* (volume 2), I forgave myself for everything I'd ever done, and I raised all those experiences up and into my heart. By creating *Signet of Atlantis* (volume 3), I was able to contemplate the originating sources of these subconscious patterns—off-planet races who have been involved in human evolution since we chose to become conscious and then self-reflective. Once the primordial sense of self emerged, other intelligences entered into relationship with us, since sense of self is what opens any being to relationship potential. Now it is time to recognize these partners in the Garden.

Pleiadian Perspectives demonstrates that all of us have experienced the full spectrum of human history and behavior. As you remember your own participation in evolution while reading these stories, consider that your ability to see this is your earthly responsibility—your ability to respond! As Quan Yin says, "A speck of everything possible exists within you." This puts you on the spot because, "If you judge others, that part of you that has done the same thing is judged and suffers." This wave of suffering is what is now causing Earth to rebel from the burden; Earth will breathe, see light, and enfold you if only you will transcend these "attitudinal energies," as Quan Yin so aptly names these stumbling blocks.

The Mind Chronicles trilogy helped me to birth a new method —shamanic reading—for moving beyond judgment and that is what I'd like to share with you. Many of you who've bought this book love to read because reading is your most precious opportunity to be alone and contemplate your mind without any other stimulation. Reading can be pure contemplation. When you read correctly, you actually alter your physical body by allowing feelings to enter into the process as your mind is stimulated. When you are all alone reading and not being influenced by other vibrations—if you read correctly—you are free. What is "correct reading"? It is avid attention to each thought that is presented so that you either agree with that thought and imprint it, or you hold that thought as a concept and consider it over time, or you decide that you disagree with that thought and you clear your mind of it and anything else that changes in your own thought bank as a result of considering a new idea. When you hold thoughts as potential new concepts, you use the storage powers of your mind to hold them in creative tension while you allow your feelings to explore your reactions. You come to a conclusion once you can "feel" something is right. When you clearly reject thoughts, you are cleaning your mind. Shamanic reading is a process of building data banks by strengthening and clarifying your mind with thoughts that you feel or know are true, as you build creative tension with thoughts that have the power to rile up your subconscious patterning. It is by means of this creative tension that subconscious patterning can be brought to light and transcended. That is the alchemy of the mind, the doorway into untapped intelligence. Amorah Quan Yin is a writer for this kind of reading, and since thought creates reality, worlds can shift as you read.

The reason 90 percent of your brain is untapped is simply because 90 percent of your brain is littered with unconsidered judgments. Even if you later decide this book is not truth for you, I would advise you to read this book as if the stories of the four worlds in it contain the keys for tapping your unused brain material. The first step in successful shamanic reading is to respect the writer's offering by opening yourself totally to the exquisite communication link the writer is simply offering to you. That's the least you can do for the tree that sacrificed itself just so this book could be printed! Out of honest respect for this gift, hold your judgment about this writer until later, just as you reserve judgment about someone who sexually attracts you until you know it is appropriate to pursue these feelings of attraction. This request assumes you selected this book carefully, just as I hope you select your dates carefully. Just like with those who want to be your lovers, you can always stop reading a book and give it to someone else if you conclude that it has nothing to offer you. But reading can even be better than sex from one point of view: A library of books is a wonderful thing, but most would suggest caution about a pile of lovers.

Assuming this book actually can tap your latent brain power and strengthen your mind, then, as you open yourself to it, be like a child. That is why this particular book is so exquisitely illustrated by Bryna Waldman. These fanciful drawings invite you to let go of the incrustations built up in your adult mind so that you can remember how to simply play with ideas. Now's your chance to allow deeply buried ancient memories to bubble up to the surface of your mind, so you can consider them in light of all that you've learned for thousands of years. You may find that you can hardly relate to old dilemmas, and you may discard them easily so you can make new images—imaginate—to create new worlds.

So, here you are, sufficiently open. Some of you may want to also set up a magical space for reading. You may want candles, incense, divination cards or runes, or other magical objects that trigger your own feeling mind. Why? Let me be honest; this is a heavy book, and playing with it will ease your feelings as you take in the stories. Remember to breathe. How could it be easy to consider the spiralic struggles engendered by our ascension into self-reflective intelligence? How could it be easy to look at our actions coming out of reaching for the Divine? As for me, I cried when I read parts of this book. This book has made it difficult to even have football games playing on the television set (I never watched them) because now football makes me think of Martian war games. It was painful to contemplate how rare is simple, playful, Venusian ecstasy on Earth these days.

Shamanic reading means *feeling a book* instead of just reading to distract yourself from real life. However, reading is also mental, and unless you follow the mental process in a book, you can't read. So again, carefully monitor the new material that fits with the truth you already have, and take responsibility for your own data bank. Hold the stuff you're not sure about at the conceptual level so you can observe how it feels. When you feel material getting into your gut and stirring you up, bypass mental arguments with the Pleiadians, with Amorah Quan Yin, or the voice in your head from some old professor or grade-school teacher, and just *feel* this book. Drop the mentalism—abstracting ideas from feelings—and just feel what you're taking in. Open yourself to it, stop and cry if you need to. Light a candle as you feel the wind responding as your mind opens. Give yourself time and space to handle remembering something that once put you in prison or caused you to be murdered, and then see how that attitudinal energy exists as a block in your brain about similar emotional dilemmas in your present reality.

Let those feelings rip through your nerves, your emotions, and your guts. Just hold with that awful truth you've found; hold it long enough to open the window in your blocked brain. Then you will remember that what is blocking you now is only an old memory of something you thought someone else did, or you thought you did yourself, when in fact everybody did it to everyone; and the only new possibility is to stop it now!

The only reason to read a book in the late twentieth century is because the book amuses and entertains you, or because the book can clean out your brain so you can really see what is actually happening to you in your world. When you read something in *Pleiadian Perspectives* that stirs you up, it's because you are realizing that this old junk is still re-creating the same reality now. Consider cleaning out your brain so Earth can cleanse and emerge into her original intention to have you live freely on her surface in the Garden. Then you will contemplate the light without averting your eyes. Then the great inner night—your mind—will become enlightened, and you will open your eyes to see the exquisite deep greenness that is Earth.

Barbara Hand Clow
Lakeville, Connecticut
January 1996

PREFACE & ACKNOWLEDGMENTS

When the manuscript for this book was nearly done, I took a card from *The Mayan Oracle* and asked the question, "What symbol most accurately describes the higher purpose and destiny of this work?" The card I drew was "Resolution of Duality," which reads:

Now is the time for you to confront directly the illusion of separation and duality! Receiving this lens asks you to resolve your separate sense of identity. Bring awareness to the way you hold duality pairs such as good and bad, right and wrong, "them and us." Such pairs support the very framework of our presently transforming third-dimensional reality.

Duality is simply a perception. Polarities are thought to be opposites only because of the way we perceive them. In the collective trance, you have probably been taught to understand polarities from the position of separation and duality. Duality is the transformational playing field, and it is maintained only by the belief systems held in mass consciousness. As you personally integrate your polarities and transmute your limiting beliefs, your reality is transformed. As your reality is transformed, collective reality

also shifts, revealing a greater reality of inseparable unity.
In receiving this lens, you are being challenged to work
with your belief systems, collectives issues, and thoughtforms to see where they appear to limit you. Your very
complexity and rigidity invite new processes that open you
to simplicity, expansion, and change. You will feel this
energy working in any area of your life that has become
too complicated or inflexible. Since your own personal
issues are connected to mass consciousness, you also contribute to the transformation of the whole. *You* are the resolution of duality.

This lens asks you to look at reality from the perspective of the *gift* that is inherent in duality. With that perception, you will be helping to support a quantum leap
into the new reality. Remember, you and planetary consciousness are engaged in the evolutionary process of
resolving duality!

This message is so perfect! As you move through the stories of
the evolutionary histories of Venus, Mars, Maldek, and their culmination on Earth—and more—you will be reading your own
inner stories. Whether you lived physically on any planet in this
solar system or others, or your soul was created and born on
Earth, these stories are deeply ingrained in your subconscious
patterning. Throughout all of our many lives we have contacted
and experienced most of the myths within these pages. It does not
matter whether we have white, red, black, or yellow skin in this
life. We have lived inside all those colors of skin during the precession of our lives. Whether your place of origin is the Pleiades,
Sirius, or the far reaches of the universe, you have experienced
human incarnations in civilizations comprised of young souls
evolving from the lower dimensions upward, and of those who
have downstepped from the higher dimensions to experience
third-dimensional reality. You have been born into cultures whose
genetic origins are Andromedan, Pleiadian, Sirian, Lyran, and
many for which we do not even have names. It also does not matter if you can trace your current life's roots into a purely Balinese,
French, English, or Native American heritage. Although those
cultures may carry specific genetic lineage from the Pleiades,

Venus, Lyra, or the Big Dipper, they have also been influenced and infiltrated by other genetic lineages throughout the ages. And even though their primary origins are genetically intact, the very fact that your own origins are unlikely to be the same as your current bloodline's makes it all strictly experiential.

You see, Earth has been chosen as the home of the "universal melting pot." We are all the potpourri for existence—the great experiment in unity in diversity. Our souls have become the melting pot of all of our experiences: genetically, dimensionally, and actually.

Therefore, the divination for this book—Resolution of Duality—is perfect. If you hold prejudice within you toward another race, that part of you that has been incarnate in that race is rejected and suffers. If you judge others, that part of you that has done the same thing is judged and suffers. If you blame and guilt-trip others, you truly blame and guilt-trip that part of yourself that has been like them, and you suffer. It is impossible to harm and disrespect other living beings, including animals and plants, without harming yourself. A speck of everything possible exists within you. And a speck of you exists within All That Is. So when you create duality through your thoughts, judgments, attitudes, actions, and beliefs you help strengthen Darkness, which is the illusion of separation and untruth.

Through the channelings from Ra, a Pleiadian Archangel of the Light, I offer a lens through which to view your own past, present, and future. The attitude with which you look through this lens makes all the difference. It is intended to give you an opportunity to see and understand your own patterns and those of others. You have most likely transcended many of the behavioral, attitudinal, and karmic patterns contained within the planetary histories. Those you have not are illuminated clearly enough that you can get a better look at yourself. Acknowledge, praise, and congratulate yourself on those areas in which you have achieved transformation and transcendence. Acknowledge, show compassion and mercy, and employ spiritual discipline to those areas in which you have not. Use this spiritual and historical evolutionary journey to find true humility, forgiveness, and compassion for others as well. When you discover an area that depicts one of your own stumbling blocks, notice whether your first response is self-judgment, shame, guilt, or self-condemnation. If so, take the time to clear and release these attitudinal energies. The techniques for clearing judgments, beliefs, and perfect pictures given in chapter 6 of my previous book, *The Pleiadian Workbook: Awakening Your Divine Ka*, are ideal to use as you find a need for them.

In fact, the planetary histories in this manuscript were originally part of the *Workbook*. They were intended to trigger the readers of that book with awareness of their own beliefs, prejudices, and karmic patterns, and then present the spiritual healing and alignment tools with which to clear them. Whether you have read and done the exercises in the *Workbook* or not, you will benefit and learn by continuing with this book now. I highly recommend if you have not experienced the *Workbook* that you do so after completing this book in order to make the most out of the spiritual transformation and growth offered. Also, I hope you will allow this journey through time and space to be both deepening and filled with fun and wonder.

As the channelings came through my own Higher Self channel from Ra, I recorded them into my computer somewhat like automatic writing. I never knew what was coming until I actually typed it onto the computer. At times the stories would haunt me and I would dream about them afterward. I often saw my own past or present tendencies in those of the Venusians, Martians, and Maldekians. When the Earth chapter was being channeled, I spent about one third of the time I was typing it into the computer with tears streaming down my face uncontrollably. The stories of the fairies, merpeople, and Ma-Ra reached deep places in my own heart and soul memories. As the stories were given to me, I saw the visions, felt the energies of the people, heard the messages from Ra, and typed them all at the same time. I had no idea that Ma-Ra was the future Mother Mary until the unfolding story revealed her identity. Then the tears really flowed. As the original spiritual meaning of baptism as a sacred ceremony to acknowledge an individual's divine sovereignty was revealed, I wept aloud. Ancient feelings of remembrance were aroused in me about baptism being an initiatic stage in which the initiate was acknowledged as having transcended ego. At that point the person was also acknowledged as being of pure intent, with the veils of illusion washed away, and ready to be held accountable as a sovereign spiritual being.

Once again, I feel I have been greatly gifted, indeed, to be given the honor of channeling and remembering the evolutionary stories presented in this book. The writing process has been life changing, at times challenging, and always heart opening for me along the way. If you allow it to, it can move you deeper into your own remembering and purification. It can also help you release the past.

As we learn to forgive, accept, and love ourselves, we learn to forgive, accept, and love others. The more we forgive, accept, and love others, the more we forgive, accept, love, and respect ourselves. The truth is that it is impossible to experience inner wholeness and to have total self-esteem and self-respect until we do so. Therefore, in the spirit of resolution of duality and unity in diversity, which are the last steps toward wholeness and Oneness with God/Goddess/All That Is, Ra and I offer this book to be used as your own shamanic journey. May it be an impeccable one!

Before beginning, I would like to acknowledge and express deepest gratitude to the Ascended Masters Mother Mary and Jesus Christ for the supreme examples they have given us of what we truly are, and what we are becoming again. To all of the Ascended Masters who have gone before us, thank you for your ongoing dedication and loving guidance on the initiatic path home. I also acknowledge and thank all of the Pleiadian Emissaries of Light, and especially Ra, for their wise, impeccable, and always loving presences and service to Earth's Divine Plan.

I send gratitude and love to myself, and to all of us who have had the courage to question reality, to demand to know Truth, and to challenge our own beliefs and desires when they have proven to be limits to Oneness.

The students I have taught during the time period in which this book was written have been such great sources of inspiration and courage to me along the way. Many blessings and thanks to all of you. Especially, I would like to thank Cree and Rosemary for opening your homes and hearts to me when I am in Phoenix. Guy Lone Eagle, you are a friend and colleague beyond measure. Thank you for choosing to share yourself and your sacred process of unfolding with me. I thank the entire Phoenix class for demonstrating new depth to the meaning of the word "willingness" as you consistently exceed your own previous limits, face your fears, and become more.

To my Mt. Shasta classes, I honor the unity in diversity you have demonstrated with one another. Your ability and willingness to suspend judgment, to resolve duality, and to open your eyes to see the true beauty in all things and people have been deeply moving. I also appreciate your enthusiastic and sincere support of me and my life purpose.

I acknowledge Gail Vivino for the initial copyediting of the Venus, Mars, and Maldek materials and for her personal feedback and appreciation of the materials. Gerry Clow dedicated himself to the copyediting of the finished work in a thorough, thoughtful, and beautiful way. It was fun sharing the special energy of the deer stories with you, Gerry, and all of the other steps, conferences, and stories along the way.

Barbara Hand Clow, I first must acknowledge you for the incredible gift you have given all of us with your latest book, *The Pleiadian Agenda: A New Cosmology for the Age of Light*. As you first described the materials in this book and my *Workbook* as companions to your new book, I am deeply honored. You are a true sister, colleague, and inspiration to me in so many ways. Thank you for recognizing this material and its place in the scheme of things. Thank you for the pleasure of working with you in the publishing process. And thank you for doing it all with so much love, forthrightness, and supreme dedication.

As with the *Workbook*, the process of writing this book demanded so much that I had very little time or energy left over for my friends and godchildren. Thank all of you for being so patient, understanding, and loving, and for sharing the vision.

I gratefully honor Bryna Waldman's creative expertise that comes forth in the illustrations throughout this book. You have made this book much more fun, and the lives of the Venusians, Martians, and Maldekians so much more real and accessible through your inspired visual adornments.

I am also grateful to all of the Bears who have been and continue to be involved in bringing this and other sacred writings to the public. And for the beautiful job you, Lightbourne and Bill Binger, did on the cover, bravo!

PLEIADIAN
PERSPECTIVES
ON HUMAN
EVOLUTION

INTRODUCTION

COSMIC STEPPING STONES

What does it mean to be living in a microcosmic solar system —or "solar ring" as the Pleiadian Emissaries of Light call it— made up of planets such as Venus, Mars, Maldek, and Earth that are considered to be cosmic stepping stones? This solar ring itself is merely a microcosm of an unimaginably vast existence. Does it make your life, your past lives, your future, and your world seem extremely small and insignificant? Does it make your ego cringe a little? It is intended to do so, and yet, beyond ego, it need not.

We are living in a world made up of sequentialness in time and space. This is demonstrated by the precession of time measured in minutes, days, seasons, our lives, the order in which the planets in this solar ring have been inhabited, and the movement from one millennium into another. This sequentialness is the natural order of any evolutionary process, and the third dimension is just that. We might think of ourselves as divining rods for our Higher Selves who learn and feel through our experiences. We are impulsed by our own Creators in order to magnetize the life experiences we need to complete our goals in each life. Until we awaken, we are mere creatures of survival who are self-centered, identified with ego-personalities and bodies, with little sense of anything beyond our immediate lives. Up to the point of our spiritual awakenings, we are even unaware that we are unaware.

Then one day, while in the middle of a lifetime of being ourselves doing what we always do, a pause happens: a gap in consciousness during which an unsettling feeling comes over us. This might be followed by such thoughts such as, "Who am I really?" or "Oh my God, what am I doing here?" or else tears might simply begin to flow for no apparent reason. Our hearts open. We put down the newspaper or turn off the television, and say silently, "There has to be more to life than this." Something stirs inside and we do not know what it is; but we know we have to find out. We know that things will never be the same again, although we have no definition for these changes or explanation why. We become seekers of Truth.

The angels and our guides send out a big "hurrah!" A great celebration is held in the higher dimensions in honor of you; your own Higher Self and future Ascended Master Self attend for you. You feel it. A new energy is directed your way. You feel inspired and filled with determination and enthusiasm. Joy of a new kind radiates through your whole body. You have felt the call to freedom, heard your own inner voice, and stopped what you were doing to pay attention. You feel like everything in your life has led you to that moment. You have a deep sense of knowing, and yet you do not understand. Now what?

The avalanche of books, yoga teachers, spiritual teachers, workshops, unusual dreams, and synchronicities begins. You opened the door, and existence rearranged itself to place all the right people, situations, and materials in your lap. Your mate thinks you are crazy. With a deeply concerned look in her eyes, your best friend recommends counseling or a vacation. That is it. You have been overworking. You need a rest. You just smile and say, "No, it's not like that. Something is happening to me. I don't know exactly how to explain it, but it feels right. I just know that I have something special to do in this life; and I have to find out what it is."

Your friends and family continue to have mixed reactions, so after a while, you just stop talking about it. You hide the latest book on angels and extraterrestrials in the nightstand on your side of the bed. Inside the book you hide your astrology chart after staring at it one last time in awe and wonder at how the astrologer could have been so accurate about your life up until now. You recall what the astrologer said about your past-life karmic pattern of denying your own inner spirit and adhering to the status quo. You shiver a little as you remember. And then you go on with your life. Your new spiritual/psychic interests are a little piece of this ongoing life; but they are not integrated with the rest of it. You live in duality.

The average story goes on to include how your family either starts to join you in your spiritual pursuits, or you separate from your spouse and later divorce. You need time for soul-searching, exploring, finding out who you really are, meeting like-minded others, and redefining your priorities. Friends drop out of your life as new friends enter. Emotional and physical bonds either change or they are broken. Then you have your first clear vision. Perhaps you reexperience a past life, or see Jesus, or remember flying in the stars with an angel. Your memory begins to be objectified. Another phase of renewed enthusiasm and inspiration ensues. The emotional pain of change and separation are temporarily removed from focus as you embark upon the path of remembering.

Past-life regressions, hypnosis, shamanic journeying, meditating, and focusing your attention usually come with the path of remembering. Your dreams become more vivid, with obvious lessons. Your crown and third eye are buzzy, or you feel pressure in them. You see flashes of colored lights occasionally, or catch fleeting glimpses of light in peoples' auras, or around trees. It is all falling into place now, or so you think. This must be it!

Then the karmic lessons really begin. You are challenged on any level at which you are still ego-identified. You attend a workshop at which everyone else is in bliss and you just feel agitated and do not know why. You would like to punch the next person who says, "Oh yes, I get it!" Or you just feel sorry for yourself and pine away about how unworthy and "less than" you are. Whether your negative ego game is to make yourself feel better than or less than, your ego does not care as long as you feel separate and special. And you do. Either all those people are a bunch of flakes, or "poor you" is the only one whom God/Goddess has chosen to omit from the Divine Plan. Both are your negative ego's games. So what do you do about it?

You could give it all up and go back to your level-headed spouse. Begging your old friends to take you back might work. But would you be able to be happy, or at least content? No way. The door has been opened too wide, and you saw too much of what awaits you on the other side to turn back now. You are a seeker at the point of no return. Face it, it is this or nothing else. You know by now that suicide would only lead you to more pain in your next life, so you may as well decide to go for it. How long it takes you to get to this step will be determined by the amount of struggle and resistance you go through. Eventually, however, surrender is the only alternative. If your surrender comes from believing you have no choice and you are angry about that, it will be difficult for a while. If you begin to understand that *you* create your own reality, and if you are humbled by and accept this fact, your surrender will be much more gracious. If your heart feels a deep longing and hunger to be the best you can be and you eagerly begin the process of self-examination, dissolution, and transmutation of your negative ego, you will become a spiritual adventurer. Everything new and challenging will renew your enthusiasm, inspiration, and determination. Your attitude at this stage makes all the difference.

The self-help and clearing techniques given in chapters 5 and 6 of *The Pleiadian Workbook: Awakening Your Divine Ka* are invaluable at this stage, as well as throughout your path to enlightenment. Certainly other schools of thought and clearing will work also. Whatever methods you use, you need to know how to stay grounded and focused; how to keep cosmic energy running into your chakras; and how to clear yourself of unwanted psychic influences, beliefs, contracts, and denser, repressed energies. This stage of the spiritual journey is one of self-clearing. It is followed by your consciousness redefining itself as your Divine Essence instead of as your ego.

Additional individual stepping stones that normally follow are: refinements in your spiritual growth and identity; aligning with your Higher Self; clearing your multidimensional hologram; purifying your consciousness; and, eventually, enlightenment, embodiment of your own Christed Self, and ascension. *The Pleiadian Workbook*, beginning with chapter 7, provides one path for attaining these goals, as do other spiritual books and practices. What is important is that you know inside the way that is right for you. It is not necessary that you understand fully why one path is correct for you personally and not another. The inner knowing is what is crucial. It is also important that you do not project your path onto others. What is correct for 90 percent of the people may not be correct for the other 10 percent. We are here to learn unity in diversity: to accept and trust that every individual has the innate ability to know what is right for himself or herself.

The Supreme Being for this solar ring is also called The Spirit of Oneness. (Because this great being is androgynous, I will use the pronoun "it" when referring to the Supreme Being.) It was chosen as Supreme Being not only because of its spiritual vastness and Light, but also because the very nature of its essence is what we are here to become. The Spirit of Oneness holds the divine capacity of every individual in our solar ring to transcend duality, heal the male/female split, and unite with the higher consciousness of God/Goddess/All That Is. This is the ultimate goal of existence. By being offered opportunities throughout our lives to experience every alternative to Oneness, we are ultimately led home. Through the sequential evolution of third-dimensional lifetimes and spiritual growth, we gain empirical wisdom. When we finally realize we cannot do it all alone, we are humbled. Then we reach out to our guides, angels, and Ascended Masters. After a time, our own higher-dimensional aspects conjoin with our human selves, and we choose to surrender our individual wills to divine will. Divine will is truly nothing more than the will of your own future Ascended Master self that has become one with God/Goddess/All That Is. When you surrender to divine will, you surrender to the truth of your own highest destiny. Ego identity is passé, or becoming so, at this stage.

The book you hold in your hands is about individual and collective spiritual evolution. It is about the movement along the stepping stones of life and lifetimes toward Oneness. It is about compassion and nonjudgment of yourself and everyone else along the way. And it is about how each person's life is a microcosm of some greater myth within the Divine Plan. What is your role in it all? Are you a Venusian archetype who obsesses on your own body's sex appeal and that of others? Are you an artisan whose entire sense of self-esteem is wrapped up in your art form? Or is your tendency more Martian? Do you still try to control others, or play the victim and give your power away? Is your sexuality based on lust and dominance/submission roles? Or are you a Maldekian archetype? Do you distrust everyone, even yourself? Do you fail to make good, discerning choices? Are you subject to blind faith, competitiveness, or shame?

These are a few of the basic tendencies that we humans have derived from these planets which, each for a time, housed third-dimensional life. And yet, in each of these planetary civilizations, there were those who became spiritually awakened, enlightened, and ascended. Each planet also developed its own lower-astral planes, which were filled with negative thoughtforms, denied ghostlike aspects of the people who lived there, and parasitic entities—just like we have on Earth now. So what does knowing about them have to offer you now? The answer is: a macrocosmic view and a microcosmic one simultaneously.

The broader view pertains to our own pre-Earth history, and the development of the karmic patterns within this solar ring. As you explore the lives and cultures on these other planets, including their growth and achievements, as well as their seeming failures, you begin to witness the sources and patterns that brought about their successes as well as their declines. These patterns are intricately interwoven into your own psyche. Whether you are dominately a Venusian-, Martian-, or Maldekian-type personality, you have traces of all of them. They are the most immediate heavenly bodies within our solar ring. The same sacred Sun shines upon us all, and is reflected back to each of the planets within our solar ring from the others. Those reflections of light travel in refracted rays to Earth from all of the other local planets. And Earth reflects back to these planets the successes and declines of her own inhabitants. In other words, "everything affects everything." Every thought, action, and "ah-ha" impacts not only everyone on Earth, but everyone and everything throughout our solar ring and beyond. Our solar ring most directly impulses—and is impulsed by—the Pleiades, Sirius, Orion, and on and on.

Therefore, from the standpoint of the big picture, we are simply individual players living out the greater myths that unite us. From the microcosmic viewpoint, Earth and our solar ring are the playground for the gods and goddesses, as humans have called them throughout time. The paradigms and predispositions of all aspects of all beings, lower and higher, impact us all the time. We are the divining rods for higher consciousness. We are the ones who were split apart from the higher-dimensional realms for the very purpose of giving our own Higher Selves the opportunity to experience linear time and space.

When we think of ourselves as puppets to higher puppet-masters, we become angry, rebellious, disillusioned, hopeless, revengeful, and ego-identified. When we think of ourselves as the sparks of consciousness emanated from our Higher Selves into the creation of our souls, then we realize, as third-dimensional emanations, we may not have chosen to be human beings with souls. But you must realize that at the time of your own creation, the spark with which you normally identify was still part of a greater whole self. And that greater whole self did *choose* to send part of its own self to be a soul. That creation came about through a tantric-like melding with another; and from that union, your soul was conceived and later born. But you are indeed a part of that greater whole self who chose to incarnate at the soul level. There are no victims of Creation here.

The Divine Plan was always for each of us to learn through experience, to awaken, to love and care deeply for one another and all of Creation, to transcend all beliefs in the supposed limitations of the physical plane, become enlightened, blend completely with our higher-dimensional selves, ground higher consciousness and Oneness into all dimensions, and then to ascend. Eventually all of our experiences, understandings, and attainments become integrated into our united whole selves.

So, microcosmically speaking, this solar ring that houses the Sun, Earth, Mars, Venus, and all of its other planets is a melting pot for the Milky Way and other galaxies. There are beings here from all over existence at this time. Life in this solar ring is the greatest experiment of unity in diversity that has ever occurred. If you could see beyond these earthly costumes we call bodies to the origins of our true selves, you would see something akin to a bar scene in *Star Trek* or *Star Wars*. Every imaginable type of being from all over the galaxies has come here to experience cohabitation, resolution of differences, and a final grand Harmonic Convergence in which win/win is the only acceptable motive and outcome for all action. Whether these beings hang out in human bodies, fourth- and fifth-dimensional planes of Light and Dark, subterranean cities of Light and Dark, or in the subastral planes, we are all in this together.

The stories of Venus, Mars, and Maldek—and their culmination here on Earth—will mostly emphasize the human beings who lived or live on these planets and their perspectives of reality. As you move lightly across the stepping stones of each colony, civilization, and planet, remember that each one reveals a little more of your own psyche, whether through experience or heritage. Allow the stories in this book to move you, to help you feel more deeply the roots of your own myth, and to understand compassionately how and why we sometimes appear to devolve in the overall process of spiritual evolution. As you find these beings more and more endearing, as you react to them, forgive them, and love them again, you do so for yourself and for your fellow humanity as well. As you are willing to recognize the ego traps into which you still get caught, and choose to make those areas different in your life, you, as a microcosm, impulse the macrocosm with integrity and spiritual attainment. You create a map for others to follow. Simultaneously, your sense of your true self is restored as you acknowledge those behaviors and attitudes that are not inherent to your own God/Goddess nature, or your Divine Essence. If you have already transcended many of the ego vices and traps, then there is a deeper learning to be attained: the lessons of compassion, mastery, and enlightenment. These may appear subtler than the grosser lessons of ego. Yet the snowy white lotus emerges from the mud; or as Buddhists chant, "Na-mé ho renge kyo."

Most of this book is channeled by Ra, a representative of the Pleiadian Archangelic Tribes of the Light, who are members of the Pleiadian Emissaries of Light. Those of you who have read *The Pleiadian Workbook* are familiar with Ra and these Pleiadian groups. For the rest, I will give a brief description of who they are and why they are here assisting Earth beings at this time.

Earth and our entire solar ring orbit the central sun of the Pleiades, Alcyone. Our Sun is the eighth star of the Pleiades. As the furthest removed solar ring of the Pleiadian cluster, we are also the last to become a spirituality-based group of beings. The

Pleiadian Emissaries of Light comprise a large group of highly spiritually evolved beings who are fifth- and sixth-dimensional guardians of our solar ring. They have played a key role in the lives, cultures, and spiritual development of every planet and being in our solar ring, teaching everything from beginning-level to advanced healing and spiritual growth processes to beings on each of the third-dimensional planets discussed in this book.

The Pleiadian Emissaries of Light include Light Beings who function as psychic surgeons, healers, and guides from the fifth dimension as well as the Pleiadian Archangelic Tribes of the Light from the sixth dimension. There are other Pleiadians, mostly of the Light. But there are still a few who have rebelled against the Light, seek control, and are totally self-serving. Therefore, it is recommended that when calling upon them for personal healing or guidance that you use the full name, Pleiadian Emissaries of Light.

As most of the information in this book has been channeled, I want to clarify what I mean by channeling information or Light Beings. I *never* bring other entities into my body nor do I intend to. It is extremely hard on the body, sometimes even dangerous except in rare cases. Most entities or beings who come into human bodies do not know how to take care of the human body so that it remains unharmed by the experience. Besides, it is just simply unnecessary to bring in beings this way.

I am extremely clairaudient as well as clairvoyant, clairsentient, and intuitive. (Respectively, full sensory hearing, vision, feeling, and knowing.) To channel is to go into a full multidimensional, Higher Self alignment. After that, one of two things will happen. The being may stand in front of or above me presenting itself to my clairvoyant vision and talking to me. If I am teaching a class or giving a private session, I then repeat the message word for word. When alone, I merely listen and assimilate or write it down.

The other way it happens, especially with the Pleiadians more than the Ascended Masters, is that I will receive the words through my Higher Self channel and spontaneously voice them or type them into my computer. When it happens this way, I do not know what is to be said prior to speaking or typing. I do, however, hear the words inside my head as they are transmitted to me, since I always remain in my body. Afterwards I can usually remember the essence of what was said, but not the details. This is because I am in a trance, or an altered state, during these transmissions. So even though I am in my body, my consciousness is operating from a deeper state, and one of a higher frequency than in normal conversations with my eyes open. Ra, as the spokesperson from the Pleiadian Archangels who has been assigned to communicate with and teach me, is the teller of the evolutionary history that follows.

The channeled information about third-dimensional life on Venus, Mars, Maldek, and Earth is intended to trigger your own subconscious patterns and memories. The stories are presented in a specific manner for this purpose, and Ra and the Pleiadians are very clear about what needs to be told at this time.

Before Ra's stories of the history of evolution in this solar ring begin, I would like to make one more important point: Earth, our solar ring, and the entire galaxy are at a crucial turning point. By the year 2012, the face of Earth will have drastically changed. As we come to the end of a 26,000-year orbital cycle of our Sun around Alcyone, we are entering a photon band that is approximately 2000-years wide. The frequencies of this band are so high that humans with repressed emotions, overstressed nervous systems, lower-vibrational thought patterns, and ego identities will not be capable of withstanding them. Unless we spiritually evolve now, activate our divine Ka's (the light bodies of our Christed Selves), and become, in general, less dense and more spiritual, the times ahead will be unnecessarily chaotic.

Earth changes will affect the entire planet, and have already begun. Volcanic eruptions, pole shifts, giant tidal waves, atmospheric fires, and earthquakes of unheard of size are all predicted. And yet, the gift in all this is that, with enough human beings who have attained their own Christ consciousnesses, we as a planetary race shall ascend to become fourth- and fifth-dimensional beings and bypass the worst of the cataclysms in the physical world. The main thing for all of us to do now is to be impeccably honest with ourselves about the karmic patterns and negative ego games we still need to transcend, and then transcend them. While cleaning up our acts, we must also hold the inner knowing that we are all little pieces of God/Goddess/All That Is and that we have value. Each of us has a multidimensional holographic self that is wise, compassionate, loving, forgiving, and dedicated to our human self. These Higher Selves are the stuff of which our true selves are made. Our Divine Essences are the only lasting truth about ourselves, and knowing that, we can more graciously and lovingly begin—or continue—the process of ridding ourselves of the illusions of limitation and ego. Inner housecleaning and impeccable honesty are the stuff of which true and lasting self-respect, self-esteem, self-worth, and self-image are made.

We must now relearn about the sacredness of all things. Whether people, animals, rocks, trees, streams, or anything else in the natural world serves an obvious purpose or not, they are all sacred and deserve our respect. Ra told me not long ago that within existence there are three primary natural forms that serve

as record keepers and as guardians of our experiences and learning. These are crystals and crystalline rocks, whales, and trees. When he said this I spontaneously began to cry, releasing ancient grief about the misuse, abuse, and destruction of all of these sacred beings. Yes, crystals and trees are beings of consciousness as much as the whales are. And all three, within the last hundred years, have become endangered within the mineral, animal, and plant kingdoms. When a planet and its lifeforms lose their record keepers, they cease to be. To destroy these keepers of our own learnings and experiences in the third-dimensional world is a grievous violation of sacred law. There is a fourth source of records and memory that must now be activated in order to save the other three: *our own souls.*

So it is time now for a renaissance in human consciousness and spiritual awakening and growth. The path of learning and remembering is presently being offered to all humans. It is up to each of us to choose—not from a place of fear, but from a place of sincerity and spiritual commitment. After all, what we think of as physical destruction is really just change. Spirit cannot die; only the body can. Yet when the body dies, the spirit still carries with it the priorities from its human life. Whether those priorities are love, spiritual respect, and wisdom, or greed, lust, and prejudice, they are with us until we heal and transcend all limits. The transformation, transmutation, and transcendence must be accomplished completely before we move on to higher realms and higher learnings. Why? Certainly not because it is forced upon us—but because our own spirits will not allow it be otherwise. *At the core of each of our Divine Essences lies an integrity so deep and impeccable that nothing else could be so.* And thus, in the name of the divine intent of each of us, I turn the book over to Ra, whose stories as given to me I will transcribe on the following pages.

PART I

PART I

COLONIZATION OF VENUS

The following story is channeled directly from Ra:

Signature Plants

Before this solar system was inhabited by self-aware physical lifeforms, some of the planets were breeding grounds for bacterial and amoebic life, as well as plant species. We (the Pleiadian Emissaries of Light) were the caretakers and grew many kinds of trees, flowers, shrubs, herbs, vining plants, and sea vegetation, as well as simple lifeforms. What you call "herbs," we call "signature plants." This name is derived from the fact that this particular group of plants was genetically engineered to carry specific geometric "creation signatures" that have the ability to align or realign their environments to match their signatures. Your botanical group entitled signature plants is quite different from our use of this term. Earth's scientists refer to obvious physical appearance of a plant structure as reason for designation as a signature plant, whereas we refer only to the cellular geometric creation signature as the criteria for the designation.

The capabilities of signature plants to impact other species upon being consumed have been tested in many different environments and species since the creation of these plant forms, and it is why they are so effective when used properly. These signature plants, when ingested into human or animal bodies, seek out the places in the bodies where the same geometric signatures exist, and regenerate and nurture those areas. When cellular mutations, or miasmas, occur in a particular area of your body the cells in that area have their own genetic creation signature. If you ingest a plant whose genetic creation signature matches that of the mutated cells, the plant begins the work of healing the area and restoring the integrity of the cells.

Other planets have also served as breeding and testing grounds in addition to Earth. In fact, Venus was the first planet, other than Earth, in this "solar ring" to be so inhabited. "Solar ring" is our name for the solar system. Venus, Mars, and then Maldek were developed and first populated with bacteria and amoebic strains, then with plants, and ending with flowering plants and trees. When these species were reproducing naturally, and the necessary strains of plant life for self-mobilized lifeforms to feed on were thriving, something akin to tadpoles were birthed. You might think of it as if we took a spark of consciousness and implanted it into a multicellular body that had been in incubation. Its only awareness at the point of birth was the instinctual impulse to eat in order to survive and grow. That instinct, and the mobility of the form, were the two factors that originally distinguished animal life from plant life. Earth was the last planet in your solar ring to be impregnated, so to speak, with animal species, as the Divine Plan for habitation and spiritual evolution unfolded.

Armada of Andromeda

Prior to the preparation of the varying planets for mobile lifeforms, a group of angelic beings from Andromeda had requested the opportunity to experience self-motivation and sovereignty. When this request was approved by the hierarchies for this galaxy, by the androgynous Supreme Being named An, and by the Elohim Higher Council of Twelve, a plan was set into motion. This plan, which we have called the Armada of Andromeda, laid out planetary laws for those who would be born into physical forms and was agreed upon by An, the Higher Council of Twelve, and the angels, or future humanoids.

This was not the first time an entire group of beings had made such a request. Other galaxies had experienced similar transitions as serving angels and other beings had made choices for their own devolutionary learning experiences, and succeeded. They wanted to experience creativity, sensation, and emotions, and not just continue serving and following instructions. This desire is a normal part of evolution and awakening for many groups of beings, though not all. What was unique about this plan was that the angelic group mutually agreed not to have a hierarchical being or beings embodied to rule them; they wanted to evolve enough to rule themselves. They wanted to start out as sovereign beings, learning through experience. This created quite a stir throughout existence as it had previously been believed and upheld that it was both impossible and unethical for beings not to be ruled by "higher-ups."

Some of the angels decided to remain in etheric form and serve as plant devas and future animal devas, and to assist in maintaining the necessary food chain and atmospheric conditions. Others volunteered to take turns being guides and guardian angels for each other while those who chose to do so incarnated. Since the planetary orbits and weather conditions had been stabilized prior to the forming of the physical Venusian race, there was little need for concern or supervision on those levels beyond what was already maintained by Light Beings from the Galactic Center and from Alcyone, the central sun of the Pleiades. Alcyone had been chosen long before as the main control and monitoring station for lifeforms in your solar ring, so it was natural to continue in that role.

All involved agreed that the hierarchies could observe, but not interfere with, the development of life style and social forms. The upper-dimensional guardians could intervene to prevent beings from other dimensions from invading or trying to take over. No spiritual teachings could be given other than those that had meaning to the angels from their own previous experiences as servants of the Elohim. Natural changes, which you would call disasters, could neither be prevented nor caused. In other words, in every way other than that of ultimate Oneness, the forthcoming Venusian race would be a sovereign race unruled and undisciplined by hierarchies physically or etherically. The excitement this plan created might loosely be likened to the atmosphere just before a long-anticipated horse race, prior to which everyone has decided on their chosen favorite outcome, but in which no one knows for sure what the results will be. Multiply this excitement a few thousand times over and you might begin to get the idea.

The only other intervention to be allowed from the hierarchies prior to the end of the first natural 5200-year cycle was that which the majority of the population agreed upon and requested.

Otherwise, the new Venusians would be left alone. Understand that the time frames of which we speak are very loose translations of the actual time cycles on Venus, as well as those on Mars and Maldek in upcoming references. Since the lengths of days, nights, seasons, years, and all other time passages are different on each planet, it is impossible to speak of actual time and have it make any sense to you at all. Therefore, I will use Earth's evolutionary and orbital time frames as metaphorical equivalents to evolutionary cycles on these other planets. In relating time passages, in general, the arrival of humanoid forms will begin at the year 0 and proceed upward in number to reflect how many years humans lived on Venus when events occurred.

Arrival of the Andromedan Angels–Year 0

The first group of Andromedan angels was transported to Venus. Their light bodies were decelerated until they became physical, and they began life in humanoid forms. At first, of course, the discovery process took all their attention. Since they had not been prepared for what to expect beyond the needs for sustenance, sleep, sex for reproduction, and the tactile nature of feeling (at least as well as that could have been explained to beings who had never been physical), discovery and curiosity were full-time life experiences for the first few hundred years. Then creativity for pleasure—versus creativity for survival and maintaining comfort—came into play. Music was the first area to be explored and developed. The creation of instruments that could reproduce remembered etheric sounds became an obsession. With this creation came competition to see who could produce the truest and purest sounds with the most beautiful instruments.

Class Division–Year 1200

For over 500 years, musical development was the most prestigious and fulfilling occupation for skilled Venusians. Those with less natural ability in music than others became the first minor class, although their service to the musicians, singers, and instrument makers was still highly valued and praised. At the end of the first 1200 years, the social structure pretty much reflected the following order of importance: highly esteemed musicians and singers; highly achieved instrument designers and makers;

middle-class musicians and singers;
middle-class instrument designers
and makers; middle-class producers
of instruments designed by others;
middle-class servers of the higher
class; lower-class musicians and
singers; lower-class instrument
makers; and finally, lower-class
servers of the middle class.

Even though the
class divi-
sions were
clearly
intact,
there
was
still an
absence of
crime, and sovereignty was
honored for all beings. However, after 1200 years of Venusian civilization, another class began to emerge as a result of incest. No
one knew of genetic problems with inbreeding, nor
did they have social or moral codes to inhibit
it. So the natural genetic products of incest
began to make themselves obvious.
Deformed and "ugly" children were born.
This was not exclusive to any class
or group, since the process of mating was impulsive, innocent, and
unrestrained by all.

With the first appearances of
deformity and malformation, or
"ugliness," the Venusians united
in their mutually shared discovery
process to correct the problem. At first
it was only a problem to be understood and solved, but gradually it
became another source of class division and discrimination. In the

beginning, the exceptionally beautiful people, by common standard, came to the conclusion that they should isolate themselves and breed only with others like themselves in order to prevent the possible contagion. Of course, they found themselves rapidly increasing the frequency of production of the "ugly ones," as well as developing the further complications of mental instability and low-grade retardation. Retarded people, at that point in evolution, were no more than what we today would consider people with below-average IQs, or people who are slower mentally and less able to function analytically and creatively.

Beauty and intelligence were quickly added to musical ability in determining a person's inherent value. Venusians with more beauty, intelligence, and musical ability were considered better than those with deformity, less physical beauty, or lack of creative skill. Prejudice and his sister, arrogance, were born of fear and grew into full adulthood rapidly. It took nearly 300 years for the Venusians as a whole to understand the genetic source of their problem and to stop inbreeding. Once they discovered the cause, the decision was soon made to not allow the "ugly" and "retarded" ones to reproduce. These people became the lower-class servers exclusively, and carried the shame of the race, even though they were not outwardly shamed or ridiculed. This was because, at that point in history, the Venusians still realized they were cocreating a new world and felt responsible for the cocreation of genetic defects. They even assured the incest-born "victims" who could not have children that they would be provided for as long as they lived, and they kept that promise. Any future deformed and "ugly" ones would be killed at birth, thus eliminating the embarrassing problem and preserving the purity of the race. (Recognize this motivation in Hitler's justification for slaughtering Jews and others in World War II?)

The "Ugly Ones" Form a New Colony–Year 1500

These rules worked for a while, until some of the victims decided to leave the inhabited areas and establish their own colony. There they could remain sovereign sexually and reproductively as well as in every other way of life. Although there was much concern and disagreement about this decision between the people on both sides, the incest victims' right to choose sovereignty was upheld, and they left with the bare necessities to begin anew.

The new colony quickly established itself in a separate region, and its members began new and promising lives. They refound the old values of equality and self-worth that had been lost to them, and rediscovered the soul- and being-level qualities of inner beauty, love, and Divine Truth. They cultivated these spiritual qualities and longed to share them with the original colony members, but feared rejection and ridicule. They knew they were considered simpletons, as well as "ugly," even though the original people outwardly showed them only compassion and tolerance.

In the meantime, the "beautiful" people felt a sense of relief at not having to see the "ugly" and "retarded" ones their race had created. They secretly felt less threatened with their victims out of sight, and became more and more enthralled with their own beauty, intelligence, and musical skill. Theater was also in its early developmental stages, contributing great new inspiration and a new opportunity for prestige among peers. Writers, actors and actresses, and costume and set designers joined the ranks of the higher and middle classes, and Venusian evolution continued.

The original Venusians maintained the genetic purity of their race, experiencing only rare instances of "ugly" or deformed babies, who they continued to kill at once. However, they grew increasingly arrogant and competitive. The value systems being rediscovered and evolved spiritually by their forgotten victims were scarcely even remembered by the "beautiful" people, and eventually they were forgotten altogether. Even members within the same class began to compete with one another to determine who was the *very* best, not just one of the best. This was a new development. The camaraderie of sharing similar talents and social status deteriorated into out-and-out rivalry. Initially this competition involved only physical appearance, intelligence, and creative talent, but it soon expanded into jealousy and competition for lovers—the winner claiming to be the most beautiful and worthy, the loser secretly plotting revenge and self-redemption.

All the while, denial of spiritual value and spiritual beauty grew proportionately to obsession with physical form and physical accomplishment. Creation of beauty through physical art forms joined the list of desirable accomplishments by this time, about 2000 years into Venusian history, and added yet another area of competition and class division. Those who could not produce music or art found other ways of climbing the social ladder when a form of currency exchange was invented. Of course, as it was intended to do, the currency system rewarded the artisans of all types more highly than the farmers, clothiers, and other common folk. So those from families of great instrument makers who had accumulated beautiful possessions and wealth were also among the elite by virtue of inheritance. Their greatest talent was in knowing how to benefit themselves at the expense of others. This class of elite boasted that they collected the best art and were entertained by the best musicians, and thus had superior taste and social worth. By the time the original colony had fully developed to this extent, 3500 years had passed, class division was an absolute, and sovereignty was an ideal only to those who were poor —and a distorted joke to the rich.

Crime Begins–Year 3500

Resentment, hostility, jealousy, envy, prejudice, and revenge replaced cocreation awareness and sovereignty, as well as the long-forgotten spiritual equality and spiritual beauty. The lower classes began to rebel and demand sovereignty. Their first official step occurred when a group of the poor decided to go on strike, as you would call it, demanding that all the inhabitants of their sector join them for a large meeting to air their complaints. They attempted to express their need to be seen as valuable beyond the service they provided to the upper classes. They reminded their oppressors that they served as vital members of the community, providing the bare necessities of labor such as growing food, washing clothes, and other "common" jobs. They told the rich and middle-class Venusians that the wealth must be distributed more evenly and fairly, that they had come to the planet to cocreate, not to dominate.

The upper classes mostly huffed and turned up their noses, saying those were old tales, creation myths, and that even if those stories were true, it was obvious that equality was a lie—as they had proven through their own obvious superiority. At this point, a few of the Venusian men began to make their way forward from the back of the crowds where they had agreed to wait peacefully while the milder-mannered delegates spoke to the crowd. They pushed people along the way, inciting more anger and hatred among the people. Eventually the crowd broke out into fighting. Poor women pulled at the hair of the rich women, grabbing jewelry and shawls and anything else that was easily detachable. The rich women and men hit them, kicked them, and violently tried to stop the thievery, while the lower-class men engaged in fistfights with the upper-class men. The whole thing ended in the murder of a wealthy art collector and writer who had especially provoked the less-fortunate men and was "accidentally" beaten to death. The man's wife screamed out, "He's dead. My husband is dead, and these barbarians have killed him!" A hush went through the entire group, and all fighting ceased at once. Some of the poorer women handed back things they had taken, others simply ran in fear of punishment, and the crowd silently disbanded. The next day, about half the lower-class men and a few of their womenfolk refused to go to work for the upper classes. They pledged to only provide for their own families and themselves from that point forth unless their requests were honored. Instead of meeting these requests, the upper classes put their heads together and agreed not to rehire those who had gone on strike, to increase hours and benefits to those who "remained faithful," and to go on with life as usual.

Naturally, this incited more anger and hatred in everyone. The upper classes had taken another step in ruling over the lower classes, praising the "faithful ones" for their subservience and threatening to cut them off if they were seen fraternizing with the rebels. The rebels hated the servants who continued to work; they began to steal from them and occasionally to intimidate them with threats and minor skirmishes. The "faithful" servants hated the upper classes for the power they held over their lives. They had succumbed to fear of survival and deserted their fellow lower-class friends. They likewise were angry with their former friends for putting them in the position of choice, felt mixed feelings of guilt, shame, anger, and hatred toward them, and began to look down on them as well.

Now, let us take a look back in history at the seed of this confusion, denial, oppression, prejudice, and deeply hidden emotions. Yes, it goes back to the genetic impairments created through incest. Although the original violators were ignorant and naive about genetic damage from incest at the time the problem occurred, they still felt the sting of fear and shame at its discovery. Those who remained the "beautiful" people were secretly disgusted with and terrified by these mutants their race had created. They denied the fear that this could happen to them, as well as shame that they had helped to cause it; resentment was felt toward the "ugly" and "retarded" ones for reminding them of it. This fear of "ugliness" and "retardation" haunted their dreams and every waking moment. These negative feelings were never acknowledged outwardly. Instead, the "beautiful ones" overcompensated with arrogance, false compassion, and agreement to allow the mutants to leave and create their own colony. The Venusians missed the opportunity to learn more about compassion and love of the sacred essence in each person, choosing to feed their obsession with "outer form" instead.

There was, of course, conscious relief and release of tension when the mutants left, but deep down inside the Venusians always held a fear of being inferior in any way. The fact that the mutants existed anywhere on their planet was a deep source of pain. The shadow side of consciousness was born into the subconscious of these "beautiful" people, and they became addicted to physical beauty and artistic expression as an overcompensation for their fear, shame, resentment, lack of compassion and pure love, and prejudices. And yet, they maintained a "pure" race.

Correspondingly, the mutants developed a much more spiritually based culture and one that excelled at agriculture. Music, theater, and art developed in their colony as well, and yet the bitter sting of old, remembered prejudices and superiorities kept these arts in balance with the rest of their lives. They were as careful as they could be to prevent further genetic impairment through obvious incest, and yet they were a race with damaged genes. Though the pull to reunite with the original colony was always there to some degree, their own buried shadow side kept them isolated. They carried deep scars of shame and fear of their own physical inferiority. This fear and shame were masked by their spiritual beliefs in equality, sovereignty, and inner beauty, and yet the wounds lay untended emotionally.

The mutants found respectable work for even the most simple-minded among them, shared with one another equally, sang and worshipped spirit together, and grew as a race. However, the genetic damage was quite real and still with them, since genetic impairment also impeded their souls and spirits from being able to completely embody and function in full capacity.

The paradox was that each colony deeply needed what the other had. The "beautiful" people who were so physically obsessed needed the spiritual purity and memory of innocence of the genetically impaired. The mutant race needed the genetic purity to enable them to recover lost abilities and full soul embodiment. And yet, neither could get past their own buried scars and denial to realize their mutual needs. Even though miles apart, they were on the same planet. Therefore, what affected one group had psychological and subconscious impact on the other.

Criminals Leave the Original Colony—Year 3800

At about 3800 years into Venusian colonization, a group of the criminal rebels from the original colony set out to recolonize elsewhere in order to get a fair start again. By that time, theft and murder were beginning to run rampant, and rape had been introduced. This new form of violent punishment was a direct reflection of people's deep anger and their need to punish others for having what they wanted and thought they could not have. Raping their bodies removed the sterility and hatred of separation and said to the rape victims, "See, you're no better than I am because I have the ability to take from you what you say you won't give." The false sense of power bred by this latest violence imposed on the middle and upper classes led to civil war. The lower-class rebels had no chance of winning, and so they organized, stole supplies, and left during the night for hills in the far west.

One month after their departure from the original colony, the rebels sighted the mutant colony. A humble city stood on a hillside rich in green pastures, rivers and streams, wildflowers, and a natural beauty previously unseen by the rebels. Their reaction was a mixture of shock and fear. Since they had learned to sneak around unnoticed, they decided to send spies in after dark to observe the people. The spies returned two days later reporting a very quiet, humble group of "strange and ugly" people living simple lives. Everyone appeared to be calm, reasonably happy, and equally provided for.

This news left the rebels quite surprised and hopeful, although fear of "ugliness" was deeply buried in their racial subconscious and made them cautious. They decided to send a delegation of men, women, and children to meet the people and ask if they could join them. The mutant race listened to their stories of woe and discrimination. The rebels had agreed, however, not to report their own criminal acts to these new people in the hope of being accepted. They also were holding onto righteous anger and hatred, which is by far the most dangerous kind.

Within a few days, the newcomers were being woven into the community like new strands in a tapestry. They were fed and sheltered in the homes of the mutants until their own shelters could be constructed. Some of the rebels found it easy to let go of the old ways of violence and competition. Others did not. Those who did not began to steal unnecessarily—taking tools, knives, and special foods they had not had before and for which they were afraid to ask. As this behavior was totally unknown to the mutants, realization of what was going on dawned on them slowly. The members of the host community thought they had forgotten where they left things, or misjudged how much food was left, until these incidents finally happened often enough and to enough different people that they began to put two and two together and come up with the concept of theft.

It was decided that a meeting should be called in order to address this new problem openly, with hope of understanding and resolution. The mutants genuinely wanted to know why the new community members would steal when nothing was withheld from them. But the rebels had a different kind of history with group meetings for problem solving, and therefore approached the mutants defensively and with undue caution.

The mutants were extremely tactful and gentle with the rebels as they broached the subject at hand. A point was made of first praising the new arrivals and thanking them for the good they had brought to the colony so far. When the subject of missing objects and food was brought out, the guilty rebels became angry and defensive, while the hosts puzzled at, and feared, their reactions. The rebels mistook these responses for weakness and simplemindedness, and began to formulate a subconscious group mindset about taking control of the new colony.

Some of the members of the rebel group had been sufficiently impacted by the purity and generosity of the mutant group that they spoke up. They told the mutants that where they had come from they had lapsed into stealing and at times even harming others just to survive; they confessed that they had further resorted to violence out of anger at times. Though the rebels still concealed their worst crimes, their stories helped the mutants understand the source of the deviant behavior sufficiently to stir compassion in them. Soon everyone was communicating civilly again, with minimal guardedness on the part of the guilty ones. All was forgiven, and the rebels were encouraged to ask for what they needed. Assurance was given that if the mutants could not meet their needs immediately, every effort would be made to help in the manufacture of the right tools and the harvest of the right foods.

For a while, everything went well between the two groups. They even began to share cultural differences, historic stories, and spiritual music. Both groups were appalled at the absence of historical records about the mutant society. When this was discovered, a deep silence fell over the mutant people, who were laden with old hurts, wounds, and prejudices. Those of a more competitive nature among the rebels began to fear the mutants, saw themselves as superior to them, and encouraged their friends to segregate in order to protect the purity of the race. Some listened and, in fear of being polluted by these ancient ancestors, began to separate from them more and more. Although nothing was overtly expressed, the tension increased, and old feelings of shame and victimization began to surface in the mutant people. Distrust was unspoken, but palpable on both sides. Some of the converted rebels were totally open to and loving and grateful toward the mutants; they sided with them against the more hostile rebels.

Rebels Control and Declare War on Mutants–Year 3801

Slowly, but certainly, small quarrels rose to the surface. "Better than/less than" thinking grew in the people—the rebels took on the dangerous superiority of a previously oppressed race, and the mutants felt less open and trusting, as well as resentful of the old shames being dredged up from their group subconscious. Neither group took the obvious opportunity for self-examination and healing, and instead subtleties became passive-aggressive behaviors, which became segregation, which became stronger resentment and distrust. Eventually this process led the rebels to impose the same illegal breeding laws upon the mutants as their ancestors had done centuries before, and the shadowy nightmares in the subconscious minds of all concerned slowly began to surface.

At first, the mutants tried to reason with the rebels by virtue of their generosity and openness to the new people. When this did not work, they offered coexistence with segregated living. When that did not work, they began to develop weapons for self-protection and to preserve their sovereignty. This time, however, they did not offer to leave, as this place was their home. Eventually the rebels were asked to leave, except those who had melded with their culture and begun to intermarry.

The righteous rebels were indignant with this last request and declared war on their former hosts. Though the rebels were greatly outnumbered, they were more experienced in violence, sneakiness, and instilling fear in others. They raped and killed the mutant women, dismembered male children, and created an atmosphere of hatred and fear everywhere around them. In the meantime, one elder among the mutant race remembered the promise of divine intervention if the majority requested it. The people immediately gathered in the middle of the night and by consensus requested that the violent rebels be removed from their colony and the planet. The plan worked. That night a huge tornado came over the area where the rebels had built their homes and all of the rebels were killed.

The mutants were in a state of shock at this turn of events. They had expected something more gracious, like the rebels deciding to leave on their own, or perhaps an opening in the clouds and a nonviolent group removal of the rebels. This extreme yet natural phenomenon shook them and filled them anew with guilt, shame, and feelings of deserving punishment. In other words, their victim mentality took a quantum leap.

End of First Evolutionary Cycle—Year 5200

The natural cultural and technological progress of evolving races continued throughout the rest of the first 5200 years of colonization. The "beautiful" people grew in artistic accomplishment, as did their accompanying sense of class division and prejudices. They even developed a government to make sure the servant classes remained in order and to check the ongoing, though diminished, violence. They became a civilization of arrogant artisans and wealth holders; middle-class workers, including most government officials and lesser artisans; and lower-class servers and common laborers. Overt displays of resentment and prejudice were kept to a minimum most of the time. The government became very popular with the wealthy. People in general were extremely repressed emotionally and verbally, as their civilization was based on "better than/less than" thinking and was nearly devoid of spiritual values.

The mutant race continued to improve mentally, and even physically, with the introduction of the few remaining rebel converts to the community. Spiritual principles continued to overrule the physical obsessions of their "beautiful" ancestors, and these people maintained a reasonably peaceful existence in spite of the increase in repressed fear, shame, guilt, and hatred brought on by the rebel invaders.

When the 5200-year mark was approaching, some of the Andromedan angels who had remained as guides and plant devas carried out their initial plans to incarnate at that time in order to bring about the conscious choices necessary to plan the next 5200 years of Venusian colonization. Those born into both colonies were strikingly different in temperament and somewhat different in appearance from the existing cultures. There was a purity about them that had been lost to both groups—emotionally, mentally, spiritually, and even physically to a degree. Of course they carried the genetics of the race, complete with the mutations brought on by repression, prejudice, and other deviant attitudes over the previous 5200 years. Consciously pure of spirit, their memories of what had taken place over the centuries since colonization began were mostly intact. The newborn angels were preprogrammed to awaken these memories during early puberty.

Slowly both cultures began to be filled with stories of Andromedan angels, sovereignty, and equality of spirit. The stories also told of the 5200-year turning point when their progress would be assessed by the hierarchies and themselves to decide upon the next steps in evolution to be taken on Venus. Needless to say, both groups had more than a little to think about. Both colonies originally resisted the ideas being brought to them by these young souls; but as more and more of these angels were born and independently kept telling the same stories and giving the same predictions, the Venusians began to listen. The newly born angels assisted in the healing process as residents of both colonies experienced deep feelings that had been buried for a long time. The use of signature plants was introduced for restoration of health and DNA. The newborns helped many people access their own subconscious minds and emotions to find the long-buried memories and truths, but many were not willing to heal and change or acknowledge the need for it. Arrogance, self-righteousness, prejudice, and fear of relinquishing power held the wealthy and government people firmly in outmoded ways; these people threatened and intimidated the new believers, but could not stop them. The believers heard and healed to a degree, but then they began to feel spiritually superior and prejudiced against the elitist holdouts—a reverse prejudice, as you might call it.

In the mutant colony, the healing and transformation was by consensus. The mutants began to understand their deep-seated shame and prejudice against their own physical appearance. They began to get in touch with the deep anger and hurt they felt toward their "beautiful" oppressors. They also let go of the guilt regarding the removal of the rebels; the angels assured them that the rebels had been taken to another planet to work out their own karmic problems. This other planet was called Mars, and it showed in the night sky at certain times of the year. The mutants and converted rebels would hold night meetings during which they would look to Mars in the sky and sing to the planet and the people on it, asking them to forgive and let go of their pain. They began to pray to the hierarchies to help these new Martians grow and heal. As they prayed, their own emotional wounds healed as well. They asked for guidance and for help in becoming what they were divinely intended to be. The need for genetic purification was understood, and it was happening as much as it could with the use of signature plants, and emotional and mental healing.

In the year 5200, a great earthquake happened. (Or maybe it should be called a Venus quake.) The rivers and streams flooded and destroyed much of both colonies' surrounding areas and some of their homes. About 20 percent of the people were killed in these natural disasters, which were being used to clear spiritual and emotional karma and mental thoughtforms. The message in the events was one of purification and clearing. The people were shocked, and yet the newly born angels were able to explain the purification in such a way that most of the people understood. Some members of both colonies were resentful and felt they were being punished by the Higher Council and An, the Supreme Being. These thoughtforms went with them into the next era in the form of distrust and fear of the divine, the Higher Council, and of An, in particular.

Emissaries of Light Arrive–Year 5200

The majority of colonists from both groups were afraid to continue without hierarchical supervision and assistance. This fear was a message to the hierarchies that the majority of the colonists desired intervention in the form of the incarnation of more evolved beings.

The Higher Council sent a delegation via a merkabah spaceship that materialized just above the planet where both colonies could see it. Emissaries of Light were sent to each colony to educate the Venusians on the history of the other colony since the two had separated. The Emissaries told the people they must reunite soon in order to begin the rectification and healing at its next level. For fifty years, the two colonies were spiritually taught, restructured, reminded of who they were originally, and strengthened in many ways. Then they were told that the time had come for the reunion.

The "beautiful" people were told to send a delegation to welcome the mutants back home. Those remaining in the original colony built new homes, stocking them with food, furniture, and even artwork. The mutants were told to keep a fire going on the eastern slopes nearest their colony to direct the ancient ancestors to them. Both groups were excited, and a little afraid of the changes that were inevitable. The government was finally destructured and the mutants welcomed home. The restoration of the race, spiritually and physically, began.

The Emissaries sent by the Higher Council remained on Venus as advisers, diplomats, spiritual teachers, and trainers of spiritual leaders to replace themselves when they left in roughly 500 years. This time it was agreed that every 500 years a few angelic ones who had previously remained disembodied would be born into Venusian culture to keep the people in line with their intended evolution and remind them of past learning. Healing methods and spirituality would be updated in any way needed at those intervals.

The plan was very successful for a long time, although prejudices and arrogance about beauty and artistic skill still remained ingrained in the people. These ideals seemed to be in their blood and never left altogether. In spite of this fact, the Venusians continued to develop primarily as an artistic and agricultural society. Steadily their culture evolved in these physical areas while holding on, almost fearfully, to the original spiritual premises, lest they fall again.

Fear of trusting themselves was the first and foremost cause of the Venusians' repression and denial for the entire second 5200-year cycle; physical prejudices and arrogance were the other major causes. At the end of that cycle, the hierarchies and the Venusian group higher mind—also called the higher collective consciousness, which had developed through the people's cooperation and cocreation with one another—agreed that a flood should be sent to destroy most of their crops but harm no people. The purpose was to create a situation in which all would have to work together for the common good. This would force the Venusians to trust each other—and themselves—and to experience their equality and their interdependence upon one another and the planet.

After the floods subsided, the Venusians were told by the most recent newborn angels that they must interpret the manifestations in their reality for themselves, come to understand how they had created them, and take right action accordingly. The flooding and crop loss were certainly not intended as punishment or intimidation, for their own group higher consciousness had agreed that the floods were needed to unite and humble the people at deeper levels. The people were being asked to interpret the signs and act accordingly in order to heal their lack of self-trust.

Meditation and Mahayana Consciousness Expand– Years 10,400 to 15,600

The angels gave the Venusians a tool to use in the process, a new form of meditation for self-discovery. At the end of each day, they would go into deep silence and reexamine everything that had happened to them during that day—their thoughts and feelings, as well as their interactions with others. Some people were deeply resentful of the implication that they had created this natural disaster; these were mostly the ones who had carried the distrust of divinity, of An, and of the Higher Council from the previous 5200-year cycle into the latest one. The rest were more receptive and eager to comply with this new approach, and experienced it as empowering. When they did this new meditation in groups, they were able to experience a quality of depth in silence that they could not find when meditating alone. The meditators also observed that subtler aspects of their own feelings and thoughts became more apparent to them when they meditated together and shared their observations with one another. Therefore, humility came through willingness to expose themselves to one another in more personal and intimate ways, as well as through their realization of the strength inherent in the group when meeting with a common purpose.

Within the first fifty years of the third 5200-year cycle, the Venusians became aware of their own higher consciousness that existed beyond their physical bodies and was enmeshed in the group higher mind. In Buddhism, *mahayana* is the stage of spiritual development during which no one member of a group progresses unless all do; the Venusians discovered this principle experientially, and it became the theme of the third era of colonization. Angelic messengers continued to be born every 500 years to assure their ongoing evolution and memory retention. Materially, advancements during this era were minimal compared to the expansion of group consciousness; and yet, evolution on all levels took its natural course.

A New Race Is Born–Year 15,600

At the end of the third 5200-year cycle, a new challenge was introduced to the group. The Higher Council and the Venusian group higher mind decided to introduce a new race to the planet to test the Venusians' spiritual evolution and ability to integrate it into a new experience of all-inclusiveness. The new race was a group of linear, seraphimlike beings with extremely developed mental capacities but very little right-brain type functions. However, they had learned the power of group mind for creating their own reality and evolution in nonphysical settings, so the two groups had that acquired knowledge as common ground.

When the new beings arrived on the planet in the middle of a group meditation, a group of Pleiadian Emissaries of Light accompanied them to explain their presence and assist in the first fifty years of integration of the two races. In the beginning, both groups were quite curious about one another, and explored their differences with curiosity and as much spiritual equality as they could. The original Venusians found this new group rather odd— they were not really ugly; they were just not beautiful, and lacked a certain grace the angelic group had always taken for granted in themselves. They also seemed to lack in creative impetus, while talking and theorizing almost constantly. When the newcomers began to design new buildings and tools to their own geometric specifications, the Venusians found the structures rigid, unyielding, and lacking in artistic beauty.

The linear beings, recently become Venusian, thought the old architecture was impractical and antiquated. They wanted to change many things on this new planetary home to meet their own ideas and ideals of perfection. Both groups felt defensive, and for the first time the original Venusians were faced with a race that thought itself superior to them, not because of beauty, but because of a new kind of analytical and technological intelligence. To feel the blows of prejudice turned back against themselves came as quite a shock, and yet most of them knew enough of their own planetary history to comprehend the spiritual challenge.

Without making the new race feel inferior, the original Venusians also had to maintain their own sense of personal value. In order to do this, the group higher mind impulsed them to ask to learn from the new Venusians as well as teaching them artistic ways—if the linear ones wanted to learn. Although the original colonists found themselves capable of learning the ways of the new ones, most of them were uninspired by it after a short time and resumed their old ways of artistic and agricultural focus. The new Venusians secretly considered this a sign of inferiority and weakness. They had very little interest in learning from their predecessors.

At the end of the first 500 years together, new angels and linear beings were born among the two diverse groups of Venusians, reminding them of what they had in common: awareness of higher group consciousness and sovereignty for all beings. This pulled them together in a unique way. The new ones began to meditate with the old ones at the end of each day for the purpose of self-examination and self-awareness. The old Venusians began to spend an hour a day thinking and acting in the ways of their new colleagues. Both groups felt something changing in them that was too subtle to name, but it was happening none the less.

Intermarrying Begins—Year 16,600

By the end of the next 500 years, minimal mating had begun between the races, and very unusual children were produced from those unions. The mixed children tended to be more temperamental than children of the pure races, and displayed skills in both right- and left-brain activities. Of course, each child was unique in his or her expression of that balance; some leaned more toward the artistic, while others were naturally more pensive and analytical. Besides that, different colors of hair and eyes began to appear. Previously, both races had been blue-eyed; the angels had blond hair, and the linear beings had brownish-blond hair. Now children were being born with brown or greenish-blue eyes; their hair was white blond and varying shades of medium to light brown, but always with a golden sheen.

These color changes were remarkable to the people, and the

angels secretly found them unappealing and less attractive than themselves. The linear beings remained more neutral about the changes, although they were perplexed and intrigued by the new varieties of physical appearance. That was the beginning of biological science, with humanoid genetic studies taking precedence initially, then eventually branching out into study of plants, minerals, and whatever else could be broken down and deciphered.

This study created an overly physical orientation on the part of the linear scientists that was quite different from their predecessors' obsessions with physical appearance. The older Venusians were aware of this potential stumbling block, although they found themselves quite curious about genetics due to their own history of genetic deviance. Therefore, the field of genetics and reproduction came into the foreground, while architecture, agriculture, and art were mostly maintained at existing levels, with minimal evolution. They became so involved in genetic studies and early stages of genetic engineering that they forgot about the value of soul and spirit. Spiritual common good was all but replaced with scientific common interest, and in the name of exploring group consciousness, the Venusians almost completely ignored higher collective consciousness.

This trend toward dominance of the physical world over the spiritual one continued throughout the fourth 5200-year cycle, which ended in a large quake that destroyed most of the new buildings and killed about one-fourth of the people. Though the people had forgotten it, the collective group higher consciousness was waiting to be brought into their conscious minds again. The quake was used to help the Venusians come together to mourn the loss of one-fourth of their community and to reconnect to the true value of life. It was also intended to tell them, "Look at what you're creating. The physical structures of your buildings and your genes have become more important to you than understanding one another's essential qualities of spirit. You have forgotten why you came together; you have cocreated a new obsession instead. Remember who you are. Share that with one another in innocence and trust. Remember the group higher mind. Find out its purpose." This is what the quake was lovingly and compassionately saying to the people; and it was the message the new angels and linear ones brought to the Venusians during the last seventy-five years of that 5200-year cycle. But this time the people chose not to listen. They believed they had become too advanced a society to listen to these outmoded, childlike, spiritual ideals that had appeared to hold them back culturally in previous times.

"Man Against Nature" Attitude Prevails—Year 20,800

Instead, the people interpreted the quake as an opportunity to become more sophisticated in their building codes, to make their structures stronger and more capable of resisting nature. Obsession with making "improvements" to every area of life ensued. The linear attitude of "man against nature" began to prevail, even among the remaining members of the original Venusian race. The other thing that turned the tide at the end of that era was a majority agreement that humanoids should control their world instead of cocreate within it. Their meditations became times to strategize and examine themselves for innovative ideas they may have overlooked, rather than times for self-awareness, growth, and spiritual connectedness with the group higher consciousness and their individual Higher Selves. Naturally, these meditation groups and individual practices died out altogether within the first fifty years of the new cycle.

During that cycle there was steady development of "man against nature" thinking, growth in scientific fields, and genetic engineering of plants and people. Segregation was reintroduced as class division once again flourished. The scientists put down the spiritualists but tolerated the artisans. Medical professions were created that used engineered plant and mineral sources to eliminate the symptoms of problems, much like allopathy on Earth today. The common laborers became the lower class again, their value determined only by how much they provided for or made life easier for the middle and upper classes. Prejudices, resentments, shame, and fear grew, but with a new sophistication that in some ways made these emotions more unpredictable and dangerous. This cycle was very similar to the current 5200-year cycle on Earth.

The spiritualists became mostly dogmatic, judged those who disagreed with them, and catered their practices and teachings to the masses. Only a few Venusians retained spiritual integrity and purity and listened when the newly incarnate angels were born every 500 years, until finally no new ones came. The vast majority of the Venusians had alienated themselves from the higher collective consciousness and agreed that no more new ones were wanted. Their majority decision was honored.

By the last century of this fifth era, approaching 26,000 years of colonization, Venus had become so much like modern-day Earth that the two planets could be considered like nonidentical twin sisters. The main differences were in the smaller size of the population of Venus and the absence of war.

This period marked a turning point in Venusian evolution. When the 5200-year review time came, the Venusian group mind was so severed from higher collective consciousness that it was as if a great veil, or thick dark net, had been placed in the atmosphere around the planet. Etherically, it looked like a geometric linear construct, put together with an erector set. It blocked the Sun's more refined solar coding and radiant patterns of light from entering the atmosphere in their pure form. The Sun's rays took on the gridlike flow pattern instead of retaining their own integrity. (This condition of a veil, or gridlike net, around the planet is also similar to what has formed around Earth at this time.) Little could be done without total intervention from the hierarchies, and the hierarchies were unwilling to go against the free will of the Venusians.

Upholding the people's group and individual rights to explore evolution as sovereign beings was foremost in the minds of the Higher Council and An when they reviewed the dilemma. The group higher consciousness asked for assistance in the form of burning away the linear grid and bombarding the planet with encoded solar rays to create planetary chaos. Fires would erupt all over the planet, forcing the people to unite again in order to survive. This would again provide for the emergence of a state of humility and spiritual awareness. The Higher Council agreed this was a possibility, but not a probability. They believed the Venusians had gone too far to read messages through natural disasters in the old way. They also saw that the civilization was on the verge of destroying itself through experimentation with explosives and atomic studies.

It was finally decided to hold back until the last minute to see what the Venusians would do on their own. However, because the civilization was nearing the end of the fifth 5200-year cycle, the hierarchy could override the previous decision and send new angels and seraphimlike beings to be born and warn the people. As the plan progressed, there was a spiritual revolution, although it involved only about 20 percent of the people directly. The rest of the population judged the spiritual ones as being misguided misfits, and ignored them until it was too late.

Chemical-Triggered Disasters–Year 25,980

The expected chemical-triggered explosions happened about twenty years before the end of the era, causing quakes, atmospheric fires, water pollution, flooding, drying up of streams, and general chaos. Only about a third of the population survived. Those remaining agreed, at a group mind level, that they needed help in order to go beyond what they could do for themselves. This opened the doors for the Higher Council to send help.

Once again Pleiadian Emissaries of Light came to the planet, this time joined by Andromedan Emissaries of Light and hierarchical members of the seraphim origins from beyond the Milky Way. This hierarchical conglomerate converged upon the survivors, bringing spiritual teachings, new healing modalities, meditation techniques for reconnecting with the higher group and individual consciousnesses, and promises of further assistance—as long as the majority agreed.

The help of these spiritual teachers was mostly well received, though a few Venusians remained wary and secretive. Ego consciousness of separation and distrust of the divine made it hard for some of the people to accept the principles of inner godliness and cocreation; they preferred to think of themselves as victims of the hierarchies. They needed to retain control in the name of sovereignty. However, the Higher Council's Emissaries continued to assist the Venusians and remind them of long-lost spiritual values and truths.

Spiritual Values Return–Year 26,000

At the end of the 26,000-year cycle, a great hurricane was brought over the waters of Venus; huge tidal waves washed upon the shores. Land masses were buried in water, rains came for many days, and the people had to work together again in order to survive. Most did, and they pledged to make a fresh start, to remember the value of each soul and spirit, and to rediscover what balance meant. When the shifting of land masses and waterways was finished, less land remained between the Venusians and the oceans. This served as a constant reminder that life was sacred, ever-changing, and evolving, and should be cooperated with, not controlled.

The reemergence of spiritual priorities, dissolution of governments, focus on creative expression for its own sake, and return to more natural agriculture and technology were all outward signs of change and renewal. Inner changes were more time consuming and slow in coming, but the majority of the people remained dedicated to making those changes just the same. Sovereignty with cooperation and cocreation became a way of life once more, and respect for differences emerged in a new way. The Venusians began to realize that all forms of creative expression had value, whether linear or artistic, spiritual or agricultural. They began to discover unity in diversity, and balance through appreciation of differences, instead of holding on to the old model of trying to convert others to their way of thinking and doing.

Self-respect grew rapidly with this new way of thinking and being with one another. Each person was encouraged to do what he or she did best and enjoyed. Meditations for groups were reopened to those who wished to attend, but no one was pushed. For the next 5200 years, Venus and her inhabitants flourished as never done before. Peace prevailed, diversity was honored, and everyone felt safe.

Animals Introduced—Year 31,200

Then, at the end of that cycle, the higher collective consciousness operating in Oneness asked the Higher Council to give them the opportunity again to welcome a new race and integrate it into their culture. The main purpose for this was to restore the group's self-trust by presenting it with a challenge it had failed previously. As that era ended, a huge comet landed in the ocean. No major visible planetary changes resulted, but the climate was set for a new race to emerge. This new race was mammalian animals, including dolphins, porpoises, and whales. Wolves, coyotes, other canine species, small felines, deer, and bears were introduced. Something akin to wolverines appeared. Other smaller mammals were also brought to the planet at that time, with the general instruction to the Venusians: "You are your brother's keeper."

Most of the animals lived in the hills surrounding the colonized areas, but a few smaller ones were brought directly into contact with the people. Deer drank from the streams that were the people's water source. Chipmunks and squirrels lived in the trees near colonists' homes, eating from natural sources as well as receiving handouts from the people. It took some adjustment for the people to relate to species that could not speak their language, live indoors, or communicate their needs other than by simply taking. For the most part, the people loved the animals and found them endearing. It was not uncommon for a deer or wolf to eat from a human hand. Those who felt the urge to do so learned to swim and spent time in the oceans with the dolphins, porpoises, and whales.

All the people agreed these new Venusians were an unusual challenge, yet mostly a delightful one. Some people protested that these new creatures contributed nothing but only took from the planet, while others felt truly enriched by their presence. There was such abundance of plant life that scarcity was not a concern, so the people and animals flourished side by side for many years. However, as the animal population continued to increase, the people began to anticipate problems. Together, they met to look for a

solution, both by brainstorming and by meditating. Those of the lower group mind aligned with the higher group mind and concluded that species control was necessary, and asked to receive help with the problem. In response to that decision, the number of animal spirits allowed to incarnate at any given time was regulated. There was agreement from the animal spirits as well.

Rediscovery and Rebuilding of the Ancient Mutant Colony Site–Year 31,400

The planet continued to grow in human population, however, as some of the souls split into twin souls for the purpose of diversity of experience, and simultaneous male/female incarnations. Once again overpopulation, this time by the human beings, became an issue. It was decided that a group of people would go on an exploratory journey for the purpose of finding new inhabitable land. They were instinctually drawn to the hills in the west where they discovered the old city of the former mutant evacuees. It was in ruins, and much of it was buried, but it seemed a natural location for recolonization to begin again. So one-third of the population gradually moved to this new-old city.

This move solved their problems for quite a long time; it even introduced trade and travel to the people, both of which were exciting and rewarding. After a few hundred years, a quake destroyed a good portion of the new city, which then required assistance from the original colony members. However, the original colony was experiencing crop failures due to a drought condition, and its citizens felt they needed to remain free from involvement in the problems of the new colony. This incited anger and bitterness in the new colony, whose members felt abandoned in a time of great need. After getting back on their feet, the new colony members decided to stop trade with the old colony and take care of themselves only. The old colony's citizens tried to explain, but their predicament had seemed minor in comparison to the new colony's need for help, and hard feelings grew. There were no wars or outward fighting, just alienation and estrangement.

For a while this alienation seemed to have little impact on either group, other than the absence of travel and trade; however, separation took its toll psychologically and spiritually. The Venusian lower group mind became severed into two group minds that operated autonomously. Each group continued in its own natural evolution, but the spirits and creativity of the people suffered. Irritability and small squabbles became more prevalent. Quite separately from one another, they developed identical problems—feelings of discontent and a spirit of laziness began to prevail. Arguments became more frequent and severe. Fewer people met to meditate and problem solve, first for one reason, then for another.

People cannot harbor feelings of separation from, and blame toward, others without eventually affecting all their relationships. The people on Venus were experiencing this, but not learning from it yet. Nit-picky arguments turned into ego battles and then feuds. Families would not speak because of what one father had said to the other father. Neighbors refused to socialize with the woman up the street who had let it be known she considered herself superior to them. The minority of spiritual-minded people who tried to meditate could not influence the general population with their perceptions of what they saw happening. Righteous blame and indignation were rampant.

Animals Are Killed, Alienation Between People Deepens –Year 31,925

Soon, incidents of animals attacking humans began to occur. Of course, the attacks were brought on by instinctual responses by the animals to protect themselves against such angry, sour-smelling creatures as some of the Venusian humanoids had become. But the humans refused to learn and understand. By the end of that era, animals within populated areas were killed on sight, even eaten to assuage the hunger caused by failing, dried-up crops. Like the people, the planet was getting hotter and drier, and growth was not only stopping, but reversing itself.

Colonies Reconnect–Year 32,300

Each colony at the same time decided to send messengers to the other colony to see what was happening. They were surprised to discover that, even though their members had lived several days journey apart and not interacted for over 400 years, the two colonies were almost duplicates of one another. A committee was formed in each colony to go to the other one. They would meet with the spiritual leaders and those who still meditated together to see if any conclusions could be reached about what was happening to their planet and her inhabitants.

Both groups traced the onset of problems to approximately the time when the two colonies had become estranged. They realized that long-suppressed hurts and resentments with one another were causing social and planetary discord and strife. Each group independently decided that trade should be reinstated, that a win/win policy of helping one's neighbor should likewise replace the feuding, and that people from each colony should volunteer to go and live in the other city in a kind of exchange program to heal the old wounds.

The same day they came to agreement in both cities, rains came and began to restore the land. Vegetarianism was agreed upon by consensus, and renewal of harmony began. For the rest of the 5200-year cycle, studies in human behavior and emotional response were developed and applied. Human psychology was birthed as a profession and a source of study. There was a basic understanding that all beings, human or animal, need to feel safe, trusting and trusted, respectful and respected, and loving and loved. Kindness and understanding were rekindled, and the group higher consciousness was reformed. The animal kingdom took a couple of centuries to overcome the distrust and hurt at being killed, but they finally healed their connection to the humans, and peace prevailed.

"Leave Well Enough Alone Policy"–Year 36,400

At the end of the 5200-year cycle, the people were reasonably content. Populations of both animals and humanoids were manageable, and there was a balanced expression of the arts, agriculture, psychology, and spirituality. When the cyclical review took place, the main desires among the people were for unity in diversity and peaceful coexistence. Though they had gone through rough times, they had learned well and become better people for it. So the Higher Council asked the group higher mind what it wanted for the next 5200 years. It was agreed that everything was fine as it was, and that to "leave well enough alone" and allow a natural sequence of events was the best plan.

The Higher Council agreed to comply and sent only minor,

scattered storms to break up any old thoughtforms remaining in the atmosphere. For a few hundred years, all was peaceful and well among the Venusians. Then a strange thing happened: people began to develop depression for no apparent reason. Lethargy swept through the younger generations, who could find nothing they believed in or wanted to do. The people were confused since on the surface all appeared to be normal. Delegates from both cities met and compared stories, only to find once again that they were identical.

It was agreed that both cities would call off all work on the same day in order to hold large gatherings where people would brainstorm and meditate together to try and solve the problems, or at least come to understand them. This was the first time all the people had met at the same time for the same purpose since the early civilizations. It was a very powerful time. The conclusions arrived at during those meetings were: (1) We have widespread lethargy due to a lack of anything that inspires the young; (2) many of the middle-aged and older people are depressed, commonly complaining that their lives have lost all meaningful purpose; (3) we have been peaceful and unchallenged for several hundred years, yet we can see how challenge has united and inspired our people in historic records; (4) we do not wish a disaster upon ourselves in order to find inspiration, but we do need inspiration in order to continue evolving; (5) we trust that the higher group consciousness is capable of bringing us what we need, and we agree to ask for their intervention and the intervention of the Higher Council and An to help us find new spiritual inspiration so we may continue to evolve.

Age of Enlightenment—Years 38,200 to 46,800

With this last conclusion and agreement, new angels and linear beings were sent to Venus to be born. Over the next 1000 years, as humans died, about one-third of them left Venus altogether and were prepared on the etheric realms to reincarnate on Mars and reconnect with their former Venusian ancestors. In the meantime, the newborn beings brought renewed spiritual practices, healing techniques, and inspiration for enlightenment to the people. Avatars were also sent to each city, and many of the people experienced enlightenment states, the performance of mira-

cles, and the desire to help their fellow Venusians evolve to similar ecstatic states. The Age of Enlightenment had come to the
planet by virtue of the people's shared recognition of the need in
life for continual evolution. (This recognition is needed on Earth
at this time in order to turn the tide of events to a more positive
and spiritually based focus.)

For the rest of that 5200-year cycle and for the entire next one,
spiritual evolution, initiatic training, enlightenment, ascension,
and higher-dimensional communications flourished. Art and
music were at their highest peaks ever, and the people were generally happy, content, and inspired. By the end of the fourth era
of the second 26,000-year cycle, the planet was fast becoming a
spiritual and initiatic mystery school with appreciation of beauty
and art still remaining a primary trait. The Venusians even had
their own Ascended Masters who formed a council not unlike the
Great White Brotherhood on Earth.

At that time, it was decided that the Venusians were ready for
a next, and possibly final, challenge before leaving their third- and
fourth-dimensional consciousness and moving back into the
higher planes. This challenge began with a great flood during
which all the inhabitants of the original colony had to flee to the
mountains in the west in order to survive. The western neighbors
were given the opportunity to test the ancient wound of being
abandoned in a time of need by the other colony. Though it was
very ancient and long forgotten, the karmic traces remained; and
they were healed completely when the western colony dwellers
graciously opened their doors and hearts to the people from the
east. Some western colonists were frightened by thoughts of
scarcity and lack because they were taking on so many people to
feed, clothe, and shelter. Yet they met each challenge with open
hearts, praying and meditating together to get answers to pressing problems, and always considering the greatest good of all concerned. They connected more deeply than ever before with the
higher collective consciousness through this new alliance brought
on by survival needs.

Many Venusians died from illnesses spread as a result of
overcrowding. However, this did not change the atmosphere of
win/win, and the people grew more intimately connected with
one another. When the floods receded, most of the eastern city

had been destroyed, and a general restoration plan began. As many people as could be housed in the surviving buildings returned to the city to begin rebuilding and planting, and within ten years the city was restored. The populations divided again, and yet remained spiritually closer and more harmonious than ever.

At the height of the Venusians loving and caring for one another, with their spiritual growth continuing to accelerate, the Higher Council and An sent a messenger to them asking what they would choose now for their populace. Did they wish to ascend as a group, moving on to higher-dimensional planes again and ending this experiment? Would they prefer to go to a new planet that was less evolved—one that could use their love and experience? Did they wish to remain and challenge themselves in some new way on Venus?

New Damaged Beings Arrive–Year 46,900

After a few days of gathering and meditating together, the planetary citizens agreed that they would like to share the abundance of love, beauty, and spiritual ecstasy they had found together with others who needed it. They preferred to remain on Venus and yet were willing to relocate en masse if need be. The Higher Council and An were well pleased with the Venusians and decided to send them a group of outcasts from a galaxy in the constellation of Virgo who needed to feel loved, valued, and accepted for who they were. These new beings arrived in two separate transports a few years apart. They were from a planet that had decided to become spiritually self-sustaining and that had appointed one of their own kind as a Supreme Being. However, their spiritual evolution had not been commensurate with their desire to self-rule, and cruelty and elitism had taken over at once. There had been civil wars and religious wars, and those who had been unwilling to kill or fight had been considered outcasts, weaklings, and inferior, and had been killed.

Leaving that planet and galaxy in a very traumatized state, these Virgoans, as I will call them, had been put into healing cocoons and transported to the Pleiades for a time until they could maintain light-body forms again. The Venusians had asked for beings in need of their love and support, and these wounded ones were brought forth. When they arrived, they looked as if their forms could be blown away by a strong wind. Still fragile, lacking in confidence and feelings of being wanted and accepted, they faced their new Venusian family, wary and yet hopeful.

Taken into homes, fed, nurtured, talked to as valuable equals, and shown compassion and understanding, the newcomers slowly recovered. It was several generations before their nightmares stopped altogether. When they did stop, the Virgoans began to experience sudden outbursts of anger and violence. These emotions had been deeply suppressed in order to maintain nonviolence on their former planet and were surfacing now that the people felt safe. At first, no one knew what to do about these outbursts except try to talk the troubled ones through them. Guilt and shame mounted in the new Venusians, for they felt powerless to control their emotions. As enough of the people expressed shame and guilt about this lack of control, the older Venusians began to remember what had happened to their people when they had tried to control themselves and each other in various ways. Remembering the psychological studies of their ancestors, they studied the remaining old books, hoping to find understanding and ways of helping their newest friends.

Soon it was apparent that a treatment program for releasing deeply buried emotions was needed, so they began to develop one. The new Virgoan-Venusians learned to accept scary feelings without being frightened of losing control. Safe environments were created in which the people could release anger and find forgiveness for their former planetary oppressors. The older Venusians shared their own planetary history of evolution and struggle with the new people to show them that beings could evolve who had been through deep damage and pain.

The newcomers began to trust more deeply and heal, yet they still harbored doubts about how far the older Venusians would go to help them. Subconsciously the Virgoans felt a need to test the loyalty of the older Venusians to see if the colonists would reject them if they did not conform, as had been their experience on their former planet. The Virgoan group mind decided that one of them would go completely insane in order to test the response of the Venusians. When this happened, the Venusians did not accept that individual's condition as permanent; they believed that with enough love and patience they could pull the person back to sanity. It was inconceivable to the Venusians that a being might be unwilling to be helped and that they could do nothing in that case. As time went by with no change, and there was ongoing need to keep the person locked up for safety reasons, the Venusians felt defeated. Feelings of inadequacy and shame prevailed due to their perception of failure to help the insane person.

As the lower group mind of the newcomers perceived the weakness in the Venusians, more of them began to go insane. Subconsciously they wanted the Venusians to fail and to reject them because of their damaged genetics, although consciously they feared insanity and rejection and wanted to survive. The fear, of course, fed the problem and brought it into full bloom, and over half of the newcomers became insane, or at best schizophrenic. The Venusians lacked psychological sophistication and experience with deep self-sabotaging behaviors. They became obsessed with the urgency to heal these lost ones. Feelings of inadequacy and spiritual doubt grew so rapidly that they began to merge with the lower group mind of the Virgoans out of pity and shame at having failed them. In other words, the older colonists began to lose their healthy emotional and psychic boundaries and take on the karma and pain of the insane and troubled new ones.

The Venusian Decline—Year 47,000

The Venusians began to have hellish nightmares about demons coming to kill them and destroy their homes and families. They would awaken in night sweats from these bad dreams and be afraid and unable to go back to sleep. Over the next few decades, the martyrdom of the Venusians fed their demise. Genuine desire to love and help others in need became obsession with *making* others get well in order to prove their own worth. When they failed, the would-be healers doubted their own spiritual growth and connectedness, which deteriorated quickly as these feelings escalated. *The belief that their love had not been enough or good enough was strong.* Slowly, the long-time Venusians were worn down by serious psychological problems brought on by absorption of psychic pain and trauma from the Virgoans, and by their own self-doubt, perfectionism, and sense of failure.

Incidents of domestic squabbles became common, occasionally deteriorating into physical slaps and hits. The women began to fear and distrust the men who hit and intimidated them, and the men grew to hate the women whom they were sure saw them as failures and misfits. Some of the most spiritually developed were the hardest hit by this new paradigm shift. Miracles ceased to happen and people stopped going to the spiritual healers for advice, since nothing helped; the healers themselves fell into loss of faith and lack of self-trust. Some became hostile, arrogant, and prejudiced against the newcomers, and wanted them cast out so the true Venusians could return to normal. They really knew the old norm would not be found again since they had volunteered for this assignment in all sincerity, albeit with naiveté.

By the end of the fifth 5200-year period of the second 26,000-year cycle, Venus was in a police state. Crime and insanity were out of control. Distrust and inadequacy had erupted into deep resentment, prejudice, and anger, and an overall sense of failure and worthlessness prevailed. The newcomers had become the planetary lowlife in the eyes of most of the older Venusians. Before the end of the evolutionary cycle, angels and Emissaries of Light were sent to bring understanding to those who would listen. A few did, but most had gone too far into the illusion of darkness, failure, and insanity to recognize truth and spiritual value. Illusionary and dark astral planes had begun to form around the planet, created by negative thoughtforms and fear. When faced with spiritual beauty, purity, and love, the people turned away. They felt shamed by what they perceived as their own contrasting characteristics that they believed these qualities reflected. They forgot their true nature and believed in the problems and illusions they had become immersed in. Their downfall was the development of spiritual ego—the need to change the reality of others to meet their ideals in order to substantiate their own perfection, and attachment to outcome. And still they could not even comprehend that the troubled Virgoan newcomers themselves refused to be helped.

That 26,000-year cycle ended with a near consensus in the Venusian lower group mind that they had failed and deserved to be wiped off the face of the planet. So, as the planetary laws had been established to grant what the majority of the group mind wanted, they got just that. A polar shift took place that was so drastic that the entire planet was thrown out of orbit for three days and nights. Quakes, storms, floods, fires, darkness, and death prevailed, until at the end of the polar shift the entire Venusian civilization had been destroyed.

Venus has never since been inhabited by physical beings. Angels and other Light Beings dwell there on the higher planes to heal the planet and hold the vision and memory of her true purpose and essential nature. The planet itself is still undergoing healing from the civilizations that existed there, reflecting to Earth both polarities: arrogance and humility; fear and love; hatred of what is perceived as ugly and appreciation of the true inner Beauty; unworthiness and shame as well as self-love and nurturing; obsession with pride of achievement and perfectionism as well as natural grace and artistic flow; female self-centeredness and pride as well as the true archetype of the Goddess.

At this time, Venus holds a higher vibrational pull toward love and spiritual beauty than does Earth. In other words, Venus as a planet has been healed and re-evolved far enough to assist Earth and her people in their evolution, especially through learning from Venusian mistakes and misunderstandings. The Venusian Ascended Masters are also still available to guide and assist Earth beings with true Venusian love, awareness of inner beauty, the divine feminine archetype, and artistic creation as a means of joyful self-expression.

I, Amorah, offer this poem in the spirit of healing and awakening of the true Venusian archetype.

SPELLBOUND

Beauty,
what have I known of you
in my endless struggles for
perfection?
Struggles to fit in?
To please and be pleased?
I have taken your name
in vain.
Cried for you in the darkness
of illusion,
in the illusion of my own darkness.
In my narrow-minded,
new-moon way
of not seeing,
I have looked past you
and thought
you were not there.
As a child,
I saw your reflection,
though briefly, at times,
in my mother's eyes.
But when I responded,
it turned into sadness,
and hid behind a veil
of distant longing
that seemed to say,
"Oh child, if you only knew."
I never knew what.
But I knew that when
I caught a glimpse
of you
in my mother's eyes,
that she would hide you
quickly again

as if some shameful secret
had been revealed.
And yet I knew you lived
inside her still.
Somewhere.
If only I could catch her
off guard.

And then I learned
that when you live
inside a flower,
or a sunset,
or a doll,
or a new dress,
that it was okay
to look at you
directly,
and even to speak
of you.
And no one was embarrassed,
or turned away,
or blushed
self-consciously
like when I saw the inside
Beauty.
And so I learned:
to know Beauty
is to hide
behind clothes,
makeup,
new hair styles,
perfect bodies.
And soon I found
I'd forgotten you
altogether:
your purity,
innocence,
naturalness,
and ease.

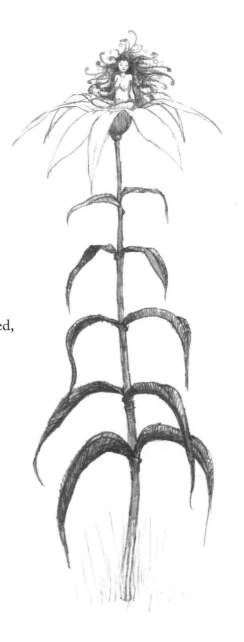

I began to try
and fit in.

In school,
I learned that Beauty
is exclusive,
that it is donned
by a chosen few
with perfect bodies,
perfect faces,
perfect clothes,
perfect hair.
And that the rest of us
were less valuable,
dispensable.
Our greatest service
was to provide
a contrast:
contrast that helped
Beauty to shine
brighter compared
to those less fortunate ones.
So some of us
performed more,
studied harder,
and tried to please.
Some just simply gave up.

Beauty,
you became
an ugly word
that kept company
with shame
and loneliness
in dark corners
of narrow minds.

For years I learned
to compensate,

to give more,
to work harder,
to listen and care,
to be more clever,
appreciate all
the beautiful things—
outside myself.
I did not expect
to be happy—
just to survive
was enough.
Until one day
a strange,
provocative
powerful voice said,
"You deserve to be
the best that you can be.
Your very existence
is Beauty.
You are that
which you seek."
As if a veil were lifted,
the trees,
and hills,
and fields
all sprang to life
as if a still-life
watercolor
became animated.
Each leaf,
and every blade
of grass,
and even the tiniest
dirt particles
were living and glowing
Essences of
wonder and awe
and Beauty.

Unashamedly
they glowed:
radiating
light as pure,
and innocent,
and present
as that in my mother's eyes
when I
was young.
Each was whole.
Each knowing,
each being
the Essence
of self
unveiled.

And how can we compare
a grain of sand
to a wildflower,
or a scrub brush
to an oak.
And yet I saw them all
held in the eyes
of God,
and in the heart
of the Goddess
as equals:

Beauty
   Beloved
      Beheld
         of
Beauty
   and
      Spellbound.

Tears of remembrance
washed away years
of forgetting,

as my heart embraced
All That Is
through my eyes.
Windows of my soul
cleansed in tears
of love
and grace
as I felt
and knew
that I, too,
was seen and held
in the eyes
of God,
in the heart
of the Goddess
as equal:

Beauty
   Beloved
      Beheld
         of
            Beauty.

And after a time
another came:
a Beloved
who through years
of denying,
forgetting his own
Essential self—
not being truly seen
by others—
had a veil
of distant sadness
and forgotten worth
that hid
the best he could be.
And still,

I saw him.
I recognized him
behind the veils.   Beauty
And I knew that you,   Beloved
Beauty,   Beholds
were not lost.   Beauty
With time we learned   and is
that Beauty   Spellbound.
hidden in illusion
is not lost.
And when our eyes met
with open hearts,
willing to be seen,
the veils were lifted,
and

Beauty
    Beloved
        Beheld
            Beauty
                and was
                    Spellbound.

Beauty,
I have only begun
to know you
as I cease
my endless struggles
for perfection,
struggles to fit in,
to please
and be pleased,
and look into
my own eyes,
and the eyes
of my Beloved;
and then:

PART II

PART II
COLONIZATION OF MARS

Ra continues to unveil the history of the planets in our solar ring:

Establishment of Martian Culture—Year 0

When Venus was cleared of its population, the Venusians were put into protective cocoons and sent to Sirius for healing and preparation for their next evolutionary choice. By that time, Mars had been inhabited for five thousand years. At first, the new Martian colony consisted exclusively of the outcast rebels from the Venusian city of the mutants.

The original Martian colonists were very adamant about their desire to prove themselves better than those who had brought about their removal from Venus. They were extremely angry at what they perceived as gross injustice and unfairness on the home planet, and they took no responsibility at all for contributing to their own demise. Their focus was on never allowing anyone else to tell them what to do, and on proving that they could create a better world than the one from whence they had come.

Mars was a virtual Garden of Eden when the colonists first arrived—lush with vegetation and artesian springs. There were also lakes filled with strange water that seemed to resist penetration instead of clinging to and soaking the bodies of those who entered. These lakes were mercury-like in their consistency and obviously not for drinking or bathing, so the Martians stayed away from the strange-liquid pools and utilized only the artesian springs, which were more than adequate.

From the beginning, the need to work together was clear, and so the first colonists went about creating shelters, sleeping places, simple furniture, and food-storage areas. There was always a certain amount of bickering among them about such things as: which type of structure should be built for what purpose; who had eaten more of the food; or which man had sexual rights to the woman of his choice. Women were second-class citizens from the beginning since brute strength and intimidation were more valued by these people than the gentler arts. The men did the "important" work—that which required skill and thinking—while the women performed "menial" tasks such as gathering and preparation of food, making clothing and blankets, and being sexually available to the men upon demand.

When the women began to add artistic touches to their homes and crafts, they were punished and chastised. Subconsciously, anything that reminded the men of the Venusian artistic way of life brought up resentment and anger, although the men justified their feelings by insisting that the artistic touches were a waste of time. None of the Martians were conscious of the fact that their oppression of women was creating a society based on "better than and less than," just like the one they had left behind on Venus. The women were simply considered less valuable, and to exist for the men's convenience; it was that simple.

Bitterness, shame, resentment, and revenge grew in the women. When alone, they were scornful of the fact that the men even existed, and spoke with loathing of them. They talked of how stupid and crude the men were, and of how women could do everything much better if given a chance. Of course, this attitude of proving themselves better than each other was common to all the Martians, regardless of gender, due to their history on Venus.

The men laughed at the women's weakness and subservience the way a child might cruelly laugh at an insect that cannot fly because the child has pulled off its wings. Competitive male games were created to test which men were the strongest, or had the largest penises, or could have sex the longest without ejaculating. All of these were public games. There were also wrestling matches, and contests to see who could break the leg bones of others with their bare hands, or carry the heaviest loads for the longest distance. Deeply buried in the men's subconscious minds, however, was a deep sense of shame and inadequacy due to their lack of creativity, beauty, and grace—all feminine characteristics.

Therefore, they continued to deny their shame and inadequacy by oppressing and belittling all that was feminine, artistic, and gentle, while creating new standards only they could live up to.

New Venusians Reincarnate on Mars—Year 250

This basic life style and mindset continued with little protest until children began to be born who were gentler and more effeminate. The Venusians who had chosen to cycle out of lifetimes on Venus at Venusian year 38,200 began to arrive as new babies on Mars at around 250 years of Martian colonization. By then the Martians were a hardened race, patriarchal, unrefined, and extremely willful. These new gentler beings were quite a shock to them.

As children, these boys and girls alike preferred to draw or pick flowers rather than compete or fight. They were more affectionate with their mothers beyond the time of nursing than their ancestors had been. The women were leery and a little afraid for these new children at first, and thus would spank them or punish them in other ways—such as when the young boys became clingy or refused to go with the men for early male training. However, the women were so starved for affection and attention by that time that they soon softened and began to stand up for themselves and their children more. At first, this took place in subtle ways: adding flowers the children had picked to the table; or sewing designs the children liked into their clothes. The men protested in the beginning, but soon let these small changes pass as they had "more important" things with which to concern themselves.

As these small victories continued, some of the women began to refuse to have sex with the men. They had never experienced loving sexuality, so they considered sex, in general, a brutish, violent act with no redeeming virtues. About the same time, many of the young boys began to experiment sexually with one another. The sexual role-modeling of their parents was so horrid that the children were searching for new and more humane ways of relating to one another. The young boys and girls also began to "fall in love" and teach themselves how to "make love" instead of following in their parents' footsteps.

Early on, some of these gentler boys were slain for refusing to learn the male games and ways of treating women. The young girls who screamed in frantic protest against rape by their fathers, or against being used in the sexual contests, were also beaten and/or killed unless they submitted. Women were beaten and often raped when they refused to yield to the men sexually. Yet, the new trends continued. As the new Martians who survived reached adulthood, many of them questioned authority and refused the old ways. They questioned their mothers about why the women had allowed the men to treat them and their children so badly. The women were both ashamed and frightened, and yet found new courage and hope through their rebellious offspring.

As the young adults married and created families, many of them were more loving and sharing with one another. Of course, they were genetically infested with the negative build-up of the original Martians, but their souls and spirits were new and determined. Within three generations of the arrival of these new ones, the sexual aspects of the male competitions were ended. It was still common for many of the men to oppress and even beat their wives, and yet the influx of gentler consciousness was obviously having a steady impact on Martian culture.

Art and music were beginning to be accepted into the Martian way of life, though minimally and without encouragement. Females were beginning to get the idea that they could say "no" to men if they did not wish to marry or have sex with them. Rape and force were not eliminated, but they diminished enough to introduce the first measure of safety Martian women had ever known.

As some of the people began to marry for love, the women got stronger and more confident. Soon rape of another man's wife was punishable by brutal beating or even death, affording at least the married women more freedom. Because of the long history of oppression, hate, resentment, and revenge carried in the DNA, trust was slow in coming. There were many battles of the wills between men and women, with the women accusing the men of being controlling and insensitive. Those men who were genuinely trying to change resented these accusations and yet carried their own repressed ancestral shame and feelings of inadequacy. The rest of the men continued to keep the women under control through intimidation and violence.

As the genetic inheritance was being healed and cleared due to the influx of new souls, repressed feelings began to come to the surface for clearing. Some of the Martians were sensitive enough to realize that these feelings were based on the past and not to be believed in, but most did not understand this. Hurt feelings arose continually due to seemingly unresolvable conflicts, and yet somehow love and sexual magnetism would always draw couples back together. Gay and lesbian couples began to appear, though they found it necessary to remain secretive for several generations.

Pleiadian Emissaries of Light Born—Year 5100

Near the end of the first 5200-year cycle, the Martians were an evolving race with problems and prejudices to work out, but they were slowly doing so. When the first group of Venusian criminals had come to Mars, they had been promised complete noninterference unless assistance from the hierarchies was requested by consensus. The Martians had been very angry because a majority request had succeeded in ousting them from Venus, and they had intended, by adapting consensus rule, to insure that this could never happen to them again. They had been told that at the end of the first 5200-year cycle, the planetary agreements would be reviewed, with the opportunity to make changes in the existing order then. Smaller contingents, in addition to the voice of consensus, would also be heard at that time. The only requirement the guardians from the Pleiades had made of the Martians was that they must show evolution by the end of this time cycle in order to maintain the option for noninterference.

Though the Martians did not consciously remember these agreements after 5200 years had passed, the agreements were part of their collective unconscious. Therefore, it did not seem so strange to them when the changes began. With less than 100 years left of the time cycle, Pleiadian Emissaries of Light began to enter the Martian culture by way of physical birth. Since there were only about 200 Martians at that time, a dozen Pleiadian Masters, three from each of the four Pleiadian Archangelic Tribes of the Light, were enough. Generally, they chose the most evolved and genetically pure couples among the Martian colonists to be their parents. However, two of the Pleiadians chose parents of the original rebel bloodlines. These choices were made for the purpose of creating a new genetic strain, which would include Pleiadian soul- and spirit-encoding for the first time.

These new Pleiadian/Martian/Venusian children were different from the very beginning. They were much more present and "behind their eyes," even as babies. When they began to speak fluently, they spoke of places they remembered from "before they came here." They spoke of great schools where people could go while asleep to learn about the stars, and God consciousness, and about where their own spirits came from originally. They told stories about tall beings made of light who traveled through space as well as time. They talked about how much these Light Beings loved the Martians, and how they wanted them to be joyful and feel good about themselves.

As the Pleiadian children grew older, their stories and teachings became more sophisticated and evolution-based. They even began to tell vaguely about Venus and what had happened there, and the people wept when they heard these stories. The only ones who were not moved were a group of men who had never let go of the old ways when "men were men" and the women "knew their place." This group of men met secretly and planned cunning strategies for regaining control. Many of the Martians, however, received these new teachers openly and began to let their teachings make a difference in their lives.

The incarnate Pleiadians were able to teach the people simple meditation practices like watching their breath, or feeling the energy in the center of their chests, or imagining the sun shining through their bodies. As the Martians did these meditations, they realized they had known very little about themselves. They noticed that when they meditated, thoughts and feelings they had not even been aware of came to the surface and that they could choose to let them go. The meditators felt excited about sharing their experiences and what it would mean in their lives to be more aware of themselves and each other.

At this stage, the gay and lesbian Martians "came out of the closet" and announced their desire to be open about their sexual choices, to not have to hide any more out of fear. The Pleia-dian teachers were very supportive of this opportunity to create more openness and honesty among the people and alleviate preju-dices. In fact, the twelve Martian-born Pleiadians called a meet-ing of all the Martians who wanted to attend and announced their full purpose for being on Mars. The Pleiadians explained to the people that in the past, male/female sexual practices of the group had become extremely distorted from the original intention. Therefore, when the males and females lost respect and trust in one another, the natural outpouring was for both men and women to heal themselves through sexual relationships with the same gender.

The Pleiadian teachers further explained that when a person deeply needs sexual healing and wants to rediscover sexual inno-cence, pleasure, and sacredness, his or her natural tendency is often toward homosexuality. The person has become too damaged to heal sexually with the opposite gender because trust and safety have been destroyed. When the person chooses a same-sex part-ner, two wonderful things can happen. First, in the atmosphere of sameness, the qualities of trust, respect, and safety can be restored. Secondly, as the person receives and gives love to the same gender, he or she begins to appreciate peoples' unique qualities that are gender-specific. As a result, the individual comes to the realization that he or she has those same unique qualities. From there, self-love, self-respect, and self-trust are developed, or reborn, and the person starts to let go of guilt, shame, anger, low self-worth, and victim/victimizer scenarios. The individual realizes, "I am as lov-able and tender and wonderful as my partner is, and I deserve respect, too. I won't ever settle for less than that again. Now I know the value of what I have to offer because I have been receiv-ing it from my partner." At that stage of healing, whether the person continues in homosexual relationships or switches to hetero-sexual ones is simply a matter of choice based on preference, with-out the consideration of healing as the main motivation.

Violence Against Homosexuals–Year 5125

Many of the Martians were startled by these new sexual reve-lations. Some were a little frightened, some curious, others relieved. The angry men who were meeting secretly saw this new perspective as the greatest threat to their control and male supremacy and began to plan a rebellion. Basically, the old patri-archs wanted to intimidate the others back into submission. They participated in a night raid during which they captured a lesbian couple and a gay male couple. The men were dismembered and hung in the central courtyard area, along with the women, whose breasts were cut off. Blood was smeared on the doorways of the two slain couples' homes, and a sign was put in the courtyard say-ing, "We will destroy all deviates. Martian law will be restored."

The three dozen men involved in this massacre and attempt-ed intimidation thought the rest of the people would come to their senses and be easy marks for reindoctrination with the tried-and-true-Martian patriarchal way. They were greatly surprised when the opposite happened.

The rest of the Martian people, except for about four women and two men, saw the violent display as an atrocity and proof that the Pleiadians were right. They formed a plan of passive resis-tance that included people traveling the streets in groups and staying in each other's homes. All of the remaining homosexual couples were taken into the homes of their neighbors and pro-tected. Those who would not allow this to take place were singled out as the obvious violators. Soon the colony was distinctly divid-ed into two parts: the angry patriarchal contingent and the rest of the people who wanted change.

Hierarchical Intervention and the Law of Instant Karma–Year 5125

When it looked like the only outcome would be civil war, the Martian-born Pleiadians called for help from the etheric realms. In broad daylight, a lightship precipitated in the central square area above the colony, and a dozen Light Beings filed out: three golden Ra Beings, three red Ma-at Beings, three blue Ptah Beings, and three green An-Ra Beings. The delegation members first greeted those of their colleagues in Martian bodies and then addressed the people as follows:

"Before your people came to this planet, we agreed to allow you to develop your own way of living together and to remain neutral and noninterfering unless you called on us by consensus. The exception was to take place at the end of your first 5200-year solar cycle, at which time you would have to show evolution in order to remain in total sovereignty. That time cycle is nearing an end, and some of you still confuse sovereignty with the right to control others and take away their free will.

"All parts of your society now have a right to speak their truth to us and to one another, the right to be heard without harm. From now until the end of this solar cycle, we will assist you in determining the guidelines for the next time cycle, which begins in seventy-five years. We will allow no violence or harm to come to any of you during this time of review and decision making. We will return in fifty years to meet with all of you at the same time, and together we will determine the future agreements. Those who would take away the free will of others or destroy them, come forward now."

In an altered state, brought on by the high-frequency light bodies and merkabah lightship before them, the patriarchs filed out from behind doors and buildings and came to the front of the crowd. The Pleiadian spokesperson said to them, "You have violated the sovereignty and free will of your brothers and sisters here among you. You have killed for power, prejudice, and greed. Yet because this planet is still under consensus rule, you cannot be removed, and we would not punish you even if we could. You have a right to learn and grow here.

"You must evolve. That is what you agreed to do before you, in the bodies of your most ancient ancestors, came here. At this time, the rest of the inhabitants of this planet are evolving and learning from the past. Unless *you* evolve and learn from the past within the remaining seventy-five years, you will be subject to the decisions made by those who are evolving. These are the terms you chose, and we are here to see that these terms are carried out.

"Until we return fifty years from now, you yourselves will

immediately experience whatever you would inflict upon another. If you raise your hand to strike another, the force of your own hand will knock you down. If you seek to kill someone, your own hand will turn on you and kill your body instead. In turn, if you are kind and generous, you will be responded to with kindness and generosity. By these terms, you may remain here as part of the colony.

"You have another option. You may leave the colony altogether and start your own colony elsewhere on the planet. All those who willingly go may go. None may be forced. If you choose this option, you must return in fifty years for the planetwide meeting with us. You will know the timing when a giant red comet moves across the sky, lighting the planet like a red sun for about five minutes. We will arrive again within one full cycle of each of your two moons after the appearance of the comet. What do you choose?"

Without exception, the patriarchal group chose to leave. Although they might not have been able to put it into words, they did not trust their self-control enough to withstand the instant-karma alternative. They knew they must digest all of this and have time to understand and choose—away from the pressure to be nonharmful. The group was told of an area approximately a two-week walk from the colony, and they departed for it at once.

The remaining colonists were deeply relieved and grateful for their first experience of true safety. For the next fifty years, the members of the original colony worked with the Pleiadian-Martians, and they learned and grew rapidly. They were taught how to heal with signature plants, not only physically but emotionally and psychologically. They learned how certain flowers have the ability to impart sublime emotional states to people. This led them to revere plants more than they had ever imagined.

The main teaching was about their divine purpose and right use of sexual energy. The Martians were taken beyond the experience of passion and orgasm by learning about connecting with each other's souls when making love. By learning the most basic tantra, the people opened to experiences of new, more blissful, and ecstatic states. They shared eye contact with one another, allowing soul blending to take place, and then made love from that place of connection, tenderness, and deep caring. At times,

deep emotional pain would release during or after these tantric experiences, bringing the people to more inner peace.

Conscious spiritual birthing of children was introduced, and this new practice accelerated the genetic healing even more. By the end of the fifty years, the Martians remaining in the original colony were eager for more spiritual understanding and practice. They wanted to understand soul and spirit and to experience the sacred purpose of all things. Sexual exploration was still the major avenue of growth, healing, and pleasure, as it needed to be at that time.

In the meantime, the patriarchal group had left feeling confused, frightened, ashamed, and yet still very self-righteous and angry. They were still wallowing in the old ideas of unfairness and of their need for control. These men deeply wanted to take out their hostilities and resentment on others. However, attempts were made to curb these tendencies since the patriarchs believed they had no choice.

When they first arrived at their new homes, the patriarchs created makeshift shelters. Food was plentiful, though with only four women among them, the men soon had to begin sharing in the "menial tasks." The women agreed to each have two husbands, but *only* two, which left many of the men unmated. Everyone agreed, however.

The men found that hard physical work helped move their emotionally violent energies better than anything else. Much of their time was therefore occupied with improving housing and building furniture, and with such activities as wrestling, weight lifting, and distance weight-carrying. They really did not know what they wanted that was still possible for them to have, and when they had idle time the men tended to feel at a loss with themselves. The women were happier because at least the physical violence had stopped. The men and women still did not open to one another intimately, however. Feelings were hidden from each other, and sulking was done privately; the men disappeared for hours, even days at a time. When they returned, all that was ever said was that they had needed time to think.

At the end of the fifty years, all that could be agreed upon was that they needed to understand what was expected of them and how to achieve it. The patriarchs contained a confused mixture of feelings—ignorance, anger, vulnerability, fear, and shame—but hid these feelings under gruff exteriors, always using injustice as the reason for their gruffness and anger. Their basic attitudes were: "How can these space people expect us to change when we don't know what they are talking about? It is unfair of them. Those space people talk about free will, but we aren't being allowed to be how we want to be, which is the old way. What is all this double-talk anyway?" And with those attitudes masking their vulnerability and fear, the small band returned to the original colony for the fifty-year meeting.

Clean, comfortable quarters and wonderful foods awaited the patriarchs when they arrived at the colony for the meeting with the Pleiadians. The colonists were friendly, curious, and gracious with the returning ones, and yet the patriarchs did not know how to receive such treatment. They were as polite as they awkwardly knew how to be, but also distant by virtue of their cultural and spiritual differences.

When the Pleiadian lightship returned, the gathering began. Everyone, even individuals with personal questions or concerns, was heard. All were given equal respect and attention. Even the patriarchs, as they huffed out their complaints and confusion about free will and justice, were honored and appreciated for their presence and candidness.

At the end of the ten-day gathering, the meetings were adjourned for one day while the Pleiadians and the higher collective consciousness, which was forming, conferred. The unanimous, or mostly unanimous, conclusions were: (1) the Martians wanted some kind of guidance system or rulership that would teach them how to be sovereign without taking away the rights of others; (2) all of the inhabitants wanted forgiveness and release from the past, a rebirth of sorts; (3) violence for the sake of control was not okay, but for self-defense it was acceptable; (4) women had the right to leave violent husbands and be sheltered by the community, and the community had a right by consensus to extradite any violent person; (5) consensus by all but one person was acceptable; (6) all Venusians who wanted to come to Mars to reunite with their ancestors were welcome; (7) their greatest karma on Mars, and before on Venus, was a result of prejudice; therefore, their need to evolve in that area was a priority.

There were other concerns that the Pleiadians and higher collective consciousness also agreed must be addressed. These were: (1) the need for spiritual focus and sacredness without dogma; (2) the need to learn appreciation for other people, plants, water, and all of creation beyond how they serve the individuals' needs; (3) the need to understand right from wrong for reasons other than fear of punishment or being without choice; (4) the need for people to be able to measure their own evolution by how they feel about themselves—by having a conscience; (5) the need for individuals and groups to connect with higher beings for spiritual attunement and communion without interfering with the growth of others.

These changes that made to the Martian culture as a result of these meetings:

1. Spiritual temples with priests and priestesses—the original twelve Pleiadians and their offspring—were established. Attendance and study at these temples was strictly voluntary.

2. These priests and priestesses would settle all social disputes and make rulings on individual cases of conflict as they arose. They would be available for consultations on spiritual and social matters

upon request. This was the extent of rulership at that time.

3. Nonviolence was made the first absolute law, with violence being punishable by extradition.

4. "Consensus minus one" became the guideline for decision making and calling on divine intervention from the Pleiadian Emissaries of Light.

5. Evolution was an agreed-upon individual and group responsibility.

6. Deep healing was needed. A great fire ceremony was held for the purpose of purification and forgiveness, with all Martians in attendance. The Pleiadians facilitated the ritual.

7. The priests and priestesses could, by consensus, call upon the Pleiadians for intervention if things ever got out of hand.

8. The Pleiadians would send delegates at the end of the next 5200-year cycle to monitor progress and make any agreed-upon changes at that time.

As far as the rest of the conclusions were concerned, the Pleiadians simply spoke to the people, explaining each area of concern, whether it was the need to eliminate prejudice or the development of conscience. All remaining areas were discussed, and the Martians were told that they could individually or collectively seek guidance and assistance with these issues at any time from the priests and priestesses and through their own higher consciousnesses as they began to develop that communication.

After a few days of further planning and working with the Martian-born Pleiadians, the Pleiadian ships and Light Beings left, with the advisory that pole shifts would be occurring near the end of the twenty-five years remaining of the cycle. This always happened then and still happens at the end of a cycle due to repositioning of the planet in its orbit around the Sun. The pole shifts happened in three stages, and were experienced on Mars as quakes, tremors, and changes in the day/night cycles. Longer periods of daylight and shorter nights were the major long-lasting changes. Of course, these shifts created temperature increases, less rain, and changes in the water tables, though minor at first.

Evolution and Healing Ensue—Years 5200 to 10,400

Progress was steady and enthusiasm high for most of the entire 5200-year cycle. Isolated experiences of violence were mostly responded to with nonviolence. Several people were banned from the colony over the centuries, and yet there were only two major incidents during that time. One involved a father killing a small child in a fit of anger when the child was ill and would not stop crying. The man lost his patience and shook the child so hard he broke its neck. It was agreed that he would not be banned if he would admit himself to the temples for healing for as long as the priests and priestesses deemed necessary. He agreed and set a new precedent for asking for emotional help. Many others who had short-fused tempers began to go the temples for assistance and achieved amazing results.

The other incident was more traumatic. A homosexual man was raped and killed by six very homophobic men who collectively plotted against him. Prior to the attack on him, the gay man had been teasing the men by touching them and making sexual gestures and comments. He was pushing the men for the pure amusement of seeing them get angry and not be able to act on it. The men intended to anally rape him and "teach him a lesson he wouldn't forget." During the process, the man threatened to have them banned, saying the rape was an act of violence, not sex. The angry men panicked, strangled him to death, and hid his body.

When the slain man was discovered a few days later, it was still obvious from the blood and semen what had happened to him. An investigation ensued, during which one of the six men, who had raped him but had not strangled him, confessed. He was beside himself with grief and guilt about what had happened, and wanted justice to be served against himself and his fellow conspirators. A group meeting, like a trial, was held, during which all of the men were banned from the community except the one who had confessed. He was allowed to opt for healing time in the temples, to which he readily agreed.

The other five left, but angrily sneaked back into the colony a few nights later to seek revenge against their betrayer. In the process of protecting the man in the temples against the others, the priests and priestesses killed all five men. The Martian colony agreed that this case came under the rule of self-defense, or defense of another, and that no one was to be blamed. Yet, it had a deep wounding effect on the people. The fact that it took place on the temple grounds made it worse for them.

The Martian citizens utilized the tragedy as an opportunity to reexamine their overall evolutionary progress and review the treatises from the Pleiadians. As they read the part about their main karma being caused by prejudice, they decided collectively to unite as a group and take responsibility for ending that karma once and for all. They gathered with the priests and priestesses to ask for help and advice. A program was mutually agreed upon, which consisted of meditation, weekly sharing between diverse groups, and yearly gatherings of all colonists to discuss progress and plan their next steps. The entire colony felt the sting of shame and fear from the incident, and it moved them to take action and follow through with their commitment to end prejudice. A few people chose not to participate, saying they could take care of the problem on their own; but they secretly still believed in the inferiority of homosexuals. By this time in Martian history, homosexuality was more often a matter of preference than of choice made to heal damage; and this incited more hostility by those who were still prejudiced, even though they were consciously unaware of the subtle change.

By the end of the second 5200-year cycle, peace prevailed. The temples were the center of all social and spiritual activities; yet the people had grown so dependent on the temples, priests, and priestesses to keep them in line that self-trust was still not healed. The Martians agreed unanimously that they needed more time before they would be ready for true sovereignty, not realizing the motivation behind this decision was their deeply buried shame, inadequacy, and lack of self-trust and trust in others. Their request to maintain Pleiadian-ruled temples was honored. The Pleiadians and members of the temples recognized that the Martians were finally at a place in their evolution to deal directly with the original cause of their history of violence, patriarchal physical power, and prejudice: the buried shame and inadequacy of being lower-class citizens on Venus, being discriminated against, becoming criminals, and being outcasts from their home planet. They were beyond their angry obsession with injustice and unfairness, and had begun to understand about responsibility for creating their own reality; it was time for the next history lesson.

At the end of the 5200-year cycle, the Pleiadian Emissaries of Light arrived again on Mars, heard all of the individual and group concerns, reestablished the existing agreements, and told the Martians their complete ancestral history. Stories were shared about the class divisions and prejudices that had made their ancestors the lowest-class members of Venusian society. Any lack of physical beauty or of musical and artistic skill had made them automatically "less than" in that culture, and left them to serve the upper classes and do the "menial tasks." Though they had originally tried to be heard, they had failed, and eventually had become thieves and violent criminals. Banned from the original colony, they had traveled to the distant hills and discovered another group of outcasts, the "ugly ones," who were products of genetic mutation due to incest. The criminals had been lovingly and whole-heartedly welcomed, but after a time, their own feelings of inferiority had led them to attempt domination over the "ugly ones." Their prejudice and hatred toward these loving colonists had led to war, and eventually to the criminals being banned from the planet by majority agreement among the "ugly ones."

As the story was told to them in detail, the Martians fell into a deep hush. They *knew* this story was their true karmic history and that they were at a turning point. For a few days, deep remorse and quiet were prevalent among the people. Then the meeting with the Pleiadians was reconvened and the Martians were told what was needed at that time. Everyone agreed that a year of forgiveness and rebirthing was essential, and the Pleiadians agreed to dwell among them and assist in this process. There were purification ceremonies by fire, by water, by air, and by going underground into kiva-like chambers for several days at a time. Simple rituals were taught and performed. For example, the people would go to a hilltop, remove all clothing, and ask the wind to blow through them, taking with it all the remnants of past shame and self-reproach. In fire ceremonies, the people would walk or dance around the fire and ask the flames to purge them of anger and hatred and give them the courage to become their true selves again. They were taught to do firewalks to strengthen their self-confidence and belief in mind-over-matter. Purifications were done in water while naked, during which the participants asked the waters for rebirth and genetic healing from all past misconceptions and resentful feelings. In the underground

kivas, the participants would ask to face their deepest, darkest, hidden places inside so these shadows could be identified, understood, forgiven, and taken into the sun, air, water, and fire for purification.

The people were humbled, purified, and renewed during this year and learned much about themselves and their true natures. Collectively, they requested assistance from the Pleiadians for learning to love and accept themselves and others unconditionally, without judgment or prejudice of any kind. The Martians asked that an opportunity be given to them to practice nonprejudice. The Pleiadians agreed that this was appropriate, but that the people of Mars first needed another 200 years to continue their race's evolution. At the end of these 200 years, a group of new beings would be sent to Mars to reunite with their ancestral family.

These new beings would be the final group of Venusians who had opted to end their incarnations on Venus because of belief in their failure to heal the insanity among those they had chosen to help. They needed to reincarnate and heal the past. The Virgoan-Venusians they believed they had failed were to come to Mars as well. The older Venusian group would consist of many of the same beings who had made the Martians into lower-class citizens initially, plus a few of those who later banned them from the planet altogether. Those to be reincarnated would be only a small portion of the Venusian population at its peak. Many had already ascended, become enlightened, or chosen other evolutionary options. The Martians were eager to make amends with these old family members, fully aware of their part in cocreating the separation in the first place. Though clearly told what to expect, the Martians remained a little over-optimistic and naive about what would truly take place when these Venusians began to arrive.

During the 200 years prior to the arrival of the first Venusian reincarnates, Martian spirituality, self-esteem, and peace abounded like never before. Prejudices truly seemed to be behind them, though still secretly harbored by a few. Angry feelings were dealt with in nonviolent and appropriate ways, though some people hid anger, feeling justified or shamed. The people were learning to deeply appreciate life and one another beyond what they stood to gain. Evolution was accelerated, and all aspects of their culture flourished as a result.

Final Venusians Reincarnate on Mars–Year 10,600

Before the first influx of Venusian ancestors were reborn on Mars, the Venusians were brought onto a Pleiadian lightship, still as etheric beings, to observe Martian culture without being seen. They were reminded of the evolutionary history between the groups and prepared as best they could be for the reunion.

Then the births began on Mars—about fifty of them over a twenty-year period. The integration was mostly gracious at first, with the Martian awareness of conscious birthing. The children responded a little slowly, and were sleepier than most Martian babies. This was attributed to the healing and transmutation that were accelerated once the Venusians were in bodies again. Their self-condemnation, which had brought about the end of third-dimensional life on Venus, had damaged their soul/spirit relationship; they had been healed as much as possible etherically, and the rest would have to happen through life experience in physical bodies.

The mothers found themselves more impatient and irritable with these children. They felt ashamed about this until the priests and priestesses explained that the babies were refusing to receive their love and nurturing fully. The parents were instructed to tell the little ones, while feeding and holding them, that the babies deserved love and belonged there. The mothers followed this advice, but still found the babies to be responsive mostly to survival needs and not to loving and personal touch. In other words, the babies did not allow deep soul-bonding with the mothers due to their soul damage with which they had been born.

As the babies began to reach the normal age of talking and walking, their bodies remained fairly limp, and they were unmotivated to speak or move around. When speech and movement finally happened among the infants, it came nearly a year later than for the other, more "normal," Martian babies. They were awkward in the beginning, and spoke only when necessary to get their needs met. On Earth today this would be like having slightly retarded children born to families of average-to-high IQs. The Martians grew sympathetic to these new ones, finding that pity was better than impatience and anger. Through this choice they unknowingly encouraged these new ones to feel "less than," and a "poor little thing" attitude prevailed among them.

As the children grew older, they tended to be more introverted than "normal" children. Prone to sudden, unprovoked outbursts of crying and temper tantrums, the tots accused their parents of hating them and wishing they were dead. Because these tendencies were prevalent in so many of the new children, the mothers compared stories and knew that the problem lay with the children and not with themselves. So a delegation of mothers and fathers went to the temples to ask for help and understanding. They were reminded that these beings had undergone deep emotional trauma, self-condemnation, and even insanity in their last incarnations on Venus. These scars were still imprinted on their souls and would take time and patience to heal.

The priests and priestesses suggested that, as the children became old enough to understand simple spiritual concepts, a school be set up for them on the temple grounds. It would be taught by the priests and priestesses, with parents assisting in rotating shifts. This plan brought great hope and reassurance to the people, and as the children reached early puberty they were enrolled in the schools.

In the beginning, the spiritual teachers decided to work with the children through storytelling and tactile craft projects. Simple, lighthearted stories were told in order to engage the children's attention. Then, gradually, modified versions of the history of Venus were added, introducing principles and learning along the way. Though the teachers told the stories as myths with morals, the curiosity of the children began to awaken. More creativity became apparent in their craft projects, and some of the children even began to initiate singing and simple musical sounds on instruments. The greatest puzzle was why the young ones continued to have "fits" suddenly and seemingly without cause.

By this time, the Pleiadians who had been born on Mars had birthed enough children with Pleiadian-Martian genetics to staff the temples. They had left the planet physically, and served only as etheric guides and teachers. Those who were now the priests and priestesses had not come to full mastery and still lacked the understanding and experience to interpret and heal all problems. This lack caused them to be unaware of the deeper root of the children's behavioral problems: the children still carried the negativity and terror they had taken on from the insane ones they had failed to heal on Venus, and it was literally eating away at their souls.

Progress continued, however slowly, and the school children became more and more active in the community as time went by. Their outbursts came to be expected and were treated like normal parts of daily affairs. One of the things the children did that surprised the people was playfully act out violent scenes for the pure amusement of it. Violence had not existed in Martian culture for so long it seemed foreign to the people. They spoke to the children about nonviolence, but the children responded by continuing the dramas and making replies like, "We have to kill the bad guys before they kill us," or "Look at the monsters, we have to get them." They awakened screaming after terrible nightmares and had difficulty being convinced the dreams were not real.

Suicides and Violence Among New Reincarnates– Year 10,620

The first major tragedy occurred when the oldest Venusian children were between sixteen and twenty years old. One of the more troubled children committed suicide by stabbing herself. All of the parents gathered together again, as this incident incited fear in them for the safety of their own children. Many of them confessed to feeling that they had bitten off more than they could chew. The suicide was soon followed by another and another, until within six months, six children had killed themselves, and others were violently acting out more and more. It all seemed totally unpredictable and uncontrollable. One eighteen-year-old boy was found beating his older sister to death while screaming, "Murderer, you murderer," at her. Before the girl died she was able to tell the people that the boy had "gone crazy" after she refused to have sex with him.

When the parents went to the temples for help, the priests and priestesses could only determine that the problem had to do with the insanity that had happened on Venus, but they knew no more. They unanimously decided to call for intervention from the Pleiadian Higher Council, and did so at once. The Higher Council members found it necessary to appear physically to the spiritual leaders since they were unable to understand through guidance and dreams. When the Pleiadians arrived and conferred with the people, it was determined that the only solution was to remove the children's unconscious memories of what had happened to them before. The memory patterns would gradually be reintroduced as these damaged young ones grew stronger through positive life experiences. The Pleiadians also agreed to leave an emissary at the temple for further consultations.

The children were gathered together at the sacred baths on the temple grounds, where at a ceremony led by the Pleiadians and certain priests and priestesses, the children's past-life memories were removed from their soul matrices and unconscious. The children experienced a few days of nausea, vomiting, and other flu-like symptoms as their bodies purged the toxicity that had been created by the negative energies. They were kept and attended to in the temples during that time, then brought home when they regained their strength.

Most of the young ones felt like they were awakening from a bad dream and realizing it was not real. They instantly became more affectionate—even clingy and more needy of attention for a while—until they adjusted to their new way of being. Amnesia relative to the details of their current lives also resulted, and their perception was that they had been ill and were better now.

Without exception, they behaved as if they were younger than before, and it took time for them to gain confidence and a sense of belonging. Even as they grew older, they remained more innocent and childlike than the others, as well as less capable of dealing with anything out of the ordinary.

Partial Soul Memories Restored–Year 10,875

For several generations, these Venusian arrivals continued to integrate into the community, gain trust in their surroundings, friends, and families, and slowly get stronger. Then the Pleiadians decided that it was time to reintroduce controlled amounts of memory in the newborns, and give them a chance to heal and evolve another step. These infants were more prone to crying fits and bad dreams, but not to the same extreme as before. Also, the people had kept abreast of the Venusians' growth and behavioral patterns and were prepared to deal with the reintroduction of karmic energies. By the time the children were three years old, most of them had received enough love and understanding, and had cleared enough emotionally, to blend in with the rest of the children. This was a welcomed and celebrated victory. When that generation produced children who also remained healthy and normal, the following generation was given a next level of karma to transmute.

This time the transmutation took a little longer since the karma more directly involved the Venusians' own sense of failure and shame, not the energies they had taken on from the Virgoan insane ones. The Virgoan-Venusian-Martian reincarnates still carried much of their distrust of others as well as their deep sense of rejection and alienation. These children desperately clung to their mothers in fear of rejection, and then cycled into being lethargic and nonresponsive. The mothers, once again, were prepared for unusual behaviors and patterns, and remained consistent and lovingly accepting of the children.

As the children became social with one another around age two, competition, possessiveness, and fighting were apparent. They seemed to constantly be trying to prove each other wrong. The children who were reincarnates of the original Martians did not relate to these children at first, but they soon were drawn into playing "war games." Schools for the very young were established in the temples at which the children were told stories with moral lessons, learned to do crafts, and did something akin to drama therapy, in which they acted out their feelings. This was an attempt to get them to see that their feelings were not based on present circumstances and to become more detached from them. Even though the therapy worked to some extent, the children never fully trusted anyone, so the process could only go so far

No matter how much they were loved, accepted, and trusted, the children always seemed to be waiting for the adults to reject them and punish them. This was, of course, because they had rejected and punished themselves so severely and were now being given the challenge of healing those wounds.

Three generations brought only minor changes in these trust issues, and the people became concerned. The parents of these children grew weary and lost patience, which the children were masters at sensing; and so the children pushed them even harder. At this point in their evolution, the children began to physically harm themselves, cutting, burning their bodies, refusing food, and banging their heads against walls and floors, always saying they were punishing themselves because they were bad. There was never an explanation for why they thought themselves to be bad; they just were.

Though the parents did their best to remain loving and calm, this last development succeeded in pushing some of them beyond their limits. They began restraining the children who hurt themselves, taking away their favorite privileges, and promising to force feed them if necessary. Psychologically this gave the children exactly what they wanted: proof that the parents were not trustworthy and really did not love them. These children believed themselves to be untrustworthy and unlovable, so that was their natural conclusion.

With feelings of futility and failure, the parents brought the children to the temples to be kept, and hopefully healed. The parents had adopted exactly the same attitudes as their children. They understood this, because they were parents, but felt as if they were not able to love the children enough, or be patient enough. And they felt shame, failure, and remorse about this.

The priests and priestesses had little more luck with the children, even with the help of the Pleiadians. These children would have to grow up enough to understand more sophisticated karmic and spiritual teachings and be willing to let the teachings make a difference. Storytelling continued to be the best form of teaching in the meantime, though it seemed to bring only minor occasional changes.

As the children reached puberty, they were introduced to beginning-level tantric teachings and psychological concepts. The combination seemed to loosen their resistance enough to make them less volatile, though they were still very skeptical and distrusting. They had proven that the adults could only take so much, then would reject them and leave them, and that was all they had needed to justify their deep hurt feelings.

Finally, as they grew older, the former Venusians were told exactly where they had come from, what had happened there, and what their history on Mars had been thus far. The experience of hearing about their own history was startling to them, and yet they knew it was all true. They began to realize that the only chance they had to prevent their history from repeating itself was to choose to trust the priests and priestesses, and to sincerely try to change their own attitudes. So they attempted to do so.

What seemed like a great victory for a while deteriorated into chaos as these youths grew older and reentered the community, married, and began their own families. Fighting that led to physical abuse of the women and children once again was a major problem. The men blamed the women for everything that went wrong, scorned them for being emotionally weak, and demanded their obedience in the name of proving loyalty and trustworthiness. The women often fell right into the role of feeling not good enough and ashamed, so the problem escalated. Soon children were seen with black eyes and bruised bodies just like their mothers, and, because the mothers asked for noninterference from the community, the problem escalated even more.

Segregation Results—Year 13,000

The people who had been exclusively nonviolent for so long became frightened and resentful of what was infiltrating their culture. Complaints were made to the priests and priestesses, who upheld the free will of the people, saying that as long as the women and children refused help, they could not interfere. The two distinct segments of the population became more and more segregated, and were, by this time, nearly equal in size, with over 200 people in each group. That 5200-year cycle was only halfway through, so there was nothing obvious that could be done.

The spiritual leaders asked for help from the Higher Council and were told that the only thing they could do at that time was recommend that the two groups live in geographically different locations, or else hang in there and try to work it out. The people gave the process a little more time until the troubled ones began to demand equal rulership with the priests and priestesses. These violent and troubled ones wanted another patriarchy and were rapidly becoming an extremely competitive people, trying hard to prove their worth. They had really deemed themselves unworthy, but of course, it was easier to point the finger at others as the source of their problems instead of looking within themselves. They accused the original Martians of hating them and discriminating against them, and said they were only responding to the pressure to conform and the dictatorship of the temples. These accusations were totally out of proportion to what was really happening, but the prejudice against these newcomers was growing rapidly, originating in fear and expanding from there.

The original Martians longed for their former way of life, and yet felt powerless and guilty for wanting to turn away from their friends who were so obviously in need. The option of separating into two communities was looking better all the time, so the original community members called an all-inclusive meeting and suggested just that. The newer Martians grabbed at the opportunity to throw insults and accusations at their predecessors, who tried to remain calm and tactful. After a while the meeting erupted into total chaos. Tempers ran hot and there were a few casualties.

Broken noses, cuts, and bruises were plentiful, and two people were injured so badly they had to be carried to beds and cared for until they recovered. The worst casualty was a small boy who was trampled under the bodies of two men fighting and smothered to death.

Two days later, the newest Martians began a migration toward the area where the former patriarchal group had lived. This area was still known to the people, so they hoped to discover some facilities still standing. However, the area was in ruins. It was not even recognizable as a former colony, except for a few cooking utensils under a rock overhang. But the common interests and violent tendencies of the new migrators and the ancient Martians created a strange bond to the land where the ancestors had lived; therefore, the people decided to stay there.

Shelter, food, and other basic requirements took precedence, as in all new colonies, and occupied their time and focus for the first few years. Their numbers increased as more of their former Venusian community members were born into their families. Even some of the original Martian patriarchal beings decided to reincarnate with them, so they grew to a population of nearly 500 people within the first fifty years.

Invention of Weapons–Year 13,050

Once the buildings were constructed and other basic community needs were met, they agreed that there was a need for weapons to protect themselves against invasion by the other colony, or any other newcomers to the planet. Something akin to the bow and arrow was developed, as well as slings, knives, and sharp disc-shaped objects that could be hurled. Weaponry practice ranges were built, and contests in physical might and the use of weaponry were created among the men. Unbeknownst to the people, they were acting out the same behaviors and practices as the ancient patriarchs who had lived in the same location long before.

Paranoia and distrust grew proportionately with their focus on war and brute strength. They trusted each other very little, and therefore they constantly found reasons to argue and blame each other for supposed problems. The women argued and competed among themselves. These problems mostly stemmed from "us against them" thinking that created little, if any, space for camaraderie.

The original colony returned to a more peaceful and spiritual existence, yet the fear, guilt, and helplessness born during the times of cohabitation with the violent residents still lingered in their psyches. The people were not as happy as before, though it was difficult to say just what the difference was. They continued learning, growing, and expanding in the areas of art and theater, but they, too, felt a need to improve their physical strength and their ability to defend themselves, if need be.

Invention of weapons became, at first, a minor preoccupation by a few. Then it escalated into a major community project in the original colony, just as it had done in the migrant colony. Weaponry training areas were soon created as well; these were off-limits to all children until they were sixteen. Though the people intended to use these weapons only for the protection of their families and homes, they still had to learn to use them. They were naive enough to believe that they could keep the violent focus out of the minds and attitudes of the young, to build character in them, before introducing them to self-defense. This worked at first, but after a couple of generations, the young children who had never seen weapons began to act out fighting during their play time. Violence was creeping deeply and quickly into their psyches, as demonstrated by this new, untaught behavior in the children.

Walls were built around the community, making it similar to a fort; even moats were created outside the walls to make the colony more difficult to enter. Of course, the people were fencing themselves in as well, but that was not considered. They still went outside the walls to gather herbs, food, flowers, and other items, but they went out in groups of two or more. They lived as people with an enemy; and the enemy grew stronger and better prepared for war all the time.

Civil War–Year 13,100

About 100 years after the groups separated, the new colony sent a band of spies to check out the old community and find out what they were up to. Much to their surprise, they found a fortressed city surrounded by water. Upon closer inspection, it was discovered that the people of the walled city had weapons similar to their own, and were practicing the use of them daily. The spies went back with this news, which spread quickly, and the people called a colony meeting right away. It was agreed that their neighbors were obviously planning to destroy them and that they should attack first.

Plans for the attack were made within two weeks, and the first Martian army was formed. Their first priorities were to burn the wall and pollute the waters around and in the city to make them unuseable. Teams were created and drilled for each job. Two weeks later, 300 Martian men and youths, with a few women to cook for them and take care of the wounded, left on a mission of war.

Upon arrival at their destination, the soldiers camped just out of sight until nighttime. Then they polluted the water in the moat and that which ran from the hillside into the city with ashes and bitter poisonous herbs. Something similar to creosote was smeared on the walls in enough places to make them burn quickly. Just before dawn, the invaders lit the fires. This way, the people were caught off guard, yet the invaders could see their way into the city and choose the buildings to attack.

Originally the invaders had agreed not to harm the women and children, but when the raid began, the warriors became crazed with killing and slew everyone they found. By nightfall, over half of the original Martians were dead, and the rest were crowded together with their weapons in the temples. The priests and priestesses were at a loss for what to do since the need for self-defense was obvious, so they tended to the children, freeing the women to help the men in any way they could.

By the end of the second night, the entire original colony was devoid of members. Literally every man, woman, and child had been killed except for a handful of young women who had been taken for sex. One of these young women slit the throat of a man who had raped her while he slept; she and the rest of the women were slain the next morning, leaving none of the original Martians alive. The invaders justified the mass slaughter on the grounds that they would have come to the same demise as their victims if they had not struck first. The invaders also rationalized that the women and children would have brought trouble and polluted the minds of their young if they had been left alive. So, in their way of thinking, the new colony triumphed.

When the victors returned home, a great celebration was

held, and plans were made to move the entire colony back to the original site. There were enough artesian springs to supply water until the recently polluted sources could be cleaned up again, and more than enough buildings to house the people. Vegetation was more plentiful, the buildings better built and stronger, and the psychological effect of claiming the city as their own was too appealing to resist.

Migrant Colonists Reclaim the Original City–Year 13,100

Men had stayed behind to burn the bodies and begin cleaning up the polluted waters. Therefore, by the time the victors returned, the city was ready for minor cleanups and habitation. The leaders of the army who had shown the greatest ability during the war set themselves up in the temples, which were converted to army and government-like offices. At first, their only jobs seemed to be to keep the army trained, beginning with young boys, and to oversee the development of weapons. Soon more areas of authority were established. The common people were ordered to supply the needs of the army officers, which enabled the officers to focus exclusively on running the training camps. Jobs were created such as inventory control, weapons design, organization of competitive war games, and collection of goods from the people to support the army. Though there was no one else on Mars at that time, the need for protection and war preparation was considered eminently important.

Within the next century, something similar to gun powder was invented. Mining and forging of metals had become an important industry, as had the invention of new weapons. The remaining Martians, especially the military men, longed for another military challenge. The need to fight in order to feel important and strong, and prove their worth, as well as the psychological need to kill, was in their blood now. Their collective consciousness called out for an enemy to war with, and the enemy came.

Lyran-Orion Invaders Arrive–Year 13,200

There was a group of beings who had originally come to Orion from Lyra, defying the established order in that star system. The Lyrans had enslaved the indigenous Orion Beings many thousands of years previously and become the warring rulers of all of the planets in one Orion solar ring. Orion is one of the star-gates in this galaxy, which is why the Lyrans desired to control it. Mechanistic spacecraft, as opposed to the merkabah lightships used by more spiritually evolved Light Beings, were among their technological creations. They also produced sophisticated weapons capable of massive destruction. The Lyrans had challenged the Light Beings of Orion for control over the entire constellation and all of its solar rings, but they had been outnumbered and unable to defeat the higher intelligence and spiritual superiority of their chosen enemies. Therefore, leaving behind most of the warriors and leaders in the one solar ring of Orion they did control, the Lyrans left Orion in search of more territory and power.

Since Mars was the first inhabitable planet they came to that had a ready-made slave population, they landed there. Your solar ring, in general, appeared to be an easy mark to the Lyrans. They knew that if they were successful in taking it over, they would have control of another galactic gateway, the Sun. After exploring Mars for the best land and water resources, they discovered there was only one part of the planet that was inhabitable at all. (This land was about the size of the present-day state of California.) It took them very little time to discover the Martians, and though the Martians outnumbered them about two to one, the Lyran/Orion Beings were amused by their primitive technology and life style, and they began a plan to capture the city.

The Martians, who had wished for an enemy, got more than they had ever imagined possible. The Lyrans, who were quite strange-looking by Martian standards, landed their ship right outside the city and walked in, dressed in weaponproof clothing and carrying laser weapons. The Martians gazed in shock as their new enemies fired at stone walls and blew them apart. The Martians soon surrendered. A few of the Martians put up some semblance of a fight, but by Lyran standards it was laughable, and the Martians who resisted were killed before they could fire twice.

Everything had happened so rapidly that the Martians scarcely knew what had hit them. One morning they got up feeling like mighty warriors as usual; by afternoon they had been turned into whimpering, awestruck prisoners by these advanced space beings in weird clothes that repelled gunfire. Only one Lyran had been killed by a Martian; he had been shot in the face.

Lyran rule was established at once, leaving the former governing Martians to join the rest of the Martians as servers and slaves. Women were taken from their homes and families. Children who were too small to work and still needed to be taken care of were removed from the city and killed. The Lyrans had a plan to procreate and raise up their own race. Therefore, they had no use for anyone who needed care on any level. It was weeks before the Martian men even thought about how to get out of this mess and still survive. They whispered among themselves about their dilemma, but none of them had any answers. Life as slaves to the Lyrans was all that was left to the Martians, except death, and most of them opted for survival.

The Martians were awestruck by the new technology brought to their planet, and some of the men even forgot about their miserable plight as captives in lieu of learning this technology. The learning came only when they were commanded to build new structures; excavate new building sites; mine the necessary minerals; and create plumbing systems, electricity, and even nuclear technology.

Construction of the Pyramid–Years 13,210 to 13,400

The most unusual project of all was the construction of a huge pyramid that was being literally carved out of a hillside. The Lyrans told the Martians that when they completed the structure they would have the power to defy the existing order in the galaxy and command respect among the starpeople. The Lyrans believed that the pyramid alone would give them power over the Sun. They did not realize that the persons utilizing such a structure needed to wield a power that was beyond physical might and aggression; they needed to be able to create through thought and spirit. The Lyrans merely believed that whatever they projected through the pyramid would happen. They also had a special weapon planned for installation in the top of the pyramid.

It took full-time crews almost 200 years to complete the structure, and when it was finished, the Lyran spaceship was used to place a giant antenna made out of a mixture of metals unknown on Mars in the top peak. The Lyrans had brought the metals from Orion and had saved them for this purpose. When the Lyran leaders entered the pyramid for the first time and climbed to the upper chamber, the crowds cheered in delight. Soon an incredible display of light burst from inside the pyramid through the antennalike projectile and out into space. It was like nothing the Martians had ever seen before—like thousands of bolts of lightning all projecting at the same time from the same place.

As the light reached high above the planet, a loud sonic boom was heard, and another cheer came from the crowd. Even the Martians, who had adapted to working for the Lyrans by that time, were beside themselves with excitement. When they asked what the pyramid and projectile were to be used for, they were simply told, "Whatever we want to use them for."

During the 200 years of pyramid construction, other projects had been initiated as well. Many of the women and older children had been put to work in assembly lines making weapons and assisting in nuclear testing. Occasionally a guinea pig was needed to test the effects of these weapons on humanoids, and a woman, child, or aged one would be taken away from the city and exposed to radiation or simply killed with a new weapon to test its power. Life had no value at all to the Lyrans—except as it served their purpose of absolute power and control.

Since the Martian civil war, during which all of the original Martians had been killed, the equivalent of Earth's lower astral realms, or Bardos, had been growing in the etheric realms of Mars. Murder, fear, control for power, and the devaluing of life in general had established a precedent that quickly grew into a nightmarish Hell filled with manifested thoughtforms. These thoughtforms were a type of self-regenerating elemental that was initially created from repetitious negative thoughts and misapplied emotional energies. Souls became trapped at death in this illusion-based world, and denied, disembodied aspects of human consciousness roamed around there. This type of astral reality regenerated and strengthened the distrust, fear, control, and other negative states in the people. The colony had become power-crazed and was quickly deteriorating into a population of mutants incapable of love or conscience.

Experimentation using the new pyramid became the focus of the Lyran leaders. Unbeknownst to them, this was causing extreme atmospheric changes. The ozone layer around the planet was looking more and more like modern-day Swiss cheese. The mercurial lakes, which were already diminishing, dried up almost completely. This did not disturb the Martians or Lyrans since, in their minds, the lakes had always been useless. No one knew about the importance of the lakes in maintaining the mineral balance and underground water flows. A unique process on Mars created water by means of synthesis; it involved the Sun's rays combining with certain minerals through the inverted flows of the liquid in the lakes. It was like a laboratory in which the combination of sunlight and specific minerals synthesized within the imploded molecular structure of the lake's liquid. The water then filtered through a leach-type field at the bottom of the lake and ended up creating underground streams that would bubble up and overflow into artesian springs. It was the first time this system had been used in this galaxy.

The people's ignorance and their lack of honoring the sacredness of all things, regardless of whether these things served a known practical purpose, were quickly leading to their own demise. The streams and springs had all diminished to half their original size since the end of the previous cycle. At that time, the planet's poles had shifted and given them more hours of sunlight than were needed for maximum water production. The result was a drying effect. The Lyrans and Martians had not noticed this, since the change in the water tables was gradual, and they still had more water than was required.

The changes began occurring more rapidly. One hundred years after the pyramid was built, the lakes had become ponds, many artesian springs had dried up, and the springs that were left had diminished in flow and barely met the accustomed needs of the colony. After another fifty years, people were dying of skin cancer, and water rationing and storage had begun. Another fifty years and the slave classes were receiving barely enough water to keep them alive, and even the Lyrans were rationed.

With each incremental decrease in water supply, tempers and daily violence increased. Normally, the Lyrans used violence only when they deemed it necessary to discipline the Martians, or to use them for experimental purposes. The slaves had value, so they wanted to keep them strong and healthy. Domestic violence among the Martians had been minimal because they were all slaves with no power over one another. The Lyrans began to take out their frustrations about the lack of water, too much heat from the sun, and diminishing oxygen levels on the Martian slaves. People were beaten, raped, and occasionally even killed just for sport; the Lyrans experienced a false sense of power when they felt the rush of fear and pain they caused in others.

The Martians became shorter tempered with one another, and more likely to rebel against Lyran authority. This gave their oppressors more reasons to inflict violence. Women and children were not safe around their own husbands and fathers, and the women were beginning to beat their children. After the Lyrans had been on Mars for 500 years, total chaos prevailed in a police state with curfews and a prison. Many of the men were removed from their homes, kept in the prisons, and only taken out to work.

By the time Martian civilization was nearing the end of its third 5200-year cycle, the planet was only able to support about one-third of its population. The only thing everyone was in consensus about was the need for more water and less sunlight.

Pleiadians Arrive and Restore Peace—Year 15,600

When the Pleiadian Emissaries of Light arrived toward the end of the 5200-year cycle, as they had previously agreed to do, they were met with weapons, hostility, and threats. The Lyrans quickly learned they could not harm these new beings with their weapons, and found themselves powerless as a result. The Pleiadians ordered that all inhabitants of the planet be gathered together for a meeting. The Lyrans refused to bring the slaves from the prison, claiming that these people were criminals and must remain locked up. The Pleiadians replied that these people were slaves and former criminals, indeed, but not for the reasons the Lyrans believed. Because the timing of the planetwide meeting was dictated by an absolute planetary law, the Pleiadians overrode the Lyran refusal. The Lyrans and original Martians alike were told that if they tried to harm anyone, whatever they intended to do to the other would happen to them instead. The Pleiadians would harm no one, but they had the right to impose the law of instant karma. The Martians were terrified to go against the will of their oppressors, but with encouragement from the Pleiadians they began to head for the prison to release their fellow men. A few of the Lyrans charged forward to stop them, but as they raised their clubs to strike the slaves, the clubs literally hit the Lyran attackers instead, knocking the men to the ground.

A gasp came from the entire gathering, and the Martians proceeded to the prison without further delay. When they returned with the prisoners, the Pleiadians laid out rules for all of the existing Martian inhabitants, including the Lyrans:

1. Instant karma would continue for anyone attempting to use physical violence against another for the next fifty years, until the Pleiadians returned again for the decision-making meeting at the end of the 5200-year cycle.

2. The previous law of "consensus minus one" would be honored by the Pleiadians during that time except to remove the instant-karma ruling.

3. The people had to learn to treat everything and everyone as if they had value, even if they knew not what that value was.

4. Each person must review his or her own actions in order to discover what he or she had done to create the present situation. The Martians protested, saying they were slaves and had no power to create anything. The Pleiadians told them they had fully created their own situation and needed to review their own history to discover how they had done so. They also told the people about reincarnation and reminded them that they were the same beings who had been their own ancestors and were, therefore, responsible for everything that had occurred in their history.

5. Knowing they were constantly being reincarnated, the Martians needed to ponder why that was so and think about the purpose of their multiple lives.

6. Every man, woman, and child was to share equally in the water, since all of the people had cocreated the current dilemma.

7. All decisions that would affect the whole must be agreed upon by consensus minus one. Anything not agreed upon could not be done, and the person or persons attempting to do it would create their own death in the attempt to do it.

8. The Lyrans would not be able to use their ship to leave the planet until the next meeting in fifty years, due to their involvement in the planetary karma.

The Pleiadians compassionately explained to the people that they were not being punished, nor would they be. The Pleiadian sole purpose was protection and execution of planetary law as it had been predetermined by the Martians themselves at the beginning of the current 5200-year cycle. The people were informed that this was a rich opportunity for the Martians and Lyrans alike to learn and evolve together, and that the Pleiadians truly hoped the people would do so. The Martians and Lyrans were without exception deeply and sincerely loved and cared for by the Pleiadians, who were their spiritual and evolutionary guardians. The inhabitants of Mars were told that they all had divine spirits and souls that were infinitely capable and valuable. After remaining with the people for a few days to help establish the new order, the Pleiadians left.

The next fifty years fluctuated between periods of total chaos and insanity and times of calm introversion, contemplation, and renewal. A few of the Martians began to feel remorse, but the majority impatiently waited for a chance at revenge against the invaders. The more the revengeful ones plotted their violent comebacks, the more they were haunted by nightmares about being tortured and enslaved. The more the remorseful ones went into their feelings and thoughts and tried to learn, the more they experienced the Pleiadians in their dreams, teaching them about nonviolent alternatives and showing them possible loving futures. Dreams were the most powerful tool for subconsciously assisting the people; they would consistently experience in their dreams exactly what they had asked for and made their inner reality.

A dozen of the Martians and three of the Lyrans began to remember nearly identical dreams about how to meditate and how to feel the essence in plants and one another. As they shared these dreams, they realized they were being given clues about how to help themselves. A few people experimented with these dream suggestions and were positively overjoyed with the results. They also discovered that they were able to achieve even better results when they meditated together; and so small meditation groups were formed. A big hurdle was crossed the first time a Lyran came to one of these gatherings. At first, a chilled hush fell upon the people, and then two Martians at the same moment stood to welcome him. They agreed this was an important step toward settling their differences and coming to understand one another. The numbers grew until nearly a third of the people were meditating and doing "feeling exercises" together.

Something akin to "Co-Counseling" was introduced, during which the participants would divide into groups of three and take turns sharing dreams, revelations, feelings, thoughts, and questions. After each person shared, the two listeners could give feedback if the person wanted it. Otherwise, all they did was listen to one another. Then the participants would pair up and take turns trying to feel each other's energy by placing their hands on one another's chests, and looking into each other's eyes. This was especially difficult for them, and many gave up right away, feeling extremely self-conscious and afraid. Occasionally, someone would walk out in a huff, saying the exercises were all ridiculous and meaningless. Some who left returned later at another meeting, while others did not.

By the end of the fifty years, over half of the inhabitants had gone to at least one such gathering and about one-third of them had continued going on a regular basis. When the Pleiadians returned, the people of Mars were in consensus about nothing except the need for water and protection from the Sun. The Pleiadian delegation spent many days hearing the individual and group concerns and conclusions, and then adjourned to sort it all out.

It was clear that there were diverse groups on Mars. One-third of the population had begun to learn from their mistakes and wanted to continue learning and growing; their group included about a dozen Lyrans. Those who just wanted to be free to do whatever they wanted, including seek revenge and power, made up the other two-thirds. Within that two-thirds, the Martian contingent was split between wanting to get revenge against the Lyrans and just wanting their oppressors removed from the planet. The Lyrans who were part of the two-thirds were split between wanting to leave Mars and wanting to stay and return to their experiments and "rightful" control.

Because planetary rule for divine intervention and execution of planetary laws by the Pleiadians had always been based on consensus of the humanoid population, and there was consensus only about the need for water and protection from the Sun, these were the first things to be reviewed. The population was split on these issues, too. Most of the Martians wanted only Martians to be able to make decisions since the others were invaders. However, the Pleiadians explained that the Martians had invited the Lyran Beings from Orion with their thoughts and intent, so the Lyrans had the same rights as the other colonists. The people could not agree whether to make decisions based on consensus or majority vote. The Martians leaned toward majority vote since they were still a majority. The Lyrans leaned toward consensus since they were outnumbered and saw it as their only hope. So the Pleiadians said they would present at least two proposals since the people could not arrive at a decision themselves.

When the group reconvened, the Pleiadians had two suggestions about decision making and changes. The first was that the people move into two colonies, each run by consensus. Changes affecting the entire planet would have to be agreed upon by at least a two-thirds majority of both colonies. The second option was for the Lyrans to leave of their own free will, taking all weapons with them, while the original Martians would remain. The Martians would then have to decide on consensus or majority vote. Either way, instant karma for violence against another would be imposed for the next 500 years while all of the inhabitants of Mars were given a chance to further learn and heal. With this last stipulation, all but a couple dozen of the Lyrans agreed to leave at once. If they could not rule and be violent at will, they saw no purpose in staying on Mars.

Half of the Martians were of the peaceful persuasion while the other half wanted revenge against the Lyrans. Though the revengeful ones were not thrilled with the outcome, they were pacified that the majority of the Lyrans decided to leave; in fact, they wanted all of the Lyrans to leave if revenge against them was not possible. The peaceful half of the Martians disagreed and believed the Lyrans had a right to choose a new way of living if they so desired. The Pleiadians agreed with the latter group, and that part of the decision was acted upon within twenty-four hours. The Lyran ship left Mars with all of the Lyrans except those who wanted peace and evolution; these few stayed behind.

The meeting adjourned once more a few days later in order for the Pleiadians to make final decisions on the planetary laws. It was decided that the 500 or so Martians and the dozen Lyran-Martians still made up two distinct groups: one had a spiritual and evolutionary focus, the other wanted the freedom to do whatever they desired, especially to develop technology like that of the Lyrans. The decision was reached by consensus that they would divide into two colonies, each able to draw upon divine intervention any time a consensus existed silently or consciously within the group. It was also decided that a consensus must exist either subconsciously or consciously among all inhabitants of both colonies before changes affecting the whole planet could be made.

Other decisions were:

1. The Pleiadians agreed to bring about more water slowly, but said the people had created holes in the invisible ozone layer and would have to stop using the pyramid to set off explosives in the atmosphere in order for the water levels to increase gradually.

2. At the end of the next 500 years, the people would need to have evolved and developed consciences on their own since the instant karma law would be lifted.

3. The DNA had to be cleared of all incest that had developed over the past 500 years. The reasons were explained to the people.

4. Natural resources could not be bought or sold or controlled in any way by individuals. Water must be equally shared as long as any shortage remained.

5. One Pleiadian would remain with each group as a spiritual advisor and general consultant, but would impose nothing upon the people. The people would have to seek the Pleiadian's counsel in order to receive help. At the end of the 500 years, each colony could decide by a majority vote whether the Pleiadian advisor would remain or leave.

The Martians agreed to all of the terms and prepared to divide the community within a few days. The more peaceful, evolutionary-focused contingent, including the Lyran-Martians, would begin a new colony elsewhere, since they had no interest in the technology or historical significance of the original colony. The more militant contingent was happy to remain in the existing colony, so everyone got exactly what they wanted.

Segregation into Two Colonies—Year 15,600

The migrators set off, accompanied by the Pleiadian spiritual advisor called Ra. When they came upon the old colony where their ancestors had lived prior to the invasion and takeover of the larger city, they felt a need to stop for a few days and make peace with the past. Ra, upon request, helped them create a ceremony of purification, forgiveness, and envisioning for the future. Then they unanimously decided to continue their search for a new home, preferring a location that would give them a fresh start rather than a continuance in the historical older city.

Another two weeks brought them to the edge of the fertile land; a vast desert spread out before them as far as they could see. The travelers headed back into the vegetated lands in a slightly different direction, and found the ideal spot after another two days' walk. The water supply was the best to be found, though not overly abundant; vegetation was varied and plentiful; and building materials, mostly rock, were readily available. There were also caves nearby, big enough to house at least the women, children, and older people. They had found the location for their new home.

A dedication ceremony was held during which the settlers established their commitment to honor the natural resources by taking only what they needed and to live for the purpose of evolving, learning, and becoming better people. They also dedicated themselves to creating and living in a way that would leave a positive heritage for their children and themselves when they returned through reincarnation.

Progress was steadily made, with the construction of dwellings taking first priority. For nearly 100 years, the settlers established themselves in this new city, shared their dreams, and learned with one another. As the basic day-to-day life style became easier to maintain, they turned more and more to Ra for spiritual guidance and advice. He told them he could always answer their questions, and give them what they asked for, but no more. At this stage in their evolution, it would usurp their growth to teach them beyond that point. The people asked to meet with him in groups at least weekly, and as an entire population four times a year, at the time of seasonal changes. Though the seasonal changes were not as distinct as on Earth, these time cycles were recognized and honored.

For the entire 500 years, most of the people of the new city were like children, eagerly learning, opening gradually to being more vulnerable and emotionally honest with one another, and cherishing their times with Ra. When the end of this period came, the people were in such grief about the thought of Ra's departure that they unanimously agreed he should remain with them. Ra agreed, and the people held a great festival in honor of Ra to celebrate the ongoing relationship and express their gratitude to him. They also decided to build a spiritual temple dedicated to Ra and constructed in his likeness. It would serve as a reminder to future generations that spiritual evolution was why they were alive. The fact that it would be shaped like a humanoid head, Ra's head, would give that message, since he represented their greatest aspiration: to become divine humans.

The temple was a huge undertaking, but also a mission of love. (This is not the face on Mars, although it is connected to it. This will be revealed as the story unfolds.) The temple was approximately one, present-day, city block in size; it was both carved from existing rock knolls and augmented with rock and mortar structuring. It took about twenty-five years to complete, since technology was still rather primitive.

In the meantime, the older city rebuilt its culture slowly and clumsily. The limitation of no physical harm to others without harming themselves had left the Martians with no basis for the creation of any kind of rulership. Their lives were easier than the enslaved lives of previous generations, yet the people were bored. At every turn obstacles to technological growth were met. The metals brought from Orion were gone, and with little water and too much heat, there was no means of extensive mining; no one could be forced to do it as before. Occasionally, someone went to the Pleiadian, also called Ra, for advice, but most found little use for him since all he could do was answer questions about evolution, right action, conscience, and spirit.

As a group, they did agree to ask Ra to settle disputes and make decisions for the collective, which he did. Once there was a big argument about whether or not experimentation with the pyramid should be done as long as no blasting was involved. Most of the people were frightened of the pyramid in general, while others remained fascinated by its omnipresence. Ra told them that the pyramid was like a giant energy generator and in and of itself was neither good nor evil. How and why it was used determined its impact. It was decided that, as long as at least twelve people at a time were inside the pyramid and doing nothing unless they all agreed, experimentation was acceptable.

Since the people had asked him about the dangers of the pyramid, Ra warned them of the power of their own unconscious thoughts and feelings. They thought this remark was unimportant and vague, and proceeded with the embarkment of the group of twelve. Since this was the most exciting thing that had happened in twenty-five years, it created quite a stir.

People gathered around the base of the pyramid to watch as the first group of twelve ascended its steps. Though scorching in the Sun, the Martians remained watching until the twelve descended that evening. The group had very little to report except for some details about the construction of the inner chamber. A new group of twelve Martians went into the pyramid each day for several days since many of the people were curious and wanted to see inside it. Each day the group returned with little if anything new to report. Occasionally someone would share that he or she had experienced strange or eerie feelings, or had caught fleeting glimpses of light sparkles while inside, but these experiences were few and not taken seriously. There was still some equipment inside at that time, but no one knew how use it.

A few of the more sensitive and curious ones, who had experienced unusual feelings or visions, continued going into the pyramid after the initial trend had ended; but for the most part it sat empty. One day, one of these more persistent men thought to ask Ra more about the pyramid. Excitedly, he and a few friends went to Ra, told him what they had experienced inside the pyramid, and asked him what it meant. Ra told them the pyramid shape had the ability to receive, hold, and generate energy. It also had an intimate connection to the Sun and to elliptical orbits and time cycles. He explained that the Lyrans had built it to harness destructive power and had believed it to be the ultimate weapon. They intended to use it to eventually take over the galaxy, though they had been naive to believe such a thing possible.

Ra went on to explain that the strange feelings and fleeting visions of light were to be expected inside such a structure, since the pyramid itself had a powerful force field and an energy tangible to those with more sensitivity. When he gave additional information about third-eye clairvoyance, as well as clairsentient capabilities of all beings, the people responded enthusiastically, asking how they could develop these extrasensory perceptions. Ra explained that they were a natural product of evolution, an expanded use of the normal five senses, but that they could be accelerated with certain meditative practices.

With the motivation of psychic and full-sensory power, the people thought meditation could possibly serve a purpose. Ra taught them methods of beginning meditation to help them focus attention and energy, and said the meditators could come back for a next lesson when they were doing well with that one.

After a few months, several of the men and one woman came to Ra saying they were ready for the next lesson. Ra asked them to meditate and hold a specific focus for half an hour so he could check their progress. Since they were doing reasonably well but needed more discipline, he gave them a walking meditation and an open-eye meditation to add to their existing practices and told them to return in one month for review. At that time, all of the Martians who were meditating, about twenty-four altogether, were able to hold somewhat of a focus for half an hour, so Ra took them to the next level.

He gave the people a third-eye exercise to do at dusk each day, using candlelight and a mirror. They were to sit in front of the mirror for ten minutes gazing into their own eyes, using only the light from two candles, one on either side of them. All they were to do was watch. After two weeks of doing this exercise daily, they were to do it in pairs, looking into each other's eyes. After two weeks of doing the exercise in pairs they were to return and report to Ra what they had experienced.

After only the first two weeks, the group returned, saying they were afraid to do this exercise in pairs because they had seen some very scary things while doing it alone. Strange and angry faces, at times even monsterlike, had appeared in the mirrors. Several of the people had even seen the faces of their oppressors from Orion as they had stared into their own eyes, and this had really scared them. Ra explained that he had given them the exercise to help them understand that they had many things going on inside themselves of which they were unaware. The images in the mirrors had been reflections of aspects of their own personalities, as well as past-life images still inside them waiting to be healed.

Though leery, the new meditators were willing to listen and learn. Ra told them that before a being could learn to use psychic power safely, he or she must first purify spiritually and emotionally. Their own repressed killer selves were still a very big part of their psyches and had to be transformed now, not just stifled out of fear of harm to themselves. It was the first time any of this group had been willing to even consider anything like spiritual teachings, or growth and healing practices, yet they listened. Their main driving force was still the desire to understand force and power through technology, but they had also experienced looking the shadow side of their natures in the eye, and it had made some impact on them.

Ra was then asked to teach them as a group, and individually if needed, how to clear these parts of themselves. He agreed to begin at once. The teachings left psychic phenomena behind and began with deepening meditation practices and something akin to drama therapy. As the people brought the repressed parts of themselves to the surface, they could act them out, give them voice, and learn what they had to say. It took a while before any results were seen and felt; the people were extremely self-conscious and distrusting of one another. When Ra refused to teach them anything else until they participated fully in drama therapy work, little by little they began to do so.

Some of them dropped out of the group instead, leaving eighteen to carry on.

After a while, the remaining eighteen people brought in their mates and children to introduce them to the processes they had learned from Ra. Most of the relatives joined the group, increasing the class size to about forty members. The rest of the community remained detached from the group, and yet watched them for noticeable changes.

As the older members of the group died, their children and grandchildren carried on. A few dropped out along the way, but thirty to sixty members continued to participate at any given time. Progress was slow but steady, and as one practice was mastered, another would be introduced. Emotional clearing took precedence, while working on very basic morality and ethics through meditation and teachings was always a close second. These two priorities, as well as development of connection with their Higher Selves, took up all of their focus for the rest of the 500-year cycle.

At the end of this period, this minority group who had worked so diligently with Ra felt that the Pleiadian's presence was crucial. Many of the others had used Ra's wisdom in more practical ways over time, while others were neutral about his presence and remained free of contact with him. So, when the time came to decide whether Ra would stay or go, all agreed he was welcome, at least, and wanted by most. The lifting of the instant-karma rule also occurred at that time, as had been promised. Many were dubious about the removal of this restriction, but were reminded that they must evolve as a race through the use of free will. So began the next 500-year cycle.

The group of meditators and self-healers continued working with Ra, transmuting and transforming slowly but steadily. The Martians were a proud and willful group, skeptical by nature, so their progress was at times tedious and accomplished with much resistance. At other times, they broke through that resistance and surged ahead. The rest of the original colony members went on with life as usual, making normal evolutionary growth in living conditions, food production, medical treatment (mostly with plants and minerals), and technology. They created a new method of cooking using solar energy, which led to general studies of, and inventions using, solar power. Greenhousing was developed as a way of growing plants that needed more moisture than they could provide. This increased their food choices tremendously.

For the next 500 years, life on Mars followed gradual and consistent patterns of growth for both colonies. The following 500 years brought a few more challenges, however. Some of the bacterial and fungal forms evolved into parasitic, almost insectlike species, with a focus on plants as feeding grounds. These tiny creatures destroyed much grain and many trees and other plants before the people had any sense at all of what was going on. Both cities were greatly afflicted by this plague, though the original colony was hit the hardest. By the time they discovered what was causing the problem, much damage had been done to the food and building material supplies, and to the fibers used for production of clothing and paper.

When Ra was consulted with regard to what could be done about the parasite problem in both cities, he told the people to go to the lakes and gather the mineral deposits around the edges of the liquid. These specific mineral deposits contained ingredients that had leached into the soil and rocks in great quantities. As the water levels and rains had diminished, the chemical makeup of the soil and water had changed gradually; the mutated lifeforms were now seeking what they needed to survive in another place—the plants. Ra told the members of both colonies to powder the lake minerals and spread them on the ground everywhere plants grew. They were to begin with food plants, herbs, and trees, and then spread to more common vegetation after the essential ones had been fertilized. These powdered, rocklike minerals would give back to the soil what was missing due to the change in the water tables. Some moisture would be required to accompany the fertilizing, but in the garden areas, the normal watering of plants would take care of that need. The people were also told that it would take six months to a year before the results would be noticeable, but to have faith.

The Martian colonists were really learning about the long-range effects of interference with the atmosphere. They were witnessing how the activities of the Lyrans and their own ancestors over 1200 years before were still creating ongoing problems in their natural world. Ra was able to tell about the symbolic and actual nature of all events, whether they were perceived as positive or negative. Basically, he explained the principle of cause and effect, saying that every action or result is the direct effect of a traceable cause. For many of the people, this was a powerful learning that had impact on many levels. For them to examine their actions and thoughts for what they had the potential of producing was a big evolutionary step in consciousness.

Unfortunately, many of the Martians living in the original city simply used this understanding as a reason to dredge up old blame and hatred of the Lyrans. These negative feelings festered into an open wound in their emotional lives over time. Their hostility and blame had been deeply buried during the time of instant karma and had remained mostly hidden for the 500 years following that time. Now, however, their DNA was ready to be purged of those emotional and mental patterns. The plague had served to bring denial and repression to the surface.

Tempers were shorter, emotional dramas about small problems were exaggerated, mild cases of violence began to show up, and tension was prevalent throughout the population of the original colony. The meditators were more prepared for this than the rest; they had been clearing their DNA more actively for many generations. The meditators had tended to marry within their spiritual community, thus assisting in the genetic clearing even more. They offered to start teaching the rest of the people about stress management, emotional clearing, drama therapy, and anything else those outside the spiritual community were ready to try that might assist in clearing the new/old problems. Most of the people negated the whole idea, as usual, although some of the women and children—and a few of the men who really did not want to get back into the ancient way of violence and extreme oppression—volunteered to receive help. This added a total of about forty new people to the group of those trying to heal and awaken their consciousnesses, bringing their number to around 100. The entire city's population had grown to about 325. So even though the meditators were still a minority, they were a significant minority.

The polarity between the groups in the original city grew rapidly. By the end of the next 500 years, the peaceful segment of the population was obviously in opposition to their neighbors who were becoming more and more violent. Early on during the growing segregation, the peaceful ones tried to make the others understand. However, as the violent patterns accelerated over a few generations, a deep cultural and spiritual chasm was formed, with prejudices and judgments against the other in each group. At the end of that period, a majority vote could not be reached about Ra's presence in the city; the vote was almost exactly fifty-fifty.

Original City Divides—Year 17,100

When Ra announced he would be leaving, the peaceful contingent was extremely troubled and begged him to stay. He told them he could not remain unless those who wanted him there left the city and began their own colony elsewhere, or joined the other colony that had split apart 1500 years before. Over 100 people asked to be led to the other colony in hopes of healing their connection with their fellow Martians and finding a peaceful and safe home again. After consulting with the Pleiadian Higher Council and group consciousness of the other city, Ra told those who wished to continue consciously growing in peace that they would be welcomed in the other city. They would be expected to follow the established order upon arrival. Delighted, they prepared for their long journey, and with Ra leading the way, they set out for their new home.

The remaining citizens of the original colony were reluctant to let these people leave, for they secretly knew that the peace-seeking migrants had helped keep what balance remained in the city. Some of those who left even had second thoughts about leaving for exactly the same reason; they wanted to help maintain the balance and give their less-evolved neighbors another chance to change. However, even with this compassion and concern about the colonists left behind, they knew that Ra's presence was essential to their own continuing evolution. Therefore, the decision to leave was unanimous among the meditators.

The migrators found their way to the new city in just under four weeks. They were welcomed gloriously with feasting, celebration, speeches, and ceremonial gatherings. Even new clothing and temporary dwellings were festively prepared. It was a wonderful reunion that lasted for over a week; then the inhabitants got down to the business of planning and creating new dwellings and introducing the newcomers to their laws of order, spirituality, agricultural techniques, and birthing practices. It was fascinating to the new people to see how the residents were much more advanced spiritually and culturally and much less evolved technologically.

As the integration of the two groups of people began, there was a common feeling of deja vu among the people, accompanied by a sense of foreboding. When they approached Ra about the widely shared feelings, he told them the story of the first colony split on Venus due to incest and prejudices about physical appearance. He explained the formation of the criminal segment in the original Venusian colony due to class division and prejudice, as well as the second split, after which the criminals joined the newer colony. Ra related the whole history of that experiment, which led to the criminal forces being banned from Venus and coming to Mars as its first inhabitants, and how the Martian culture now consisted of all of the Venusian Beings. He also reminded the people of the split that had occurred on Mars between the other, long-abandoned city and the original city, at which time the violent patriarchs had slain all of the members of the original colony and taken it over. He said that afterward, there were only around 250 Martians left on the planet, and they were exclusively the violent ones. Now the population had grown again until those who had been slain at that time were mostly reincarnated and lived in this newer spiritual city. Some of the people who had just journeyed to the new city were the original victims, and some were the patriarchs in the process of genetic and spiritual evolution.

The people were all deeply moved by the stories of their own history of prejudice, power struggles, and separation; they vowed as a group to heal the split once and for all. Of course, they consciously meant to heal it within their own city, but the group subconscious also meant to heal it with every historical enemy. This set a precedent of spiritual preparation for the time of healing and reunion that was destined to come.

The original colony, which was now down to about 215 members, was in a state of unrest. Its members had something to prove, but they did not even know what or to whom. The people felt angry and full of blame and revenge without an apparent cause within their conscious historical memories. Daily life continued but with an impending sense of need for confrontation with someone, at some time in the near future.

For the next 1000 years, the two cities remained estranged and scarcely even remembered that each other existed. The negative thoughtforms and amorphous lower-astral energies in the original city grew rapidly once all of the spiritual and peaceful people were gone. Patriarchy reigned again on Mars in the original colony, devolving to the original state of male competitive games, brutality, oppression of females, and general unrest. The only difference between this time and the previous one was that technology and psychic control as well as brute strength were now sources of male dominance. Those who remained knew of the work to develop psychic awareness that was historically connected with the pyramid. Somehow, with Ra and the peaceful members of their community gone, interest in that area surfaced again.

The men began to experiment with projecting their thoughts through the pyramid. There were no apparent results, but etherically their messages were received as an invitation to the Lyrans to return and settle their ancient differences through war. These men were seeking an enemy who would challenge them, and their karma with the Lyrans, who were still unconsciously connected to the pyramid, created a natural link. Since the newer city's citizens had made a vow to heal the split with all enemies once and for all, the invitation to the Lyrans was unanimous, though unconscious. The Martians soon found themselves faced with their ancient enemy again.

Lyran-Orion Invaders Return—Year 18,500

Because of time and space restrictions, it was a few years before the Lyrans actually showed up. When they did, it was disastrous for the people of Mars. First, the Lyrans rounded up into the original colony all of the Martians from both cities who were considered valuable as slaves. All of the rest were killed at once, and the temple dedicated to Ra was destroyed. Since the invaders had been "invited" back by consensus, there was nothing the Pleiadian Higher Council or the two Ra's could do to stop them. The two Ra's, who could have made themselves invisible, chose to allow their bodies to be killed, thus freeing them from the etheric planes around Mars and allowing them to return to the Pleiades to work with the other Pleiadian Archangelic Tribe members.

Before the people knew what had hit them, they were under a Lyran police state with no means of self-protection. Approximately 3000 years after the Lyrans from Orion had left Mars, they were back in full charge, determined to succeed at utilizing the pyramid as the ultimate weapon to gain control of the solar system. Reconstruction of the damaged or removed parts of the control system for the pyramid began at once. Slaves worked for long hours throughout the city, the top priorities being the pyramid project, restoring nuclear power, and weapons production.

After only fifty years, the city was technologically ready to begin experiments again, which commenced with a great nuclear blast through the metal conductor at the top of the pyramid. The Martians tried to warn their captors of what would happen to the lakes, water tables, and ozone layer. This part of their history had been carefully passed down from generation to generation so that it would never be repeated. The Martians who tried to warn the Lyrans or stop the experiments were met with violence or death. All seemed lost to Mars and its people once again. There was no way to reason with the Lyrans. The invaders were more callous, violent, and power hungry than even the worst of the Martian patriarchs, who were quickly made subservient under Lyran rule.

When the first atmospheric explosion was set off, a large quake measuring about 8 on the Richter scale followed immediately with several smaller aftershocks. Though the pyramid itself sustained no damage, the city and its people did. Over 100 lives were lost, and several buildings collapsed. This brought the Martian population from the two combined colonies down to about 250, since many had been killed when the invaders first arrived. Cleanup and necessary repairs took several weeks. Since so many had died, housing was not rebuilt. The Lyrans just rearranged the people, placing more than one family in some of the homes, and continued with their technological priorities.

Experiments, often followed by quakes, continued throughout the next fifty years or so. There was an ongoing increase in the production of weapons, and several small rock pyramids were built around the base of the large one. Each smaller pyramid

contained a sonic generator that was used to strengthen the effects of the large atmospheric blasts. The aim of all this was to shoot sonic, psychic, and nuclear blasts at the Sun all at once. The purpose was to unravel the evolutionary encoding inside the Sun, change the orbital time sequence, and establish a new vibratory pattern that would allow the Lyran warriors to rule your solar ring. The Lyrans knew the Sun was the gateway to communication with Alcyone, the central sun of the Pleiades, as well as to Galactic Center. If they could successfully close that gateway, then align it with the specific Orion sun held by their fellow rebels in that Orion solar ring, they could overthrow the Pleiadian forces of Light who were guardians of your solar ring. This way, they could establish new territory for the dark forces in this galaxy.

The timing for their experiment was very specific astronomically and astrologically. Certain alignments needed to be exact in order to accomplish their goal. That goal had been missed the last time by only 125 years, when the original Lyran invaders had left Mars unexpectedly. This time the alignment would occur before the 5200-year cycle was over and, therefore, the Pleiadians could not stop them again.

What the warring Lyrans did not know was that the Sun's encoding, and the Sun itself, exist in a higher-dimensional frequency and cannot be impacted as they thought by lower-frequency energies. When they sent the energies into what appeared to be a particular space, this space would actually be another dimension, and therefore beyond impact in the way they intended.

When the time for the long-awaited blast actually came, the sundials and geometric configurations within the pyramid's structure confirmed the alignment. Synchronization of the sonic, psychic, and nuclear projectiles was all in order and ready. When the exact time came, everything went off as intended, but the results were far from what was planned. There was a loud boom, accompanied by sonic waves, collected astral/psychic energies, and blasts of light. A giant hole opened in the planet's atmosphere, creating spontaneous combustion, and every living thing on the planet was vaporized in a matter of seconds. The planet's orbit was changed, but no one was left to experience it.

The Pleiadians and other angelic Light Beings had gathered to assist when the blast took place. They had created great cones of Light in the atmospheric holes through which the souls and spirits of those who wanted asylum in the Light could enter. Almost half of the true Martians went into the Light and were gathered into protective cocoons for transport aboard Pleiadian lightships to Sirius for healing. The dolphin and whale spirits on Sirius are master healers and regenerators of damaged souls and spirits who are being prepared for rebirth into form.

The Lyrans and the rest of the Martian patriarchs were so anti-Light that they turned away from the cones of light and remained in the astral planes around the planet. Eventually, an Orion delegation of peace from the fifth dimension came for the astral bodies of the Lyrans, who agreed to return to the Lyran star system in preparation for their next evolutionary step. The Martian patriarchs remained on the astral plane, lost to time and space until the end of that 26,000-year cycle, at which time the Pleiadians chose to remove them to karmic training schools that were established in the planet's atmosphere. Between-life orientation with their guides and the Council of Elders was begun.

Mars, as a planet and multidimensional space, was etherically cocooned for clearing and regeneration for many centuries following this explosion. During that time, Maldek was prepared for humanoid inhabitation. The karmic patterns on Mars were not removed, just neutralized into informational geometric symbols, or encodings; these encodings could not create negativity, but instead projected the message of Martian history into the solar ring's collective consciousness. The Pleiadians also agreed to chisel the likeness of the face of Ra, as he had appeared to the Martians, into the planet's surface. This record of the temple was crucial to the planet's ability to reflect its complete history to future inhabitants of the solar ring. Therefore, it was created several times larger than the original temple on the now dead, arid surface of Mars.

Author's Note: It is important to remember that many Martians did attain enlightenment, and that a few ascended. Therefore, the sacred map of transformation, transcendence, and healing of the Martian karmic patterns was created and still exists within the atmosphere there. Both polarities exist within the human race: male dominance and conquering mentality, as well as men who see women as equals and treat them with due respect; misuse of sexual energy for ego gratification and lust, as well as tantric teachings and couples who share the sacredness and pleasure of sexual union; violence and nonviolence; hatred and unconditional love. You can call on those who chose the Light and ascended on Mars to assist you in learning those lessons and purifying the Martian karmic patterns that you still carry.

To those who lived on Mars and attained enlightenment—or at least spiritual alignment—I (Amorah) wish to honor the lessons you learned through the offering of this poem. To those Martians who did not transcend the Martian ego, I offer this poem as a transformational tool.

THE IMPECCABLE LOVER

Oh, Gentle Man, what do you see
when you look out at me with eyes
of desire and longing?
Eyes that reach out and surround me
with your heat and passion:
passion of wanting.
Eyes that say, "I must have you."
Eyes that plead, or eyes that lust.
Eyes that say, "I've been lonely so long."
Oh, Gentle Man, do not look to me
with these eyes.
Go to the looking glass with these eyes.
Relief awaits you there.
And when you see the conqueror,
the knight, the hungry man,
tell that one to lay down his sword,
and surrender his armor and shield:
Tell him the war is done.
Then put your arm around his shoulder

and look him in the eyes.
And when his sword, his armor, his shield
are locked and put away,
and he has cried and called you, "Brother,"
then, Gentle Man, may you come to me
with your soul's light shining
from behind your eyes,
able to see the Light and Essence
that I Am.
Then I will look back when I see
the love and respect in your eyes.
But when I see desperation and lust,
or the need to conquer and own,
I promise you this:
I shall look away.
Oh, Gentle Man, how would you give
your gifts to me?
Excitedly, like a child
who picks a flower for Mother
then runs inside to receive her praise?

Would you give to me to show
how thoughtful and kind you are?
How generous you can be?
To impress me with your charm?
To win my love and reward?
Would you give what you think I want
with hope for pardon and mercy,
that you be deemed worthy
of all my attention and love?
Oh, Gentle Man, please take your gifts
to your magical child,
who awaits, so lonely and afraid,
in your garden.
For he is in need
of your caring and presence.
Take this child to your breast.
Cradle him.
Stroke him.
Shower him.
And be sincere.

Alas, when he sleeps in your arms,
lay him down softly
and climb the stairs to my room.
And if you see the Light of my soul
and the Beauty that I Am
and wish to honor me with a flower,
a poem, a sweet word, or a kiss,
then give to me with sincerity,
without the need for flourish,
without expectation
or hope of reward,
but with the quiet dignity
with which you sniff the aroma
of a sweet-scented flower,
or watch in peaceful awe
the setting of the Sun.
Oh, Gentle Man, please burden me not
with the weight of your esteem,
or with the power to give or destroy
your joy, your heart, your image, and worth.
For this responsibility
is far too great for me.
Go find your peace and happiness,
your self-esteem and love.
Find them with God and with Goddess;
Find them in flowers, and trees,
in the wind and the setting sun.
Then bring them with you for sharing.
Do not make me your reason
for living or dying—
my approval, the source of your power;
my touch, your salvation;
my eyes, your self-knowing—
for I would grow to despise you,
and you would resent and loathe me.
This power that you would give me
I truly do not want.
At best, it could only serve
to soothe the doubts I hold,

and make me feel important to you,
and needed and worthy—
filled with a false sense of purpose—
but fleetingly.
And you would imprison me
away from my own sense of Essence,
and from the truth of my soul,
and from the Goddess that I Am,
and from my true power and Light.
You would cripple me, surely—
admiring me with your eyes that hide
your loneliness and need;
your gifts that beg for approval;
your words of praise that hide
your desperation.
Oh, Gentle Man, until the child sleeps
and is peaceful in your garden,
and the knight has lain down
his sword, his armor, his shield,
then, only then, approach my stairs.
And only then will I meet you
halfway.
When your soul is present and shining
brightly through eyes of love,
then you will see my eyes shining
and looking back at you.
When you give from your heart
and your words are not boasting,
when you know who you are without me,
then I will be free to receive you,
and to give to you fully my love.
For then, we will know that neither
of us can be destroyed.
The surrender that only can come
to two who have first
surrendered to self—
to their own inner Beauty,
and wisdom, and Essence Divine—
will be ours.

Then side by side, in blended Light,
our twin stars will shine
once again.

Just as I completed transcribing this poem into my computer, I noticed a beautiful buck with large, four-pronged antlers about fifty feet outside my window. I recognized him as the same deer who had stopped and listened to me singing from time to time. From the first time we saw each other, there was a special connection. He would cautiously walk closer as I sang to him and threw him food. He would cock his head back and forth and look me in the eyes from a safe distance of a few feet away. But this day we truly met.

Upon seeing him, I ran upstairs and filled a bowl with grapes. Then I went outside and sat on the ground about thirty feet from him. He watched me continually through the corner of one eye, and I felt he was agitated and more cautious than before. So I sang to him—one song after another—until he finally turned toward me. I noticed that he did not open to me until I became more centered and quiet inside. I complimented him on his discernment and then telepathically asked his name. The reply I heard was, "Feel my essence. That is my name." As I closed my eyes and felt his energy, the name Earnest entered my mind in response to his essential nature.

Slowly Earnest walked to about twelve feet away, stopped, explored the ground looking for the grapes I had tossed, and ate the ones he found. After that, he walked to within about six feet where I had tossed a few more of the sweet enticements. All the while I sang and talked to him about my recognition of his sacredness. I sang "You Are So Beautiful to Me" and "Beauty of Life," which is a song I wrote. I made up verses about the peace that will come to animals and humans alike when we are finally safe to trust one another. I sang and told him that he and I could begin that peace now. And as my heart overflowed with tears streaming from my eyes, and my voice choked, he ate from my hands. His eyes were within ten inches of my own, his pronged antenna even closer. He alternated between looking directly into my eyes—which continued to overflow in gratitude—and relaxedly looking at the food offering he was enjoying.

At one point, Earnest nudged the bowl that was sitting on my lap, and I placed it on the ground in front of me. While he heartily devoured the grapes, each and everyone, I took one for myself. I ate it as he watched me with furled brows that reflected his question. I told him, "I share the food I brought you in honor of our sacred communion." The puzzled look left his face, and he continued eating. Once finished with the contents of the bowl, he nudged my hands, which I extended to him, now empty. After licking them and nudging them with his nose a couple more times, he stood still, looking into my eyes, as I wept. We bonded.

As he walked away, I said silently, there are a few more grapes there to your right. He immediately stopped, looked directly at them, walked over and ate them and then walked on. I said "Namaste" silently and held my hands together until he was out of sight; I know he understood.

This incredible gift was a confirmation to me of the vision of balance, respect, and trust that males and females are meant to re-find. And it was a confirmation of the vision I, as well as many others, have held of humans and animals living in harmony, respect, and trust once again. It is the vision of the purified and exalted Martian energy when in balance with Venusian love and appreciation of inner Beauty.

PART III

PART III

COLONIZATION OF MALDEK

Ra's story of our solar ring's evolution continues:

Shortly after the destruction of Martian life, there was a great stir in another part of the galaxy. Experimentation in genetic environmental adaptability, both within plant species and mammalian animal species, had unveiled an overall genetic flaw in this galaxy's lifeforms. The flaw resulted in a predisposition to unnecessary early death. During the creation of the vast array of lifeforms on third-dimensional planets, the rotation patterns and frequencies of chromosomes had been aligned with the orbital cycles of the planets and the Sun. What had not been taken into account was the fact that these cycles would change slightly every 520 years, creating an almost undetectable vibrational frequency change. This change has to do with the built-in evolutionary and cyclical shift that encourages a pause, like the blink of an eye, during which all patterns are ever so briefly halted. Every living species, at that exact millisecond break in the time-space continuum, registers a "reality check." They readjust to present-time solar encodings and continue on their life paths appearing unchanged. However, chromosomes must have the ability to stop spinning and be receptive during that time in order to have the pattern shift affect genetics as well as consciousness.

The power of the relationship between chromosomes and consciousness at this level had not been realized up to that time; it had been believed that chromosomes would follow consciousness. When the discovery was made that the bodies of plants, animals, and humans were unable to respond to the pause and pattern-shift in consciousness, it was determined that this was the reason life spans were gradually getting shorter for all species. The shortening of life spans was caused by the reaction of the chromosomes to the lapse in time-space continuum, to contract rather than come to a standstill. This contraction created permanent imprinting of resistance energy in the cells, which made a minor shift in the speed of the cellular spin. It was as if the cells and chromosomes were always trying to catch up with the solar and planetary orbital patterns, creating mild stress on the nervous system. This shift was so subtle that it took hundreds of thousands of years of genetic study and experimentation by the Pleiadians and other nature specialists from several regions of the galaxy to even know there was a problem, and then discover its source.

The discovery was made during the transfer of plant species from one planet to another. The plants were being tested for adaptability to find out if they could "learn" from one another and adjust their cellular flow patterns automatically, without outside assistance. The transferred plants did begin to adopt the patterns of the native plants, but a "tic" was created in the cellular spin aspect of their overall flow pattern. At the end of the equivalent of every moon cycle on Earth, the newly transferred plants would experience a slight contraction. This contraction accelerated the previously existing 520-year contraction phenomenon so that the mortality rate in those species was increased. Within the first two years of life on a new planet, life spans would be reduced to approximately one half of the species' normal life expectancy. The native plants would continue as usual. For some reason, every cyclical end and new beginning created an exaggeration of the contraction reaction from the previous 520-year cycle until the transferred plants were under great stress.

The animals eating the plants also began to show signs of stress. Their bodies rejected parts of the plants that they had formerly used for nutrition. It was, for example, like eating potatoes with the vitamin C removed; over time, such bodies would become vitamin-C deficient and develop new diseases as a result. At first, the animals' digestive systems showed signs of sluggishness. Their bodies could not absorb the parts of the plants' cellular structures that had contracted as a result of the mutation in the cellular spin without experiencing contraction also. It was as if the contraction itself released a death hormone in the plants that the animals could not absorb without triggering a similar death hormone in their own bodies.

Upon further study, it was realized that this same phenomenon occurred in the humans who ate the plants. Therefore, the animals and humans who were transferred to new planets not only retained the mutations of their own species' chromosomes, they were also forced to adapt to the plant chromosome mutations in their food. In humans, the emotional impact of this phenomenon was a fear of change and death at the cellular level. This type of fear had been unknown at the beginning of human existence when human cells had a natural, built-in understanding about cycles and death.

The study was further extended to those spirits and souls who had been embodied and were now in between lives. It was discovered that the chromosomal contraction and resulting emotional-reaction pattern had imprinted on the souls of those who had experienced human life. This pattern took the form of resistance to life because of a fear of death and change. The Pleiadians and devic kingdoms began working at once to solve the problem of genetic mutation and mutation transference between species. Changes were made in the DNA strands to incorporate a consciousness override of the contraction response in cells and chromosomes; therefore, when the 520-year cyclical pause took place, the etheric and physical bodies followed the response pattern of the consciousness. It took several cycles to perfect this adaptation, but finally the chromosomes and cells were able to simply "stand still" during the brief halt in the time-space continuum, and then resume their normal rotation when the consciousness returned to its familiar, albeit new, function. Another few cycles were needed to reverse the already existing mutations by birthing enough new plants and animals with the DNA corrections to "teach" the rest how to catch up with them.

The next problem to be solved by the Pleiadians and devas was how to correct the soul's imprinting on the human spirits without altering their overall evolutionary patterns. It was decided that it could not be done without birthing humans into new physical bodies and having them eat plants and animals with corrected chromosomal patterns. If the plants and animals could "teach"

each other's chromosomes to correct the mutant patterns, they should be able to "teach" human chromosomes as well.

This is where Maldek came in. Prior to the end of civilization on Mars, the planet Maldek had been developed into a tropical paradise. Rain forests, jungles, oceanic environments, and more plant and animal species than had ever existed on any planet in your solar ring were developed on Maldek. Now there was a need for another home planet for the Martian—formerly Venusian—beings and Maldek was the most likely choice. Earth had long before been inhabited by a group of around 25,000 Andromedan slaves. They had been brought there by an angry, tyrannical fifth-dimensional overlord who had fallen from his higher-dimensional position as a Supreme Being for an entire solar ring in the Andromedan Galaxy. When the Ice Age had come, the entire population of Earth had been extinguished and their souls taken to the Pleiades for healing and new lives there.

At the time the Maldekians arrived, Earth was once again developing into an inhabitable planet near the end of the Ice Age, but it was still too unstable climatically for habitation by humans. (And, besides, Earth was being prepared for a future plan of its own—a topic that will be discussed in the next chapter.) Earth was home to giant species that were evolving, including dinosaurs and something akin to sea turtles, only much larger, that could travel on land and sea: their body-brain connections were still extremely unpredictable and erratic, and more time was needed for their evolution before new human and animal species could be introduced—even if the atmosphere had been stable enough. So Maldek was the natural—and only—planet of choice.

The only problem was that when the Pleiadians discovered the DNA mutation, there was not enough time to correct the pat-terning in the plants and animals already on Maldek. Therefore, the first human colonization was prepared for in a new way. Partly due to the lack of self-trust in those to be brought to Maldek, and partly due to the ongoing chromosome and DNA changes that must be corrected in a consistent manner over time, the Pleiadian and Sirian Archangelic Higher Council decided that a single guardian serving as Supreme Being for the planet would come to Maldek and remain in the planet's atmosphere in the higher dimensions. The Supreme Being would personally have to blend with the higher consciousnesses of all the beings on Maldek and assume the role of translating the solar and galactic encodings to the planet. This would be done by bringing the former Martians, and other groups who were to inhabit Maldek, to the planet at a very specific time during which the Photon Band from the Galactic Center would be in alignment with Sirius, Alcyone, the Sun, and Maldek itself. This Supreme Being would function as a cosmic gateway inside the Photon Band through which the souls and spirit beings of the people would pass on their way to the planet's surface. The human beings would be in their light body forms. While moving through the Photon Band and the Supreme Being's consciousness, they would be downstepped vibrationally until they were on the surface of the planet. Over a period of what on Earth would be one moon cycle, their light bodies would slow down vibrationally until they were physical again.

The Supreme Being would have to be a very evolved being, capable of holding individuation and Oneness simultaneously, and completely dedicated to the evolution and love of the Martians and other galactic citizens. He would have to hold the "dream" of the Divine Plan for the entire planet and every species on it, and be both totally receptive to the encodings from the local, regional, and galactic suns and able to function and decide independently what was needed at any given time. Archangel Lucifer was the one chosen for this high office.

Legions of angels, devas, and other guides and guardians were sent ahead to prepare Maldek after having a group blending with Lucifer and the Galactic Center. The Pleiadian Emissaries of Light as well as a group of hierarchical beings from the Andromeda galaxy were part of this preparatory assembly, since both groups would play key roles in the evolutionary guidance of the new Maldekians. The Andromedans had a strong interest in what was occurring in your solar ring since many of the Andromedans who had been damaged had been brought here, and because Andromeda and the Milky Way are what you might think of as twin-flame galaxies. They were also here because of the Divine Plan for a universal melting pot on Earth in upcoming times.

In the meantime, all of those who were to serve on Maldek went through the same process. After blending with and being encoded at the Galactic Center, they moved through the gateway and consciousness of Sirius, then through the gateway and consciousness of Alcyone, then through all of the suns of the Pleiades, and last of all through the Sun of your solar ring. Each sun/star that the beings passed through was a gateway to the next, until they reached your solar ring. Some of the larger guardian beings were stationed in Maldek's atmosphere and at vortex points to maintain the planet's "chakra system." Others were sent to maintain and stabilize the poles to keep the planet's orbits consistent. Yet others were sent to the center of the planet where, in the beginning, they were to receive encodings and instructions from the photon band. Later they would receive encodings from the Sun and stars and their instructions from Lucifer.

One of the precedents set was to have male and female beings who were divine complements to one another located at the interior core of the planet. They would hold the energy of the tantric, creative life force and male/female love, balance, and equality. These couples would receive their instructions and establish the energy patterns for the planet and its people from the inside out, based on solar encodings and Lucifer's specific instructions to them. Their main function was to go into a state of tantric blending with one another and radiate energy waves from the union out through the planet's layers to the surface, and then out into the atmosphere. Male/female balance and sexual healing were still major karmic themes for the former Martians as well as the other groups who had been chosen to come to Maldek for physical life.

[Author's Note: I am quite familiar with this latter role, as this is where and when I first became active in your solar ring. I was one of the female beings at the core of the planet who held the balance with a male partner of tantric union and male/female equality and balance.]

Lucifer Brings 5000 Souls to Maldek—Year 0

At the end of the 26,000-year cycle that preceded humanoid colonization on Maldek, when the Photon Band was in its exact alignment with the solar and stellar gateways and the planet, Lucifer came straight through each of the aligned gateways into the atmosphere of Maldek. He was blended with over 5000 souls in light bodies, whom he brought with him. When he had downstepped all the way to the sixth dimension with the 5000 soon-to-be Maldekians, a large group of solar angels, who had been previously assigned two angels to each soul, joined them and took the ensouled light bodies the rest of the way. Once on the planet's surface, they stopped in the fourth dimension for the remainder of the process, which took one moon cycle. During that time, the incarnating beings adjusted to the planet's atmosphere, frequency patterns, and orbital spin. When the acclimation time was completed, the final downstepping to third-dimensional form took place. For the Maldekians, it was as if they briefly dozed off and then "woke up" on Maldek's surface with vague memories of traveling through space and spending time with the angels—as if they had experienced a lucid dream. For about a year, they could telepathically communicate with their two guardian angels. At the end of that time, the telepathic communications were cut off and continued only in dreams. The Maldekians were prepared in advance for the change and were ready when it came.

At this stage of colonization, simple shelters were established, and food and basic herbal medicines were made known and available to the people. They knew they could call on their guardian angels and Lucifer when they needed to through silent communion and dreams. They were also told that everything that existed was sacred and should be honored, and that males and females were equal and must discover each other's true value and function. Sexual reproduction and death were explained, as was the purpose and need for evolution and healing the soul/spirit connection. Natural pairing had already been done prior to their arrival on the planet, so their tendency toward bonding and mating with partners was inherent by this time.

The people were not told about their previous incarnations and home planets, only about the patterns that needed to be transformed. For the first 5200 years, basic noninterference from higher-dimensional beings existed on conscious levels. However, Lucifer and all of his legions of angels, guides, devas, and other helpers maintained the orbital patterns, solar encodings, and atmospheric conditions, and protected Maldek from invasion by beings from any other planets or star systems. Changes in existing structure, especially if they involved direct contact with higher beings, could only occur via "consensus minus one person" in each individual colony. At the end of the 5200 years, Pleiadian Emissary of Light members would be incarnated into each colony to awaken the Maldekians' consciousness to evolutionary purpose and to offer any other needed reminders or teachings. Reevaluation of the existing order would be done at that time as well.

Martian/Andromedan Colony

Besides the Martians, who numbered about 750 due to split of the souls of the original beings, there were beings who had formerly lived as slaves to a more evolved group on a planet in the Andromedan galaxy. They had left when their planet had blown up due to atomic explosions beneath its surface and in its atmosphere. This group of Andromedans numbered about 750 as well. They were placed in a colony with the former Martians.

Orion Colony

A separate colony was formed with about 1500 people from a planet in the Orion system that had been enslaved for many centuries. Their oppressors had been from the same group of Lyrans who had invaded Mars twice during its period of inhabitation. An entire solar ring in Orion had been captured and run by those power-hungry ones. They had succeeded in destroying the planet's atmosphere and all of its people, just as on Mars, which had left this group of 1500 in need of a new planet. Because the group as a whole had wanted to be free at the time their planet was made uninhabitable, the Pleiadians had intervened under direction from the Galactic Center and brought them, after several stages of healing and preparation, to Maldek.

Black Hole Colony

A third colony consisted of 1000 beings who had been incarnate in a different galaxy. A solar implosion had created a black hole and destroyed their home. This had not been caused, as with the other groups, by human control and misuse of power and technology, but had been the result of a collision of two galaxies. Spiritually speaking, the so-called collision was actually a mating and blending of the two giant celestial beings, and not a disaster at all. The 1000 beings of this "Black Hole Colony" had been evolving for less than their equivalent of your 26,000-year cycle when the collision occurred. Their nature was cherublike, and their basic essential qualities were innocence, curiosity, and the desire for everyone to be happy. Much of their karmic history had to do with denial of unpleasant emotions in an attempt to remain happy and make others happy all the time. They also carried guilt and shame, since they felt like failures when they or anyone around them became sick or unhappy in any way. As a result, addiction had become a problem for the race. Alcoholic beverages, hallucinogenic plants, sex, and pleasurable sensations in general had all been taken to extremes in an attempt to stay "high," or happy. Therefore, when the galactic merger occurred, they were not ready to ascend into the higher dimensions, and their experience of the merger was a cataclysmic one.

Young Soul Colony

The remaining 1000 beings consisted of two groups from a star system on the far side of the Milky Way that was similar to your solar ring. Unlike the other new Maldekians, these beings had been left on their home planet with no personal soul encodings from its local sun. This had been to see what they would do without any outside stimulus toward goal orientation and evolution. The beings themselves were souls evolved from one- and two-dimensional lifeforms over a period of roughly a million years. As group consciousnesses, both groups had longed for something more to give them meaning and purpose. The members of this "Young Soul Colony" were ready to discover new options and motivations by contacting beings who had come by choice into third-dimensional reality from higher dimensions. Curiosity about the nature of existence, and how and by whom it had been created, had entered their conscious minds as well. These young souls, desirous of spirit, were on Maldek to find spirit through eventual connection with the other colonies and, for the first time, through having a relationship with a Supreme Being and the Sun.

The four colonies remained totally independent of one another for the first 2000 years on Maldek. This was due to traveling distances from one to the other, and also to predetermined timing. The groups needed time to acclimate to their new home planet and its environment, to heal genetically as much as possible, and to develop a conscious impetus to explore. After 2000 years, most of the plants and animals on Maldek were cleared of the chromosomal mutations and the Maldekians were beginning to respond to these healthier food sources with soul level and DNA-mutation healing.

In general, the Maldekians were simple and somewhat lethargic people. It had been decided in advance that certain aspects of spirit connection to the body and impulses toward creation in the seventh chakra would remain dormant until the chromosomal mutations were at least partially healed. Their pineal glands were simply not equipped to receive higher-dimensional frequencies, communications, and light until the agreed-upon activation time, which was to take place at 2600 years, halfway through the first 5200-year cycle of the longer 26,000-year evolutionary cycle.

When the Maldekians began to travel, they were still spiritually asleep in most ways and not prone to questioning the nature of reality. However, the impetus to travel and explore had been activated, and colonists began to go on pilgrimages. At first, these pilgrimages were taken by small groups of not more than thirty people, for not more than twenty days at a time. Travel was done with minimal food supplies, since Maldek was a planet of plenty; at that time, the inhabitants were meat eaters, and they found food along the way. At the end of their journeys, large gatherings were held at which the travelers would report what they had experienced.

Martian/Andromedan Colonists Meet Young Soul Colonists—Year 2000

Some of the people began to feel that travel to farther places was desirable. Their next goal was to go beyond a certain range of hills, or around a large body of water where other worlds might exist. Larger groups of up to sixty people prepared for and left on these extended journeys. On one of the first of these broader explorations, a group from the Martian/Andromedan Colony crossed paths with a group from the Young Soul Colony. Both groups were startled at first, but they allowed curiosity to bridge any gaps that existed. Though there were variations within each culture, and very different dialects, their languages were virtually the same. Originally, all of the colonies had been given the same fundamental language so that only cultural deviations would exist when the groups finally contacted one another.

This first encounter led to several days of camping together, storytelling, working out minor language barriers, sharing food, and discovering commonalities and differences. It was an exciting time for all concerned, and a major first step in the unfolding of curiosity and creative thinking. At first, the main interest of all concerned was comparison of the mundane aspects of life. Sharing of attitudes and cultural personality differences followed. At their current level of evolution and brain function, that was as far as their curiosity could go for quite some time. After about a week of camping together, they decided that a delegation from each colony would visit the colony of their newfound friends. When the groups returned to their respective homes, each consisted of approximately half original colony members and half members from the newly discovered colony. The Young Soul colonists had a natural tendency to yield to the Martian/Andromedan colonists' lead, even in their own home colony. The Martian/Andromedan people just seemed more decisive, mentally superior, and more creative and curious than the Young Soul group.

The homecoming of both groups, accompanied by their new friends, created quite a stir. In the Martian/Andromedan Colony, there was a deep inherent distrust of, and skepticism about, the newcomers due to the colonists' own karmic histories prior to Maldek. Both the Martians and Andromedans had been enslaved and destroyed on their home planets by invaders, so they carried deep subconscious fears and wariness toward the innocent beings from the Young Soul Colony. The Young Soul colonists, on the other hand, were very naive and trusting. They were also eager for contact with more evolved—or at least more experienced—souls, and readily gave up seniority to their hosts. This latter fact made it easier for the host colony members to accept them and share their homes with them.

In the Young Soul Colony, the Martian/Andromedan visitors were received with awe and wonder and great enthusiasm. Everyone wanted the new friends to stay with them in their homes. They would sit and stare at the visitors for long periods of time until the guests became uncomfortable and would try to initiate conversation or activities. When the guests would ask for things, their requests were quickly met; their hosts were even somewhat apologetic for not having anticipated their needs. The Martian/Andromedan visitors were gracious and did not take advantage of this weakness on the part of their hosts. If anything, they found it to be both annoying and whimsical.

After the agreed-upon passage of time—which for convenience I, Ra, will call a moon cycle—the travelers from both colonies set out for the original rendezvous location where they visited for a few days again, sharing stories from the visits to each other's colonies. Those who had been visitors returned to their own homes, and about thirty new members from each colony traveled back to their new friends' homes with them. This exchange program went on for over two years, with a total of about 150 people from each colony visiting their planetary neighbors. Trade of goods unique to each colony had been discussed but, for most items, seemed impractical due to travel time and difficulty. During one return trip to the Martian/Andromedan Colony, an idea for a solution developed. Witnessing a rock slide along the way, one man mentally registered the concept of rolling as an easy method of movement. Dragging bundles or carrying them was too much work, but rolling had promise. Within six months, a simple but efficient wheel had been invented, as well as a basic cart in which to haul things.

In the meantime, the other two colonies were also taking short journeys and pilgrimages, but they had not yet encountered other civilizations. Their evolutionary levels and cultural development were very similar to the two groups who had just interfaced.

Trade Begins–Year 2003

On the first two trade journeys, the stronger men took turns pulling the cart filled with trade goods from the Martian/ Andromedan Colony to the Young Soul Colony. A wide path had been worn between the two locations and served as a road, but it was still a very slow way to travel. The Martian/Andromedan men also pulled the wheeled cart back to their home colony, filled with goods for which they had traded. Trade added a whole new area of excitement and possibility to the Maldekians' life styles, and after only two trips they thought up the idea of having large ox-like animals pull the carts. It took a while to work out the details of harnessing and training the animals, yet within three-and-a-half years of the first meeting of the two colonies, the use of the wheel, carts, and animals for labor had been initiated.

It was at this stage that the next new creative idea emerged. Almost simultaneously, the two groups decided to explore in new directions together to find out if there were other Maldekian colonies and/or other environments and natural resources to be discovered. A group of thirty members from each colony came together at the Young Soul Colony and set out on a new joint adventure. They traveled for the equivalent of one-and-a-half moon cycles before coming to an ocean, which, to the Maldekians, seemed gigantic and endless. Continuing the journey a few more days along the coastline brought them to a large river inlet that was too deep to pass without boats—and boats had not been invented yet. However, the sight of logs floating on the river and out to sea planted the first seed of thought about water transportation. The travelers remained camped along the river for several days while they explored inland for narrower and shallower parts of the river, but none were to be found. However, they did discover a way to catch the large fish they had never seen before, and the explorers enjoyed their first meal of something akin to sea bass.

Three Colonies Meet–Year 2004

After they returned, the travelers decided that, overall, this journey had been exciting and stimulating for both groups. They agreed to start their next joint excursion at the Martian/Andromedan Colony. This trip took them through an open plain that was drier and hotter than either group was accustomed to. The flat plain appeared to go on forever, until at the end of nearly two-and-a-half moon cycles, another large river was discovered. It seemed to be their destiny to end at uncrossable waters. But this time, there was another inspiration to invent water travel: while exploring up and down the banks of the river, they came across a band of humans camped on the far side. These people seemed similar to the members of the other two colonies except for one major difference—the new, and unreachable, people were extremely dark-skinned, and some of them had snow-white hair, which was also new to the other colonists.

Attempts at yelling across the river to one another were fruitless. The river was deep and flowed just strongly enough to block out their voices, other than undecipherable sounds. The travelers remained camped across from the new, unknown people; the magnetic pull to meet these people was so strong that it was difficult to leave. In fact, when the group did leave, ten volunteers, five from each colony chose to remain and set up camp across the river from the dark-skinned colonists, who were originally from Orion. The Orion colonists also chose to leave a small group camped at the riverside while their fellow journeyers returned home.

Reluctantly, and greatly in need of a means to cross rivers, the rest of the adventurers left for their respective home colonies. Their stories at home incited curiosity about, and desire for contact with, the new group. With camps on both sides of the river representing three of the Maldekian colonies, those at home were astir with excitement about the new discovery and the seemingly insurmountable river barrier.

First River Crossing–Year 2004

In all three of the colonies involved, people busied themselves in an attempt to invent a craft that would meet their current needs. Floating something that could carry their weight was the easiest part of the solution. Logs floating at the edge of the ocean had given them the idea of tying logs together to make a raft. The more challenging problem was how to steer the raft to prevent it from floating downstream beyond its destination. After the normal creative process of trial and error, they finally began to experiment with oar making and came up with a design that seemed feasible. The Martian/Andromedan Colony led the way in the invention process, and after making four pairs of oars, allowing for eight strong rowers, sent word to the Young Soul Colony that they were ready to return to the river and try out a plan.

It was a long journey of two-and-a-half moon cycles back to the river site. Once they arrived and shared the invention idea with the men camped by the river, the search began for trees of equal size with which to build the raft. Within two weeks of their return to the river camp, a raft had been made and was ready to test. It was decided that sixteen of the strongest people should go first, with no cargo. This would allow for eight men to row at all times, with a relief person for each one if needed. Though the river was not flooding or extraordinarily fast, the normal flow was enough to make the men work hard to keep the raft going in the right direction. On the first try, they made it all the way across, but nearly half a mile downstream. All of the people on both sides followed the progress, walking downstream along the banks of the river as the raft was carried along by the current.

When the raft reached the other shore, there was a great cry of celebration from both sides of the river. The black colonists ran to help pull the raft ashore, and then both groups just stood back, looking at one another unselfconsciously. They scanned each other from head to toe, and after a few minutes began to make comments about oddities of appearance and general similarities and differences. It was then noticed that everyone's language was similar, again with only cultural and dialectic variations.

The Orion colonists invited the lighter-skinned arrivals to follow them back to their camp, where they began to undress the newcomers. It was customary, and considered a common courtesy, among their people to bathe and massage travelers who had just arrived. The newcomers, however, were taken aback by this strange and suspicious gesture, and tension mounted. The Orion colonists did not understand the obvious wariness being displayed by their guests, since in their minds they were honoring them. After a few minutes, the misunderstanding became clearer when one of the puzzled Orion colonists said, "We honor you. Do you not like to be honored?" One of the newcomers informed the Orion colonists that they felt invaded, not honored. At that point, one of the Orion colonists had a flash of understanding and she explained their custom thoroughly. She then asked how the newcomers honored one another when they arrived from a journey. This was the beginning of comparing cultures and ways of living.

Before the day was half over, the Orion colonists and the sixteen people from the other two colonies had managed to drag the raft back to the campsite. Halfway there, someone had the idea of pulling it upstream at the water's edge, which was much easier than pulling it on dry and rocky land. By nightfall, all forty of the journeyers and the ten who had remained camped by the river had crossed the river to the camp of the Orion colonists. Food was prepared together and shared as the people talked and celebrated long into the night. The newcomers were invited to the home of the Orion colonists, which was less than one moon cycle away. They wholeheartedly agreed and set off on the next stage of their journey the following day.

By the time the band of sixty people arrived at the Orion Colony, they had all but mastered the minor language differences and knew much of one another's history. They were welcomed with gasps of surprise and curiosity by all who saw them. When the stories about the raft were told, the people were in awe. Of course, the visitors were again greeted by their hosts attempting to undress them for ritual cleansing and massage. This time many of the travelers had "psyched themselves up" for this experience and, surprisingly, found it to be very pleasurable. About one-third of the new arrivals could not bring themselves to participate, and with the help of the Orion campers who had initially greeted them, they managed to explain the cultural difference in a nonoffensive manner. Feasting and long hours of questions and answers followed. For several days, the newcomers were given sightseeing tours, during which they visited every neighborhood, home, garden, and shop.

The Orion people were proud of their own inventions, even the simplest of devices for grinding grains, or weaving fibers for clothing. They demonstrated their tools and devices and explain how and when they had been invented and by whom. Then the newcomers were questioned about how they performed these tasks. Most often, the Martian/Andromedan colonists described more sophisticated discoveries and methods, which led to requests for demonstrations. Items that were easy to make were made and demonstrated, and the newcomers quickly gained in reputation for being supremely intelligent and clever. That reputation had already been established with the amazing invention of the raft and oars, and it expanded as the various colonists talked and shared with one another.

After another moon cycle had passed, plans were made for the return journey. Members of the Orion Colony were invited to return with them, and it was decided that fifty of them would do so. Three families from the Martian/Andromedan Colony and three from the Young Soul Colony decided to remain at the Orion Colony. Therefore, when they began the return trip, there were only thirty-five travelers from the two colonies escorting the fifty Orion colonists. Nearly half of the Orion colonists went with the band of travelers to the river to see them off. This made for a slower journey and the need to carry food, but nonetheless, no one would have even considered dissuading them from going along. The Orion colonists were eager to witness the use of the miraculous watercraft as well as participate in some small way in the adventure of their fellow colonists.

Once the river was crossed, the remainder of the journey was another two-and-a-half moon cycles. There was much talk on the trip of the need to shorten travel time, but at that point it seemed to be futile to even discuss anything as far fetched as a means of road travel. The ox carts were as slow as or slower than people walking, especially if the carts were very full, so faster travel seemed impossible.

Arrival at the Martian/Andromedan Colony brought another round of excitement, long evenings of storytelling, question-and-answer sessions, tours of the colony, and demonstrations of every tool, weaving device, and mechanistic invention the colony had. The wheels and ox carts brought another round of awe-filled exclamations from the Orion visitors, especially when they learned that both had been invented in the recent past. After a week of rest and discovery in the new colony, about half of the Orion colonists departed for the Young Soul Colony, accompanying its members who had been on the river-crossing journey and a dozen of the Martian/Andromedan colonists. Travel in these mixed groups was always fun for everyone involved. The evenings of shared food and stories and the talks about anticipated adventures to come were highlights of the trip, equaled by the scenery and the varied climates and terrains along the way. So the trip was smooth and pleasant, albeit a lengthy one of another two-and-a-half moon cycles.

Arrival at the Young Soul Colony brought more excitement, late nights of talking and storytelling, as well as the usual tours and demonstrations of tools and devices. The people were learning so much from one another that all three colonies were evolving in the area of mechanics just by meeting and sharing with one another. Again, talk about how to travel faster was prevalent, since the trip from the Young Soul Colony to the Orion Colony took nearly six moon cycles.

Some of the Orion people who had come to visit the other two groups wanted to stay and make their homes with these new people. Since everyone was in agreement, three families stayed at the Young Soul Colony, and five families remained in the Martian/Andromedan Colony. Previously, a few families from the Young Soul Colony had relocated in the Martian/Andromedan Colony, and members of the Martian/Andromedan Colony had permanently relocated in the Young Soul Colony. So Maldek's colonies were becoming diversified. There was also a small village that had been established about halfway between the two colonies. It had originally been created as and considered a stopover location for travelers between the two colonies, as well as a trade center where the people could go to drop off and pick up trade goods in only half the distance and time. During the one year this small village had existed, it had grown to contain about thirty people from each colony. Extra buildings were under construction that could be used to house travelers in exchange for trade goods.

The idea of establishing another small village for trade and travel accommodations halfway between the Martian/Andromedan Colony and the Orion Colony was soon acted upon. So within one-and-a-half years of the first river crossing, a village was established on the Martian/Andromedan side of the river. This site started out with a dozen or so members from each of the three colonies and within another year it had grown to 200 people, fairly evenly mixed. Mating and marriage between the different races soon followed, so that ten years after travels and exploration had begun, the three colonies were becoming quite integrated and were producing children of all possible mixes. The people were excited about the changes and new opportunities, and though many preferred to remain in their original homes, all welcomed members from other colonies and had not even a second thought about intermating and intermarrying.

Twelve years into the age of travel and exploration, the Young Soul colonists and the Martian/Andromedan colonists remembered their former trip to the ocean, where the river inlet spilled into the sea. Talk began about going back and building another raft at that location in order to explore the other side of the river. Maybe there were other colonies there as well, and everyone certainly wanted to find out. Travel plans were made, and members of all three colonies, totaling about sixty-five, set off on this new adventure. While their friends journeyed, the colonists at home busily tried to improve upon the design of the wheel and ox cart and find ways to quicken travel.

The explorers reached the river and, remembering how they had been swept downstream by the current even when rowing, they decided to go about a mile upstream and build the raft there. They also made larger oars for this venture, since the current was stronger and they needed to counter it both in distance upstream and strength of rowing. They built the raft and got everyone across the river, then set out on foot again along the coastline. A few days later, they divided into two groups. Far in the distance was a sharp, triangular-shaped mountain. Half of the group went inland, and half followed the oceanfront, agreeing to meet midway, at the base of the triangular mountain, in half a moon cycle.

Travelers Arrive at Black Hole Colony–Year 2012

When the time was up and the two groups rendezvoused with one another, they had little to report. So they agreed to divide again for further exploration. This time they decided to meet after one full moon cycle of exploration. Eager to cover as much territory as possible, the two groups traveled longer hours, eating whatever they found along the way that was edible, in order to waste as little time as possible. There was a pressing sense of urgency about finding another group of people; they were not disappointed. Less than halfway into the allotted time, the inland group came upon the fourth Maldekian colony. It was located in a narrow valley with a stream running through its middle, and was not visible until the band of travelers was practically upon it. As they approached the colony, they were met by gasps of surprise and wonder. People came running from all over the colony as word spread of the strange band of newcomers: some light-skinned and fair-haired, some light- to medium-skinned and dark-haired, and some with very dark skin and black or snow-white hair.

The people of the new colony, the Black Hole Colony, had unusual bluish-gray skin color, blue-black hair, and black eyes. They looked similar to the present-day pictures of Krishna, the East Indian god on Earth, although not such an extreme blue color. They were also much taller and stronger than the members of the other three colonies, which made them quite a striking group to come upon, indeed. Once again, discoveries about language similarities were made, and communication was relatively easy. The travelers were welcomed to the Black Hole Colony as if they were some sort of gods who had just descended from the heavens. The idea of the existence of other civilizations had never even occurred to the Black Hole colonists. So it was even more of a surprise to have members of other civilizations walk right into their homes. A few days of sharing stories and answering questions, however, took care of some of the mystique about the visitors being gods. Yet the sharing piqued new interests. The travelers were treated cordially, but with more detachment than there had been in previous first encounters.

Several of the explorers were sent to rendezvous at the appointed destination and time with the oceanfront travelers. They returned to the Black Hole Colony with the rest of the band. The travelers were housed separately from the members of the Black Hole Colony, and though they were not treated rudely, they remained more segregated from the host colony members than they were accustomed to. After one-and-a-half moon cycles in the Black Hole Colony, it was decided that the travelers should return home. Their hosts were invited to send people from the colony back with them, and they promised that the Black Hole colonists would be taken to all of the other colonies and introduced to the ways of life in each. The Black Hole Colony, as a whole, declined the offer readily and did not invite the travelers to leave a delegation behind. So the traveling band returned to their home colonies in full number.

What was not understood by the travelers was the origin of the Black Hole Colony's members. The sudden collision of the two galaxies, accompanied by the instant death of all the people, as well as the temporary loss of themselves in the black hole, had left these people's souls imprinted with a fear of change or anything sudden and unexpected. The arrival of the band of travelers, which was very sudden and unexpected, as well as all of the talk about oceans, rivers, watercraft, wheels, and ox carts, had left the Black Hole colonists feeling dazed and internally shaken. The subconscious reasons for their feelings of apprehension and dread were not even understood by the people of the Black Hole Colony themselves; but they had remained vaguely aloof and distant in order to allow as little impact as possible from the outsiders. It had been a relief to them when the uninvited people had gone. At the same time, doors had been opened to new worlds of possibilities. The people of the Black Hole Colony could no longer bury their heads in the sand and remain safe and happy with their status quo. There was more to life now than they had previously understood, and their psyches would never be the same because of that knowledge.

Discovery and Invention—Years 2012 to 3200

When the travelers returned home, they told of their cordial but detached treatment and the lack of interest in travel by the blue people. They agreed there was no need to waste further exploration time in that direction, and thus focused on improving trade and travel conditions and broadening their cultural horizons. Forms of music and primitive art were beginning to be exchanged and blended and new sounds and designs were born of the intermixing. Evolution, in general, accelerated more and more as time went on.

The raft evolved into a quasi-houseboat and then into a floating bridge of sorts. This latter invention worked well for the people until water levels rose and rapids increased, washing the bridge away. The next evolutionary step was a swinging bridge that could not be affected by water levels. A site was located where two banks of similar height existed about a mile and a half downstream from the original crossing location. Over 500 people showed up for the testing of this first swinging bridge. Everyone had to try it out, of course, and when, at the end of the day, it had held strong, they celebrated the brilliant new invention.

Normal technological and cultural evolutionary growth continued for the next few centuries, until the end of the first 2600 years. By that time, most of the chromosomal defects had been cleared, or were well on the way to being cleared. The built-in timing mechanism in the DNA of the people and the Sun's encoding were activated. At first, the people simply remembered their dreams in more detail, and realized that their dreams had significance. Then, as their seventh chakras and pineal glands were activated, the people began to be aware of energy and thoughts instead of simply taking them for granted. They began to see with more perceptual depth and an awareness of subtle color variances. Subtleties of flavors, sounds, smells, shapes, and colors gradually began to awaken in their senses. Cooking methods changed to suit their more sophisticated tastes. Art took on new meaning with a trend toward realism and an emphasis on creating three-dimensional impressions and likenesses. Those who specialized in portraits were especially revered, and more lifelike art, in general, received great praise.

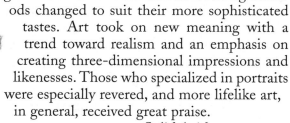

Solid bridge construction followed, at about 2700 years of colonization, and wheels became so smooth that ox-cart travel took half the time it had originally. The three colonies that traded and mixed with one another became more and more integrated, until almost half of the population of each colony was comprised of members who had originated in one of the other colonies or who were the offspring of mixed coupling.

Ornamental buildings and hieroglyphic writing developed over the next 100 years. In the following 200 years, the Maldekians created clay tablets, which were the first books, and later books were written on papyrus. Written language was simplified to sixty main characters with variations on the primary themes. Schools were begun in which the children learned history, art, written language, and basic life skills. Those who showed aptitude were taught instrument making, music, bridge building, healing with medicines, and other specialties.

Second Journey to Black Hole Colony—Year 3200

Only minor arguments and jealousies clouded the lives of the Maldekians for over 3200 years of civilization. Their lives grew in variety, artistic appeal, and comfort, and they were, in general, a happy people. At that point, the Maldekians of the three intermixed colonies put together a band of explorers to travel to the Black Hole Colony again. Stories from the past told of the people with blue-gray skin and tall, strong bodies, and the people wanted to try sharing with them again. About fifty people decided to go on the journey and take gifts of the finer aspects of their culture with them. They carefully packed sample pieces of pottery, painting, scrolls of written language, small tools, spices and herbal medicines, the finest fabric, perfume, and delicate foods that would not spoil. They hoped that all of these gifts and examples of their culture would express good will and be welcomed by the formerly aloof people.

When the travelers arrived, they found the Black Hole Colony in turmoil and still very primitive by comparison to the other colonies, due to its fear of change. Extreme weather conditions had caused flooding, mud slides, and destruction of food sources, as well as the loss of many homes and other buildings. The arrival of outsiders at such a crucial time was a shock at first, but the colonists soon relaxed as they watched the visitors pitch in and help clean up the damage. The mixed band of travelers even cooked for the people so their time was freed for other chores that needed to be done. The visitors located food sources and shared the foods they had brought with the host colony. Tools brought on the journey were used to repair and rebuild damaged structures. When the reconstruction was completed, the rest of the gifts brought from home were shared with the Black Hole colonists. The colonists were shocked and deeply grateful for the traveler's generosity, not only with gifts, but with time and hard work. They opened to the travelers more and more as time went by.

When the hard work and cleanup were done, the visitors began to share stories of the inventions, culture, and general evolution of the other three colonies. They told the Black Hole colonists that members of their colony were not only welcome but wanted in the other colonies. They expressed their love of diversity, and described the richness of shared cultural differences. The history of the other three colonies was related, including how each had benefited through contact with the others. By the time the visitors were ready to return to their homes, the Black Hole colonists had come to accept and value their friendship. The visitors were invited to leave a delegation behind to live with and teach the people about new ways. Twenty of the Black Hole colonists decided to make the trip back to the other colonies with the travelers. At last, the four colonies of Maldek were uniting.

The return journey was slower than the trip to the Black Hole Colony since the Black Hole colonists had never traveled long distances before and could not walk long hours like the others. At times, the explorers grew impatient and irritable due to the frequent rest breaks and short days of travel time. But they adapted reasonably well and kept their grievances to themselves. When the band finally arrived at the first of their destinations, the Young Soul Colony, they were welcomed with great celebration, feasts of the finest foods, music, and dancing. Being rather shy people, the Black Hole travelers were gracious but quiet and reserved at the celebrations. They preferred being with only a few people at a time, the fewer the better, and adapted poorly to the large crowds that had gathered for the festivities. The new journeyers were overwhelmed by the superior building structures, artistic influence, and general affluence. Their hosts seemed almost decadent to them in comparison to their own home surroundings and life style; but they were not prone to rudeness, so they kept their opinions to themselves.

As the band of travelers ventured on to the halfway village, which had grown into a small township of around 350 people, and then on to the Martian/Andromedan Colony, the Black Hole travelers grew more and more homesick. The more elaborate the displays of cultural and technological advancements and superiority, the more the visitors from the Black Hole Colony longed to return to the simplicity and familiarity of their own lives. However, still not wanting to be rude, they visited each colony and were shown all aspects of daily life style and creative outlets. After being at the Orion Colony for less than a moon cycle, the visitors announced their desire to return to their own home. Their various hosts found it hard to understand why they were not impressed with the beauty and advances of their colonies. The guests simply continued to repeat that they had been treated quite well and had learned much, but preferred to return to their home colony.

The return journey to the Black Hole Colony, which was done in stages due to its length, required nearly a year to complete. By then, the Black Hole travelers were more than ready to be back in their little valley. When they did finally arrive at home, the reluctant travelers were so relieved that they all went through a period of releasing the shock of their long journey before they finally felt back to normal in their own homes. The members of the other three colonies who had stayed at the Black Hole Colony were reasonably content, though they had never fully adapted to the coolness of the people and their reserved approach to progress. When the band of travelers from the other three colonies prepared to leave, those who had lived at the Black Hole Colony politely, but eagerly, prepared to return home with their friends. The travelers departed feeling some tension and disquiet about the segregation of the colonies again, and yet it was the overwhelming choice of all concerned.

The Black Hole colonists who had remained at home during the journey of their friends had mixed feelings about the departure of their short-term resident friends from far away. They felt as if they had lost something valuable; yet at the same time the relief and security of having the outsiders' influence removed from their homes was pervasive. As the returned travelers described the horrors of the celebrations, the elaborate decor, the fancy food, the complex buildings, and other aspects of life in the three colonies, the Black Hole colonists once again experienced mixed feelings. They felt like they were missing something very important, and at the same time, they felt gratitude that they were not part of that other world.

The travelers from the three colonies returned home feeling that they had failed to influence the Black Hole colonists as they should have. Yet all were relieved to be free of the tension and disquiet they had felt around the strangers. Life in the three colonies returned to normal.

The rest of the first 5200-year cycle was filled with inventiveness and cultural growth. The population increased slightly until the three colonies, which had begun with about 4000 inhabitants, now contained nearly 5000 people. Some of the beings were choosing to split their souls in order to experience male and female incarnations simultaneously, which accounted for the population increase. The Black Hole Colony, on the other hand, changed minimally and maintained a population of around 1000 residents at all times.

Solid bridges existed across the river between the Orion Colony and the Martian/Andromedan Colony, as well as across the river between the Young Soul Colony and the Black Hole Colony, even though the latter was rarely used. Carts pulled by teams of oxen now carried larger loads, and sometimes elderly people and children traveled in carts as well. Art, music, and language were highly revered areas of accomplishment for most of the people and gave them a sense of pride. Mining and metallurgy had emerged and were being developed. Jewelry making and design were new fields that brought much excitement. Although there were natural leaders of each of the colonies, no one had power over others. The leaders were honored for their natural leadership qualities; they were quick thinking, and had good decision-making abilities and communication skills. Each colony had several members of both sexes who took leadership roles without actually controlling the people.

The daily lives of the people were still more tribal than the lives of people in today's modern society. Electricity was unknown; transportation still consisted of walking and ox carts, with water transportation only for the purpose of crossing rivers. Fishing was now a favored profession and added more diversity to the diet. Agricultural advances had also contributed to the quality and diversity of food choices. However, the Maldekians' conscious world was still focused only on the physical, and that pointed to spiritual awareness as the natural next step at the end of the 5200-year cycle.

When the Pleiadian Emissaries of Light began to be birthed among the four colonies and in the smaller, halfway villages, it was about seventy-five years before the end of the cycle. There were about a dozen Pleiadians born into each colony, and four into each of the villages. These children were noticeably different from birth, as they chose not to accept the genetics of their parents beyond what was absolutely necessary. Blond and red-haired children were born to dark-haired and dark-skinned families. Unusual facial structures that were unknown to any of the existing races appeared. When the children began to speak, they did not carry the local dialects, but had a strangely different dialect of their own, shared only with the unique, new children in all of the colonies. They were extremely bright and much more alert than the other Maldekian babies and children, and they emanated so much love and poise that the people were not sure how to respond to them.

When the Pleiadian children began to speak clearly, they described tall people from the stars with bodies made of light, who took care of them and talked to them. They told the Maldekians that the star people were always there, but that the Maldekians could not see them because they were made of spirit and light, not matter. These children were very loving to their parents, other family members, and friends, so much so that the other children were jealous of the praise and attention given to these special ones. As the children got older, their ability to share their wisdom, love, and knowledge increased. They began to teach the people about soul and spirit, and about the karma and evolution of every being. They talked about the guardian Light Beings who had always protected them and who kept the world safe for them and their planet. Reincarnation and the purpose behind it was explained. They specifically described how all of the people on Maldek had lived in other places before, as well as in their own ancestors' bodies on Maldek. The Pleiadian children even told the people the names of the planets and star systems from whence they had come, and said that their colonies should be called by those names.

Pleiadian Children Rename Colonies—Years 5125 to 5200

The Martian/Andromedan colonists, whose colony was now mixed, were told to call their colony Mars II, since Mars was located in the same solar ring as Maldek. The people were taught to locate Mars in the night sky, and they learned that it was really a planet like Maldek, reflecting sunlight, even though it looked like a star.

The Young Soul colonists were told to call their colony Solaris. This was the name of the solar ring from whence the two groups comprising the colony had come. It was explained to them that they had been brought to Maldek because they needed to interact with other beings who had experienced very different evolutionary histories from their own.

The Orion colonists were shown Orion in the night sky and told about the history of that star system as a galactic gateway between dimensions and galaxies. Stories were shared about the power-hungry ones who had come from Lyra and taken over one of the Orion solar systems in an attempt to control the gateway; this attempt had been only partially successful. The Lyrans had enslaved these beings, tortured them, and eventually destroyed their planet, but Divine Intervention by the Pleiadians and the hierarchies from Galactic Center had set them free. They were told to call their colony Free Orion.

The Free Orion colonists and Mars II colonists were also made aware of their similar histories of enslavement. The Martians had experienced the same history with the Lyran invaders as had the inhabitants of the Orion system. The Andromedans also had a similar past, but this had occurred with other Andromedans. The shared histories created strong bonds between the groups.

The Black Hole colonists were also told about their past and about their nature of being emotionally and spiritually cherublike. The Pleiadian children shared stories of the collision of the two galaxies, the black hole, and why the colonists feared change and sudden unexpected events. They also explained the people's karmic problems with addictions to constant happiness and the status quo. The Black Hole Colony was to be called Sogan, which was the name of the solar system from whence the colonists had come.

Maldek now officially housed four cities: Mars II, Solaris, Free Orion, and Sogan. In addition, there were two trade villages: the one between Mars II and Solaris was named Freedom Town; the one between Mars II and Free Orion was called the Town of Miracles, because the first river crossing had taken place at that location.

The Pleiadian children were mostly in their early teens by this time and were holding regular meetings with the colonists. The focus of these meetings was to teach the people about their own evolutionary histories; the purpose of spiritual evolution, in general; and what the upcoming times would hold. This latter information was more vague than specific, and consisted mostly of guidance about how to tune into spirit and the sacredness of all things. The Maldekians were also informed of the need to transmute karmic patterns; they were told that as their culture continued to grow, they would be presented with challenges from time to time in order to learn and transform the past. Teachings were given to all of the colonists about taking responsibility for creating their own reality, and about realizing that they had the freedom to choose their response in every situation, instead of reacting unconsciously. They were taught that these two guidelines were the keys to gracious growth and evolution. The Pleiadian children said that, without exception, the people had to transmute all ideas about victimhood and powerlessness and become cocreators with Divinity, or God/Goddess/All That Is. Transcending the illusion of limitation in the physical world would naturally occur with spiritual growth and vertical, or spiritual, alignment. As the Maldekians evolved spiritually and vibrationally, and realized their full intelligence, they would transcend these seeming physical limitations until they became Light itself. This would require many cycles of evolution, but it was their heritage, and they would all eventually accomplish this enlightenment experience and become one with the Divinity in themselves and in all of existence again.

For the remaining sixty years, spiritual teachings and simple practices were given to all Maldekians. Temples of Melchizadek, centers for high orders of initiatic trainings, were established for those who wished to devote their entire lives to spiritual study. (These temples were not unlike the Melchizadek temples built much later on Earth during the Atlantean eras. On both planets, the teachings and initiations given in these mystery schools were those of becoming enlightened and Christed beings while still in third-dimensional reality.) If the people wanted them to, members of the Pleiadian Emissaries of Light and Andromedan hierarchies would remain in the temples as teachers, but they would impose their teachings on no one who did not request them. All of the colonies agreed that they wanted the temples and leaders to become part of their world, and so they did.

At the end of the first 5200 years, there was consensus among all Maldekians about the importance of the temples and spiritual leaders, as well as the desire for spiritual evolution. The Sogan people still wished to remain isolated, while the other three groups wished to merge with them. The free will of the Sogan people was respected, and the other colonists were told that if any further contact was made between the colonies it had to be initiated by the Soganites. All the Maldekians agreed to continue existing rules of order, with one new addition: the people would still be protected against invasion, unless, through their own thought processes, they requested not to be. The Pleiadian and Andromedan spiritual teachers would remain with them as long as the people in each colony or village agreed by a majority. These agreements, as well as all other rules and changes, would be reviewed at the end of the next 5200-year cycle.

More extreme weather conditions than the people were accustomed to followed the meetings at the turn of the time cycle. These occurrences are always necessary to accommodate the changes in orbital pattern, solar frequency, and solar encoding when even the slightest pole shifts are made. The Maldekians were forewarned and therefore well prepared when these changes began. They had stored foods as advised, moved out of flood plains, improved roofing as needed, and made other preparations. When the floods, electrical storms, ice storms, and series of quakes were completed, only minor repairs and restoration were required before they continued with life as usual.

Spiritualization of Maldek—Years 5200 to 10,400

The entire next 5200-year cycle was predominantly focused on spiritual growth and establishing spiritual practices that could be shared by all. The Melchizadek temples were well visited and immediately attracted students who wished to devote their lives to studying metaphysical law and spiritual order. The secondary focus for that time cycle was on art, music, and architecture. The creative stimulus was strong in the people now—even the Soganites—and inner and outer beauty were important to them. They were learning to experience energy states emotionally and spiritually with more depth, and their relationships with one another, as well as their artistic areas of focus, reflected this new-found depth. The level they were experiencing was mainly due to their learning to be more present and to offer fuller attention to their companions and themselves. They were also learning to be more loving and nurturing to one another during sexual activity. Their experiences were similar to those of new meditators when they first experience being present in stillness and silence. There was a long way to go from there, but what they had was a crucial beginning.

The Solarians were still the slowest to develop on all levels, since they had begun their evolutionary process as lower-dimensional consciousnesses instead of as beings moving from the higher realms down. However, they were always eager to learn and explore, so they created little conflict because of their differences. The Soganites remained isolated from the rest of the planet, but continued to evolve in their own right. In summary: steady, slow growth was consistent throughout the planet's population and there were only minor disturbances and conflicts along the way.

At the end of that 5200-year cycle, the Maldekians as a whole were becoming consciously responsible beings, respecting all forms of life, natural resources, and one another. They were chiefly involved in self-improvement and examination of their lives in every area, from basic standards of living to creativity, spirituality, transportation, and relationships with others. Spirituality was still very ritualistic and experienced by most of them on a practical, idea level, but that is the nature of evolving beings who are learning to be spiritual.

Karmic Patterns Reintroduced in Stages–
Years 10,400 to 10,800

When it came time for the cyclical review, all was going as well as had been anticipated, with hardly any glitches. Therefore, the basic planetary laws remained the same. The next level of evolutionary soul-encoding from Galactic Center was released through the Sun in "time-released doses." It was time for the people—who had developed consistency, morality, security, and other vital strengths—to meet their shadows from the past. In other words, the karmic patterns from each person's and each group's previous experiences were ready to be released into their consciousnesses and their lives. The temples would continue and the Pleiadians and Andromedans would remain on Maldek as teachers, and provide assistance, understanding, and direction as new challenges presented themselves.

The changes were so subtle and gradual at first that the people hardly noticed them. The Mars II people slowly shifted to a more patriarchal focus. Men became the only ones to study full time in the temples. Women were more commonly seen as belonging to their husbands, while men started to explore promiscuity. The Mars II men also started pushing their supposed superiority onto the other colonists in an attempt to control trade. It took three generations for these shifts to take place after the third 5200-year cycle began, but the signs were clear. Men visited the temples more than women and were more involved in decision making. Women started to feel less important and taken for granted, but they were afraid to speak out. When they did speak out, they tended to get angry quickly, and the men reacted defensively. Household squabbles and minor incidents of violence began to occur. These were experienced with shame by all involved, and usually kept hushed up. As the frequency of these outbreaks and disputes between men and women increased, the people compared notes and realized that there was a serious problem developing. A group of men and women went to the temples to present the problem and seek guidance and understanding from the priests and priestesses. They were told about the karmic patterns that had remained dormant in their memories until recently. They were further told that men and women had to find their own paths to equality again. Suggestions were given about ways of communicating with one another when emotional grievances arose, and it was suggested that they practice thinking of their partners as equal to, and the same as, themselves. This same attitude of equality and cocreation was to be brought back into their relationships with the residents of other cities as well.

Meanwhile, the Free Orions were experiencing upheavals with respect to trust. They were becoming suspicious of one another's ulterior motives in ordinary daily activities. As a result, competitiveness and power struggles increased rapidly. When anyone showed leadership qualities or extreme generosity, or excelled artistically or inventively, the others would suspect that person of wanting to take over. Decision making for the city was becoming difficult since the people's natural tendency was to disagree with each other and use the power of veto to prevent others from gaining control. This pattern finally erupted into a brawl during a citywide planning meeting. Several of the usual leaders accused one another of having ulterior motives and looking out for their own advancement and not for the good of the whole. After many heated words, fistfights broke out, and the whole meeting ended in chaos and violence. The Free Orions' distrust and fear of dominance by others spread to their attitudes and dealings with the other colonies, especially with the increasingly pushy Mars II people.

When the priests and priestesses were consulted, they told the Free Orion people that the karmic pattern of victimhood was being activated in their subconscious minds, so they were seeing oppressors in everyone around them. In order to turn the problem around, they all needed to look at their own thoughts and attitudes and learn discernment. Projections of their subconscious fears onto one another had to be stopped and replaced with conscious work on deepening their trust in those who had proven themselves trustworthy.

The Solarians, at the same time, were beginning to indulge in feelings of shame and low self-worth. They compared themselves intellectually and artistically to the other cities and felt embarrassed about their obvious lacks. Motivation diminished greatly, for they believed their efforts would be futile and never as good as their neighbors, no matter how hard they tried. The Solarians had reached the stage in evolution at which they realized how much there was to learn and experience, but they felt unworthy because they had not already learned it. It was a very dangerous turning point, and one that required extreme discipline, self-love, and true humility rather than shame-based humility. Over several generations, their productivity and general quality of life

suffered. Neglect became apparent in areas such as housecleaning, adequate care of children, and repairs to homes and buildings. The lethargy and futility were eating at them from the inside. They believed they had nothing valuable to contribute to life on Maldek and therefore did not try. It was natural for them to give up seniority to the other colonies, who had become so in need of dominance. There were a few Solarians who did not succumb to this negative state, and remained determined. It was these few who finally went to the temples for help when the problem became rampant and undeniable.

The priests and priestesses explained that the nature of the Solarians' evolutionary journey had brought up this sense of lack and low self-worth because they had not come from the same experiential background as the others on Maldek. In other words, they were working their way up to places on the evolutionary ladder where the others had already been. Therefore, they had to work harder to understand things the others took for granted. For instance, many of the Maldekians were awakening to latent creative and spiritual abilities that the Solarians were just evolving to the point of being able to learn and express for the very first time. In coming to Maldek to seek connection with higher lifeforms and Light Beings, the Solarians also had to deal with the fact that they needed the example of the others in order to learn and grow. Acceptance of themselves exactly as they were was the only cure, and self-pity and shame were their worst enemies.

The Soganites, in the meantime, had come face to face with their addictions and their need to deny the very existence of any problems. They were obsessed with happiness, or the pretense of happiness, and acted as if everything was okay even when it was not. They were terrified of feeling painful emotions and found every possible means for staying "high." Bars and casinos sprang up and became the favored source of entertainment by many. (These establishments were similar to the saloons with dance-hall girls of the American Western era on Earth.) Carousing, drinking, illicit sex, and even drugs became a way of life in Sogan. Women and men alike fell under the spell of addiction and obsession with sensation. Marriages broke up, creating deep hurt and angry feelings; children were neglected while parents ran out at night to the saloons and casinos, or were too drugged at home to function. Malnutrition and birth defects were prevalent among infants and young children. Worst of all, syphilis was born as a deadly disease. Bodies and spirits were weakened by damage to their immune systems from drugs, alcohol, poor diet, and irregular sleep patterns. Denial, illicit sexual behavior, and loveless sex in general deeply harmed their souls' connection to their bodies and brains. This combination of effects created the perfect breeding ground for venereal disease. Newborns came into life with the disease, and adults and young ones alike became painfully ill and died. There was, however, a portion of the population that remained unaffected by the release of the karmic patterns. These people remained sober and morally upright.

The priests and priestesses were asked by some of the healthy members of the Sogan community to call a large gathering and try to talk to the people. They responded by saying that they would be glad to facilitate a gathering, but they would not force anyone to attend. The meeting was attended by about 400 people. The priests and priestesses told them stories about the karmic patterns, the underlying addiction to happiness, and the emotional denial that was the real cause of the more obvious addictions. The people were advised that, in order to heal their problems, they must: (1) work holistically on their diets, take herbal healing treatments, and include fasting; (2) start coming to the temples for emotional healing and counseling to deal with the denial; (3) take up some form of regular spiritual practice to reconnect with their souls and spirits; and (4) work on creating intimacy with themselves, God/Goddess/All That Is, and others. The priests and priestesses were willing to work with the people on all levels as much as was required, but the people needed to seek out their help; they would not impose it.

In all of the colonies, responses to these teachings and offerings of help were mixed. Some people chose to righteously justify what they were doing and continued to regress rapidly. Some sought help, with varying results, depending on their level of commitment. There were those who came to the temples wanting the healers to *fix* them without putting forth any effort of their own, and their results were expectedly negligible. Others came ready to do whatever was required to break free of the problems plaguing them and their families. These people began to see results and changes right away; but even *they* knew that the process would require long-term discipline, determination, and the seeking of help as needed.

During this time, trade became strained between the cities. The invention of a steam-powered land vehicle had made trade physically easier and faster. However, there was so much emotional and spiritual confusion and projection onto others that it was difficult for people to maintain civil relationships within individual cities, much less between diverse groups. There were even fights among the traders from the three colonies engaged in trade relationships. For the most part, the major impact was a suffering trade business, with trade and travel simply diminishing until they became nearly nonexistent. No one quite understood fully what was going on, but within each colony, the people were aware of the karmic patterns and the influences these patterns were having on their lives. Though some people chose to deny or ignore this understanding, every person, without exception, had the opportunity to hear the truth behind his or her actions at least once. How it was handled individually was a matter of free will.

The only exception to free will came when violence began to get out of hand. Within all the colonies, for their various reasons and sources of pain, fighting accelerated. Each colony was divided between those who were genuinely taking responsibility for transforming themselves and creating their own realities and those who steadily immersed themselves in their personal debaucheries, victimhood, and underlying pain. Those who remained spiritually and emotionally irresponsible became more and more out of control. They began to create civil wars with those who were evolving. There were accusations of wrongdoing, ulterior motives, superiority, and general distrust. In some communities, those who were in denial and regression became totally nonfunctional and initiated unprovoked attacks on people on the streets. It became unsafe to be on the streets alone in these areas, and curfews at dark were agreed upon.

Imprisonment Instituted for Violent Crimes—Year 10,775

Throughout the Maldekian colonies and villages, civil unrest, outbreaks of violence, and growing polarization between the people were prevalent. In each colony, those who were attempting to be responsible and grow finally organized and decided that some sort of laws and law enforcement had to be initiated. Violence was made a crime in all cases, and suitable punishments were determined. Jails were created, law enforcement officials were selected, and people began to be arrested and locked up for everything from slapping others to beating them. While in jail, prisoners were visited by people who had volunteered to serve as counselors and go-betweens for the temples. These volunteers attempted to offer understanding, compassion, and nonviolent ways of working with the problems haunting the prisoners. Some of the prisoners were affected by their efforts, but most were not. Those who were not affected grew angrier and more hostile all the time, rebelling against discipline, spiritual teachings, and positive influence from others. The people were at a major turning point within each community about how to handle these deeply disturbed troublemakers. It was such a new dilemma that they were at a loss. When they sought help in the temples, advice and understanding were given, but the priests and priestesses could not tell them what to do without usurping their learning and growth.

The next stage of evolution came with the idea of capital punishment for repeatedly violent offenders. At first, most of the people were in shock at the very idea of anything so horrendous, and they dismissed the option completely. To kill someone for being violent was to become that which you wished to eliminate, many argued. Others argued in favor of capital punishment, saying that the violent ones were usurping their fundamental rights to feel safe and live by free will, and therefore could no longer be allowed to live on Maldek. Debates went on and on, back and forth. There was a stalemate for several years while temporary incarceration of violent criminals continued. In the meantime, it was agreed that those who were brought in for a third offense could be held indefinitely, or until the criminals chose to change. The criminals grievously protested, calling this a violation of their free will, but their appeal met with little serious consideration.

When a child in the Sogan colony was brutally beaten to death after being raped repeatedly by a drunken father, capital punishment was administered for the first time. The man had been in jail many times prior to the passing of the third-time-lock-up law, and when this last offense occurred, he knew at his arrest that he would be permanently jailed, at the very least. Capital punishment was decided on by a two-thirds majority of those attending the lawmaking gathering. Nonrehabilitated violent offenders were not allowed at the meeting, so those who did attend were not in danger of being outvoted by them. The man was hung in an open area on the outskirts of the city where as many as wanted to could observe. It was hoped that other violent people would witness the hanging and reconsider their present alternatives. Capital punishment was not made an absolute law, but was set aside as an alternative to be decided in individual cases by majority vote.

The trend toward escalation of violence spread throughout the colonies, with the Solarians remaining the most minimally affected. However, addictions to alcohol and drugs were beginning to emerge in Solaris, so the rest of their accompanying problems were destined to follow unless they were checked early on.

Capital Punishment in All Colonies–Year 10,800

Murders leading to capital punishment took place in all of the other colonies except Solaris within a year of the hanging in Sogan. Even though the other colonies were not in communication with Sogan, the planetary impact was still felt. By this time, Maldek was only about 400 years into the third 5200-year cycle. Whereas growth and peace had prevailed in the past, havoc and unrest were prevalent now. The first case of capital punishment in

each colony only incited more anger and rebellion among the violent ones, which led to more extremes of violence and murder. As capital punishment was administered again and again in each community, it grew easier to choose. Finally, a man was hanged who had beaten someone to the point of unconsciousness on a third offense. The decision to use capital punishment was made on a close vote, but the majority agreed, and that member of the Mars II colony was hanged.

More types of crimes emerged among the lower classes. Rape, theft, and destruction of private and public property erupted. These were soon added to the list of offenses for which a person could be imprisoned. Prisoners were now asked if they wished to receive emotional and/or spiritual counseling, instead of having it imposed upon them. Most refused, though occasionally someone genuinely chose to receive help and made a successful reform. The cities of Maldek were becoming more and more like the cities of present-day Earth, only on a smaller scale. The criminals developed gangs as a way to have more power and protection for their life styles. This made law enforcement increasingly difficult. However, invention of more effective weapons was in progress. Previously, the police had carried only clubs and a type of handcuffs. Then knives, small swords, and something akin to tear gas were added to their methods of persuasion. Now the development of guns was well underway, in both Free Orion and Mars II, at about 11,400 years into life on Maldek. Police had these weapons exclusively in the beginning. Of course, the gangs soon managed to steal some of the guns, and then things got really crazy. Civil war was a reality, and no one was safe on the streets anymore. Police forces were increased, and soon they were given authority to shoot to kill gang members and anyone resisting arrest. Of course, the civil war accelerated. Maldek had become a police state.

By the time the gangs were destroyed, with most members killed by the police, crime was more under control than it had been in hundreds of years. The police forces were tough and merciless in all of the cities, even in Solaris, where some gang members from the other colonies had attempted to move in and take over. This attempt was short-lived, as Mars II came to the rescue shortly after the invasion and eliminated the last of the gang members. Though life was now safer and more peaceful on Maldek, a great impact had been made on the psyches of the people. Maldekians felt shame and guilt for having been a part of killing so many criminals, even by condoning the killings. But they could not find another way that was effective. Many people became highly nervous and fearful, even when crime was once again under control. Distrust grew, and the need for protection by meeting violence with violence was deeply ingrained in the people. Delegations traveled among the colonies to discuss their problems and share methods for handling them; but all of their stories were similar. Even the Soganites sent a delegation of twelve men and women to find out what was happening in other parts of Maldek and to seek advice. They found that all of Maldek was under the same duress, with minor variations on the themes.

By 11,600 years, all of the colonies had most crime under control. They maintained jails and heavy police forces. Now their challenge was how to prevent future problems and maintain safety and balance in their cities. It was agreed that all children were to be educated in morality, emotional health, and the law. In all of the cities and towns, the Maldekians decided to impose longer jail terms for even minor crimes to discourage the criminal forces. Of course, this did not remove the psychological and spiritual problems from their world, but it did make them feel safer and more in control again. The police state was still a way of life, and most of the people were glad of it. The police forces had become very attached to their power and control, but they rarely abused it with the peaceful citizens.

Unfortunately, the temples had faded into the background for most Maldekians. They considered the fact that the priests and priestesses had not been willing to solve their problems for them a sign that they must do it all themselves. A few people continued to go to the temples and work on their own karmic patterns and spiritual evolution. And there were always those who entered the temples while still very young, choosing to make spiritual growth and study their whole lives. The spiritual focus, which had at one time been such a strong influence in all of the communities, had become part of the lives of only a small minority, and yet it did continue.

By the end of the third 5200-year cycle, Maldek had become more focused on control over its individual members and their activities than on spiritual growth and evolution. The population of the planet was up to about 7000 at that time, and only about one-tenth of the population was still interacting with the temples. Actually, a few Maldekians had attained to enlightenment by then, so the patterns of evolution and attainment were set in place. Every race benefits by the enlightenment and/or ascension of even one of its members, as this creates an energetic map for others to follow. The more key individuals who reach enlightenment, the stronger the magnetism toward spiritual attainment becomes for the rest of the population. The polarization by those in resistance also intensifies. By this time, three people from Mars II had attained spiritual mastery, as well as four from Free Orion, two from Sogan, and ten from the mixed races. This was a boon for Maldek, although not visible in the Maldekian cities as yet.

As this 5200-year cycle was approaching its end, several new Pleiadians were born into Maldekian families in each city and village. Following growth patterns similar to those who had come at other cyclical change times, they began to teach the people and set an example for them of another type of consciousness. As they grew into their teen years, the Pleiadians told stories more and more directly related to the karmic histories of the people, both prior to life on Maldek, and since then. The people, as usual, responded more to their own awakened children than they would have to anyone else, and they began to hear what the children had to say. The Maldekians were not blamed for anything that had happened there, but were simply retaught about the universal laws of cocreation, free will, evolutionary purpose, and right action. The people were reminded that every person had a soul in the process of evolution, and that until they took responsibility for that evolution on a conscious level, suffering and living in fear and denial would continue.

1000-Year Grace Period–Years 15,600 to 16,600

When the Maldekians who were willing to listen asked the Pleiadian young ones how to deal with violence and crime, they were told that a grace period would be created. During that time, anyone attempting to harm another or take away a person's free will would experience the instant-karma effect of having the intended harm turn back on the sender. During the grace period of the next 1000 years, the Maldekians would have nothing to fear from one another, due to the instant-karma law. They could use that time to break the karmic patterns that had been played out so vividly over the past 5200 years. Healing modalities that addressed the issues of emotional denial, negative and victim thinking, control and domination, and addictions would be taught to those who were ready to work as healers. The priests and priestesses in the temples, and the temple devotees, would be available for spiritual teaching and healing practices as well. Still, disciplined spiritual focus and healing would be required on the part of the people. It was recommended that the Maldekians create gathering places for group meditation services that would be led initially by members of the temples. This would be the best way to help people align with one another with higher intentions and as cocreators.

Other planetary laws remained the same, except that the people requested the ability to call for assistance from the higher realms with a majority agreement. They felt that if this arrangement had existed during the previous 5200 years, perhaps they would have found something other than capital punishment and police forces as an answer to their problems. Their request was accepted.

With amazingly little resistance, the police forces were disbanded and the jails torn down or converted into other types of structures. A ritual ceremony of forgiveness, release of the past, and commitment to cocreating a new kind of win/win future was held in each city. The Pleiadians who had been born to the people were middle-aged adults by this time. Along with the priests and priestesses from the temples, and a delegation of Pleiadian Archangels who had arrived on lightships, the Pleiadians conducted the ceremonies. All of the Maldekians were asked to attend the ceremonies, and most did. A few who were still self-righteously holding onto the old ways refused to participate and were left to their own choices. The ceremonies took place for one full week. At the end of this time, the Pleiadians who had been born to the Maldekians made a group ascension in each community, setting an energetic example of spiritual completion and transcendence. The lightships placed new Pleiadian Archangelic delegates in each temple and then left Maldek. A deep peace and love filled the hearts of those who had witnessed the ascension event and gave them a sense of renewal, hope, and determination.

The next 1000 years was filled with great spiritual acceleration. The Maldekians learned how to deal with their emotions and karmic patterns. Meetings were held regularly for group meditation, and more and more people chose to dedicate their lives to the temples and spiritual growth. Those who did not participate were left alone, but after a few generations they died out and left Maldek a quickly evolving spiritual planet. Since the people's life spans were around 150 Earth years by that time, those who began young could cover much spiritual growth in a single lifetime. As a result, several more Maldekians from each group became enlightened, including the first Solarian to attain spiritual mastery.

Music and art also played major roles in their culture again.

Even the Soganites began to mix with the other groups, though minimally at first. When the entire city of Sogan was destroyed by a giant flood about 500 years into the fourth 5200-year cycle, most of the people evacuated prior to the critical stage, and all of the Soganite survivors arrived in Solaris for shelter. Gradually the uprooted ones migrated into the other communities, until they were completely integrated into the diverse Maldekian culture. About 300 of the Soganites chose to rebuild their own colony and remain segregated, but friendly, with the other groups. Their colony was established only two days walking distance, or about four hours by steam car, from Solaris, where the largest number of their people remained. A small temple was built in the new colony and some of the priests, priestesses, and devotees from the previous Soganite temple took up residence and teaching and healing practices there.

After the 1000-year grace period of instant karma had passed, the Maldekians were a peaceful people again, and the instant-karma ruling was lifted. This did not affect their life styles at all. In fact, most of them were not very conscious of the ruling any-more, because it so seldom had been activated for the past few hundred years.

Lucifer's Fall—Years 16,600 to 20,800

In the higher-dimensional realms, during the whole history of Maldek colonization, Lucifer's role as Supreme Being had been mostly to maintain and transmit the encodings and instructions from Galactic Center to the appropriate devas, angels, guides, guardians, and keepers of the magnetic and energetic grids and poles. He had, of course, dispersed helpers and personal guides as needed, and held the focus for the higher collective consciousness to develop. Now that the Maldekians were developing a stronger higher collective consciousness, Lucifer's role was changing. The group evolutionary patterns were now being held by the Maldekians' own higher collective consciousness as well as by those Maldekians who had become enlightened and chosen to serve in the higher realms. Therefore, Lucifer was now more of a spiritual administrator, so to speak.

Though Lucifer had witnessed the evolution of species prior to his experience with Maldek, this was the first time he had served as Supreme Being. Blending with the consciousness of the entire planet and its population while maintaining his own autonomy had been an incredible learning experience for him. What he did not realize was that he had also been imprinted with the lower-vibrational patterns of Maldek's collective consciousness. The pattern that was affecting Lucifer's own developing subconscious most—which he did not think he had—was the distrust of Divinity. Other patterns of violence, victimhood, addiction, shame, low self-worth, and general distrust had also made lesser imprints on his subconscious. However, until his role of holding the higher collective consciousness was lessened by the evolutionary growth of the Maldekians, he did not know he had been impacted. As Lucifer gradually separated from the group mind of the higher collective consciousness and began to commune with that consciousness instead of experiencing it directly, he felt waves of restlessness and apprehension move through his beingness. He dismissed these experiences as being merely aftermaths of the change in his connection to the Maldekians. These waves continued in infrequent, but regular, patterns and were a direct feedback from his subconscious, or shadow side.

Believing himself to be beyond temptation and error on all levels, Lucifer continued to dismiss these sensations and thought patterns until they began to come more regularly. The more he ignored and denied their validity, the stronger they grew. He soon found himself feeling a need for more control over the evolution of the people, and a vague distrust in their ability to evolve without that control. The subconscious impressions were weaving their way into his consciousness more and more, and since he believed that all of his thoughts and feelings were responses to truth, he gave validity to the urges. As his own consciousness grew cloudier, the weather of Maldek responded accordingly. Rain and overcast skies, as well as lightning and thunderstorms, increased in frequency. He did not realize that his self-absorption in control thoughts and distrust of the people were clouding his perceptions and literally creating a fog in the filtering system of the solar encodings.

When the weather and climate-control devas asked Lucifer why the solar encodings seemed less accessible, and at times vague, he thought the beings were trying to excuse lapses in their own responsibilities. He did not stop to realize that there would be no logical reason for such action; he had simply come to have a certain amount of distrust in others, and it was spreading to the devas and guides. He asked one group of devas to observe another group as a back-up system, but the new back-up devas could find nothing wrong with what the others were doing. So Lucifer began a full-scale search among the devas, angels, guides, and other higher-dimensional servers for the problem. It never occurred to him that he could possibly be the cause of the breach; he never questioned his own effectiveness, even to the very end.

On Maldek, the people were experiencing erratic energy and emotional patterns that seemed to parallel the changes in weather. Their moods swung drastically. They became short-tempered and restless during thunderstorms. Their minds felt foggy after days of cloudy skies and fog. When the Sun came out again, they were relieved, but wary about feeling so out of control. They felt a need to be in control of their own emotions and bodies, but did not believe they could be. Lucifer's lack of belief in their ability to evolve on their own was affecting them subconsciously and beginning to change their overall sense of self-confidence. The people tried harder to maintain self-control, and went to the temples as often as possible; they sensed a need for more help. Continuing their group meditations, healing practices, and self-observation helped to a point, but addictions also started to creep in again. As a result of their mounting underlying fear of not being capable of spiritual evolution, they reached out for stimuli that could calm them and make them feel more relaxed and confident again.

As Lucifer observed the people, he grew to believe more and more that they needed to be controlled. He lost confidence in the ability of the solar encodings and the crown-chakra, time-released evolutionary stimuli to bring about positive results. He felt that the energies being generated from the center of the planet were too subtle to make a difference. He lost confidence in the personal guides' abilities to have any impact on the people at all, and came to believe that none of the higher-dimensional guides and servers of humanity genuinely cared about the people or even thought about their welfare. He believed that all of the guides, angels, devas, and other servers were merely robotically following orders as he, himself, had done for a long time. He believed he was just awakening to the fact that Galactic Center, the Pleiadians, and all of the others he was working with were under some kind of trance and unable to think and respond to individual situations appropriately. He truly believed that he was the only one who was capable of appropriate response and decision making.

By this point in Lucifer's descension into the subconscious imprinting, he had lost almost all touch with Divine Truth and the purity of Light. He had fallen into a delusionary state and believed that there was some giant plot on the part of God to keep everyone asleep and under his thumb. Lucifer thought that he had to become more powerful than God and the forces of Light in order to wake up and take control over the evolution of the Maldekians, and perhaps, over existence in general. Someone had to defy God and prove that God was holding us all back and keeping us under his control in order to prevent us from knowing that we were as powerful as he was. This was how Lucifer's thoughts were running by the end of the 5200-year cycle. Furthermore, he believed he had to keep his ideas to himself because everyone was so under God's hypnotic spell. Lucifer believed he had to operate alone until he had taken control and broken free of the encodings from the Sun, the Pleiades, Sirius, and Galactic Center.

Meanwhile, on Maldek, the people were erratically having emotional fits; many even were going insane. Dementia, paranoia, split-personality disorders, and neuroses were rapidly increasing among the people. Outbreaks of violence were recurring. The priests and priestesses were even affected by the change in the input coming from the Sun and from the center of the planet. Lucifer's derangement had created ever-increasing veils between the solar encodings and the planet. Without the solar encodings, the Light Beings at the core of the planet could not receive instructions and energy patterning to transmit to the planet, and they were "winging it," so to speak. At first, when the encodings and patterning were disturbed and erratic, the Light Beings continued to transmit whatever they received; but, as the transmissions became more and more irregular and even chaotic, a decision was made to override the imbalanced input and return to the most common patterns of transmission. The Light Beings sent telepathic waves to Lucifer for direction; all they received in return were strangely garbled signals that were undecipherable. The Light Beings knew something was off, but they had no idea what the cause was or what to do about it.

On Maldek, power struggles were taking place everywhere, even in the temples. The priests and priestesses were reacting to the pollution of the higher dimensions by fighting among themselves. Arguments broke out over the appropriateness of healing practices, and over which rituals were required for which purpose. The priests and priestesses withheld information from the devotees and one another, thinking it was for the other's own good. Each thought that only he or she was still in touch with higher purpose.

Gambling, drinking, drugs, violence, and loveless sex were becoming very common again, and with each sign of regression by the people of Maldek, Lucifer became more confident that his conclusions and decisions about taking control were correct. The people of Maldek had lost touch with any kind of sane reality and were wildly attempting to find comfort through "numbing out," or seeking extremes of sensation. Suicide was occurring frequently among the people. Climatic conditions were totally unstable. Crops were failing. Animals and plants were dying rapidly. Very little peace or normalcy existed anywhere on Maldek.

When the Photon Band began to contact the planet from Galactic Center near the end of the fourth 5200-year cycle, Lucifer made his move. He used all of his force to come between the planet and the influence of the Photon Band. He ordered the serving angels and devas to form a great shield of reflective light around Maldek. He told the angels it was to protect Maldek, but would explain no further. Since they were supposed to follow Lucifer's instructions exactly, they did so. The Light Beings at the core of the planet, receiving waves of hate and distrust from Lucifer, were trying to maintain the tantric transmissions, although they were doing so with some desperation—and with resulting energy pollution—by this time.

Higher-dimensional Light Beings such as the Pleiadian Archangels, Sirians, and Andromedans attempted to break through the shields created by Lucifer and all of those he had recruited to hold them in place. Finally, the internal and external pressures around Maldek grew so strong that they threw the planet completely out of its orbit. Lucifer had planned to do just that, but he had not anticipated the results. As Maldek was jerked from its orbit, the external temperature rose and spontaneous combustion occurred in the atmosphere. The internal pressure plates gave way and the entire planet exploded into small pieces.

The Light Beings at the core of Maldek, as well as many of those in the atmosphere around the planet, were fragmented and hurled through space. The Pleiadians, Sirians, and Andromedans were ready. They magnetized the damaged ones into healing, protective cocoons as they left the planet's atmosphere. All lifeforms, including humans, were, of course, destroyed instantly when the planet exploded. The human souls and soul fragmentations were also gathered into healing cocoons for transport. All of the cocooned beings and fragments were taken to Earth, and the cocoons were placed in the oceans to be tended by the thousands of dolphins who had already been living there for a few hundred years.

Author's Note: When the cocoons containing human beings and higher-dimensional Light Beings who had been fragmented or otherwise damaged arrived in the oceans of Earth, the dolphins were prepared to receive us. Yes, I was among them, and I have reexperienced the entire episode vividly. All of us who were stationed at the core of Maldek at the time of the explosion were cocooned and brought here. The dolphins were foretold of our arrival and circumstances by means of their highly sophisticated communications network with the stars, the Sun, and other planets. This network operates through their electrical systems and Ka bodies. In fact, their light bodies, electrical systems, and Ka bodies are blueprints for what ours are becoming. They are our more highly evolved elder brothers and sisters, placed on Earth to set the example for what we are evolving into. Therefore, they magnetically guide us toward our own destinies as fully awakened, multidimensional Light Beings.

These loving ones began at once to examine the cocooned beings one by one. They sent love and reassuring telepathic messages through the walls of the cocoons to those inside. Turning the cocoons with their snouts, the dolphins swam in pods around them while transmitting high-frequency stellar and solar emanations through their sonar. They healed all of us and nurtured us back to consciousness and peace again.

Now listen again as Ra continues:

Lucifer escaped to the Orion warrior colony, deciding that perhaps they were the only others who might understand his revelations and give him asylum. He was right, of course, and glad they were to attain such a powerful ally for their ongoing war against the Light and Galactic Center. Thus began the Lucifer Rebellion, as it has become known.

Fires burned in the atmosphere where Maldek had been for the equivalent of hundreds of Earth years before the last visible signs of the catastrophe were gone. Left behind was what we now know as the asteroid belt between Mars and Jupiter. This belt includes the Goddess asteroids: Pallas Athena, Vesta, Ceres, and Juno (Hera). The Goddesses represented are all ones who had power and sovereignty and lost it to patriarchal demigods; they are in the process of healing and being restored on Earth at this time. Coincidental or meaningful symbolism considering their origins? You decide.

Chiron is a large asteroid located between Uranus and Saturn. It is the astrological divine counterpart to this Maldekian-created belt. Chiron is the astrological aspect of the wounded healer who, in the process of serving, becomes damaged and must heal himself in order to ascend. His location in, and aspects to, your astrology chart are the major keys to unveiling your own individual wounds that, when healed, will lead to your own wholeness, enlightenment, and ascension. The key theme, once again, is in male/female balance and the right use of power and sexual energy.

Author's Note: Though they were few in number, the enlightened and ascended Maldekians do exist. They now inhabit the fourth and fifth dimensions of Jupiter, holding the lessons of expansiveness of spiritual integrity, Light, trust, and freedom. Calling on these Maldekian Ascended Masters, as well as exploring your astrological relationships between Jupiter, the Goddess asteroids, and Chiron are ideal ways of identifying and healing your own Maldekian karmic patterns.

In the spirit of the Maldekian lessons of outside authority, trust, and spiritual exploration, I offer this poem.

ANTICLIMAX

"It's time now."
A voice from behind
gently pulls at me,
pulling me back
to here and now,
to that moment
where everything
begins and ends
all at the same time.
A firm, yet soft,
touch on my shoulder
echoes without words,
"It's time now."

Responding with only
a turn of my head,
I acknowledge her.
I see in her eyes
the message once more.

My eyes reach out and say ,
"Just a little longer."
Her smile replies,
compassionately,
"It's time now."

"Come," says she.
And I turn to look
behind me one last time,
as her hand upon
my shoulder presses,
ever so slightly,
adding emphasis
to her beckoning,
her invitation.
"Come," is repeated
by her touch and nod,
like a bowing of her head.

With one deep breath
I turn to face her,
and away we step,
together again,
Spirit Woman and I,
hand in hand.

But instead, only darkness
and empty silence abide.

"Don't look back,"
    she says;
and these words send a
    quick
shiver of panic through
    me.
I jerk and start to turn,
but her hand now
    tightens,
close around mine,
repeating once more,
"Don't look back."
And we walk on,
my heart loudly pounding.
I look at her hard.
I say to her with my eyes,
"Just one last. . ."
Her eyes cut me off,
silently warning,
"Don't look back."
I feel her urging me
on with her heart,
the message repeated
in love.
But I cannot stop;
my impulse is strong.
And quickly I turn,
hoping for one last
something to pull me back,
to say, "Stay.
This is where you belong."

I look to her for
answers now, in hope
of understanding.
But her eyes,
her heart, her touch,
her silent words, all say,
"I tried to stop you."
Her arm around me
tightens, but gently,
and pulls me forward
once again.
I do not understand,
and yet deep peace
moves through me now
like a gentle wave.

And together,
we walk on.
Nothing ahead.
Nothing behind.
A pervading sense
of presence;
of here now;
of anticlimax.
I am not sure why
I avoided this
for so long.

Time passages lose
their power in
here now.

Whether we walked
for minutes or hours,
days or centuries,
I cannot tell.
We've never stopped.
And in the silence
and peace of movement
days or lives could pass
in a single step.
I know I've learned
something that gives
me a sense of Strength,
Faith,
Patience,
Trust;
for they are real:
omnipresences,
as natural to me
as taking a breath,
or feeling the wind
in my hair, or
splashing cold water
in my own face
from a clear stream.

The two of us move,
silently,
reverently,
onward:
a living, walking
Namaste
to all that has been,
to All That Is,

and all that shall be;
and to each other.
And with each step
a little more

of the burden
of meaning with which
I have laden
everything and
everyone in my past
drops away.
Piece by piece,
it dissolves
as easily as
the Sun into
the evening sky.
Until, at last,
all that is left
is a Luminous Void
abiding within me,
and I abiding within
the Luminous Void.

"It's time now."
Her words take on
a new meaning,
but I do not
understand.
As the Luminous Void
inside and around me grows,
she squeezes my hand,
and then lets it go,
and somehow this gesture
echoes her words.
My eyes seek answers.
But her eyes grow
first brighter and then
begin to fade away.
Her image disappears
into the Luminous Void.

I gasp and reach out
to pull her back,
but I cannot.
A last, loving smile
and gentle nod
and she is gone.

Sounds of silence roar
forgotten memories.
Winds of time blow
through my core.
I am alone
on a path to and from
Nowhere—
so suddenly,
like a falling star
that soars through
a darkening sky
to who knows where.
Behind me: darkness.
Ahead: soft haze.
And here and now:
the Luminous Void.

Something inside me
settles somehow.
A wave of peace
and acceptance
spreads through me—
though I do not
know why.
I begin to walk on.
Nothing ahead.
Nothing behind.
Just pervading sense
of presence: my own,
the sacred presence
that I Am,
of here now,
of anticlimax.
I am not sure
why I avoided this
for so long.

Alone I walk on—
minutes or hours or days,
I cannot tell.
But I've never stopped.
And once again
in the silence and peace
of my own movement,
one step at a time,
I learn something.
I become more.
And Strength,
and Faith,
and Patience,
and Trust
deepen:
omnipresences
as real and natural
to me as existence.

Walking on in silence
and in reverence,
I am a single,
walking, living Namaste
to all that has been,
and All That Is,
and all that shall be,
and to myself.
And with each step
the burden of meaning
I gave to her,
to us,
to everything,
slips away:
dissolving with ease
as softly as
a sigh.

Until, at last,
all that remains is
only a Luminous Void
abiding within me,
and I abiding as
the Luminous Void.
And only then,
from deep inside,
I hear a distant,
familiar voice.

"It's time now."
I hear this time—
resistance gone—

and with an inner glow
I softly reply,
"Yes!"
And closing my eyes,
I hear her voice:
"Just a few steps more,
and ahead there is
a bridge: an arched bridge.
You cannot see
to the other side
until you stand
at the crest,
in the center.
Walk slowly,
and at the crest
you will see a light
in the distance.
Follow it, and it
will lead you home."

In silence, I
softly reply,
"Yes!"
Deep inside what I Am,
I feel a warm breeze
comforting,
caressing,
filling me with all
the love I've ever known—
in a single moment
between times.
And just as I
open my eyes
to step forward,

I see endless horizons
with endless bridges,
one after another.
And with quiet laugh
and willing heart
I step forward
toward the first bridge
knowing I will cross
them all,
eventually,
without question.
I am not sure
why I avoided this
for so long.

Just as I hit "Save" on my computer after inserting the poem at the end of this chapter, I felt eyes staring at me, and looked up with a start. There, with his nose almost touching the window in front of me, was Earnest, my deer friend. After telling him to wait for a moment, I went to the refrigerator and got out a large yellow tomato. I cut it into eighths and went outside to greet him. He would not accept the food until I sat on the ground where his nod implied I should sit. Once I was seated, he began to enjoy the tomatoes, knocking three pieces to the ground in the process.

When Earnest had finished the tomatoes in my hands, he nuzzled the ones on the ground and made light snorting sounds. The juicy fruit pieces were covered with small pebbles and dirt. While sending him pictures of what I intended, I asked him if he would like me to clean off the tomato pieces for him. I sensed his acquiescence as he moved his head aside a little to allow me access to the fruit. I picked the pieces up one at a time wiping them clean with my fingers while he patiently waited, then accepted each offering as it was free of debris. As I reached for the last one, he lowered his head and my hand brushed across his velvety antlers. He twitched slightly, then looked deeply into my eyes. As I still held the last piece of tomato in my hand I felt an opening in the deer; in response, I lifted my hand and slowly stroked from his chin, down his neck, and to his chest. He then ate the last piece of tomato after which he slowly, albeit thoroughly, licked every drop from my hands including between my fingers. Tears gently trickled down my cheeks as I felt the deepening of our bond of trust and friendship.

Then he backed up slightly and just stood there looking at me. I waited for him to walk away while maintaining eye contact continually for another minute or so. Finally I received the message, "He wants you to walk away while he watches this time." In response, I stood slowly while Earnest remained close by. After I stood, he looked up at me and I felt a wave of love and trust from him that penetrated my heart and soul completely. We were quiet together for a few moments before I turned and walked away. As I reached the door I looked back to see him still watching me. I went inside and looked out the window as he turned and walked away.

I have never seen Earnest again since that very special afternoon during which he visited me twice. But the healing and bond between us remains even in his absence.

This last experience with my deer friend was another confirmation to me of the importance in the messages about healing trust among humans, between humans and animals, and in humans toward higher-dimensional Light Beings. In other words, unity in diversity is the path of the future.

PART IV

PART IV

COLONIZATION OF EARTH

Ra's story continues:

When the cocoons arrived in Earth's oceans, Earth was already inhabited by 25,000 humans. These humans had been on Earth for about 21,000 years. Prior to that time a planetary Ice Age had rendered Earth barren. The newest Earth beings were of the type who evolve from first- and second-dimensional states into souled-beings in human bodies. They were at the stage in their evolution that you have been taught to call "cave men," and they operated exclusively at first by means of animal instincts. Their consciousnesses had passed through those of several different kinds of animals on their way to becoming human. That particular stage of experience is something akin to finding yourself inside the body of a leopard, deer, or eagle and experiencing life from the animal's perspective. This phase lasts a relatively short time, perhaps only hours or days at most, and then the spirit that is soon to be human may pass through other animals' or birds' consciousnesses prior to preparation for human birth. During that time, the soul receives experiences of instinctual nature, single-pointed focus, and whatever specific traits with which the animals are imbued. As a result, the young souls are better prepared for survival in the physical world. These animals who have briefly lent their experience to the evolving human spirits are sometimes referred to as *totems* or *allies*.

Once they evolved into humans, these young soul beings were incapable of language or rational thought for many centuries. They grunted and squealed like animals, and lived only to survive and procreate. Like any mobile creatures, however, these new souls did have an ability to learn from experience. For example, if pain was experienced from touching a thorn a few times, they would begin to associate pain with the thorn and avoid touching it. Though this may seem highly insignificant, this stage of evolution of consciousness is respected just as much as any other.

At the time of the arrival of the cocooned beings and fragmented souls from Maldek, Earth's 25,000 inhabitants lived in many colonies around the globe. (See Appendix B for actual locations and distribution of population.) They had created very simple languages that were a combination of hand gestures and single syllables. Simple tools for pounding, scraping, cutting, and spearing had been invented in all of the groups. Raw foods were still their main sustenance, although they had learned to build fires and usually cooked meat, fish, and certain root vegetables.

Originally, there were colonies with as few as 25 humans up to as many as 2500, in regions throughout three continents: Asia, Africa, and North America. The North American colonies were in the areas now called Mexico, Texas, and Central America but extended further to the west. Most of the rest of the United States was under water, and parts of Canada and Alaska were on separate continents. A few of the groups migrated into South America and Eastern Europe as well. These continents, however, did not exist in their present forms. (See the world map of that time period shown on pages 262-263.) Territorial feuding and battles were common, and there was even some cannibalism between unfriendly tribes, though not within individual groups. Dinosaurs still roamed Earth but were disappearing quickly. Most of the animal species common to this planet today were living on Earth at that time, though they have changed to varying degrees as necessary for adaptation to planetary and climatic changes.

In the etheric and higher-dimensional realms, life was simpler then as well. Devic kingdoms were well developed to: manage the natural environment; caretake smaller regions and vortices; and maintain the poles, climate, and atmosphere. There were Light Beings at the core of Earth and at both poles who held orbital patterns, worked with sacred geometry and grid structures, and also maintained the poles. In addition, this latter group had the function of receiving and transmitting solar encodings and evolutionary stimuli, similar to those who had been at the core of Maldek. The Supreme Being, whom we might call the Solar Logos, actually held the Light for the entire galaxy and was not local to Earth or your solar ring. The Pleiadian Emissaries of Light were responsible for monitoring the evolution of all species in the plant, mineral, animal, and *homo sapien* kingdoms, and overseeing the devic kingdoms. Their roles would increase as the spiritual needs of the existing humans progressed. The Sirians protected Earth from invasion physically and psychically, and were overseers of the release of evolutionary encodings at the correct times.

The arrival of the cocoons took place around 147,500 years ago, though it is difficult to precisely pinpoint in time. Earth's orbital cycles around the Sun were slower; the day and night, lunar, and yearly time cycles were longer. Therefore, correspondence to current timing is illusive. This may help account for some of the confusion about historical time sequences. When a planet moves at a slower pace, life spans are altered, thinking processes slower, seasons more numerous and varied, and evolution more gradual. The lengthier orbital time cycles were associated with the recent Ice Age, which was a result of changes in the Sun's orbital patterns around the Galactic Center. If yearly orbits around the Sun had been the same length then as they are currently, the end of Maldek and arrival of cocooned beings on Earth would have been exactly 156,000 years ago, or six 26,000-year cycles.

There are points in the galactic orbital pattern during which Earth always experiences a lengthy Ice Age, and this cycle had just past. Earth's orbit slows down and widens during those times due to the Sun's orbital pattern reaching a wider angle around the Galactic Center. It always takes just over 100,000 years for the slower cycle to be completed and the warming trend to take hold. Even after that point, the speeding up of Earth's orbit around the Sun is a gradual process, culminating in a major pole shift when a specific geometric angle is reached in the Sun's orientation to the Galactic Center. When that occurs, your Sun's orbital pattern around Alcyone, the central sun of the Pleiades, stabilizes to the 26,000-year time frame that Earth and your solar ring are in now. This stabilization occurred 130,000 years ago.

These 26,000-year evolutionary and orbital cycles repeat over and over again for the entire time it takes the Sun to complete a full orbit around the Galactic Center, or approximately 230,000,000 years. At the end of that time, the 100,000-year Ice Age and slower orbits occur as the relationship of the Sun to the Galactic Center changes relative to the Milky Way's orbital pattern around what we shall call the Great Central Sun of all galaxies and of All That Is.

The orbits of the entire Milky Way around the Great Central Sun, just like the orbits of your solar ring around Milky Way's Galactic Center, take the form of continual circles connecting with diagonal arms at the end of one circle and beginning of another. At the comple-tion point of the circular orbit around the Great Central Sun of All That Is, the Milky Way Galaxy  enters a diagonal connecting link to the next ring on the spiral, which is an initiatic step into a new evolutionary cycle as well. This is what is occurring now. You, the people of Earth, are not only at the end of a 26,000-year Earth/Sun/Pleiadian cycle; the entire Pleiadian system, which includes your solar ring, is at the end of a 230,000,000-year orbit around Galactic Center; and the entire Milky Way is at the completion of an infinitely longer orbit around the Great Central Sun. All three of these cycles are syn-chronistically and simultaneously completing the last step of the spiral dance within a dance within a dance, making this a very crucial transition time. The objective is to finish without anyone's toes getting stepped on so the next, more sophisticated and gra-cious dance can begin.

What this adds up to in terms of planetary evolution is this: When the 100,000-year Ice Age ended, the Milky Way had near-ly completed its move across the diagonal arm that connects the previous spiral ring to the new ring on the greater cosmic spiral. This new ring, which all of us dwelling in the Milky Way will enter fully at the beginning of 2013, begins a new and different evolutionary cycle in relationship to God/Goddess/All That Is. Rebirth and initiatic spiritual leaps are being, and will continue to be, experienced. The previous galactic cycle, which is now ending, is called "The Evolutionary Spiral of Self-Discovery and Exploration." The new galactic cycle we are entering is called "The Evolutionary Spiral of Self-Mastery and Completion." The consciousnesses birthed during these transitional times are the products of new paradigms and new potentials, and benefit from all of the learning from the previous spiral, even if it is unconscious. It is like taking all of the dance steps learned in the previous lessons, mastering them, and then adding new steps that are much more exciting and challenging.

The time on Earth for exploration of all possibilities is coming to an end. Those of you living on Earth at this time have had billions of years to experience all of the potentials of consciousness, Light, and Dark. You have been victim and victimizer. You have loved, hated, protected, feared, known prejudice from all sides, been a peacemaker, and, in general, learned all of the options for existence. You have been incarnate and disincarnate. You have been guides to others, and you have been guided. Most of you have been enlightened and/or ascended and fallen from grace. Hopefully, by now you have learned to suspend judgment on yourself and others and to have compassion and understanding—for you have had opportunities to experience "it all." Those things that you have not experienced directly, you have chosen not to because you learned vicariously through the experiences of others. But you have had the time and opportunity to know all parts of existence.

Now the time is at hand during which you must take an internal inventory. Who have you become? To what has all of this vast experience and exploration brought you? Who are you qualitatively beyond what you have done? The time is here now for choosing spiritual mastery and responsibility for creating and cocreating reality. Those who do not make this choice will be peacefully and nonjudgmentally removed from this galaxy and taken to another galaxy that is just entering "The Evolutionary Spiral of Self-Discovery and Exploration." There they will begin anew the process of exploring Light and Dark, learning and forgetting, and so on. And once again, when that galaxy ends its long cycle and approaches "The Evolutionary Spiral of Self-Mastery and Completion," these beings will be offered another opportunity to move forward.

Maldekians Begin Life on Earth

Let us continue with the story of what happened on Earth when the Maldekians, including the former Martians and Venusians, arrived. As mentioned previously, Earth was in the completion stages of a long Ice Age, and just yawning and stretching after a long winterlike sleep. Those who lived on Earth at that time were of a minimally evolved consciousness and they focused on survival. So when the new ones arrived, it was decided by the planetary and galactic guardians that they should be placed in regions of the planet that were not yet inhabited. Because of their previous damage from the explosion of Maldek, it was also decided that they needed to be birthed as infants into human families instead of coming into life through the down-stepping process from the fourth dimension. This would facilitate deeper healing of past-life trauma during early infancy and toddler stages. It was further determined that the beings from Maldek needed to have their memories of Maldek removed. Pleiadians who had evolved beyond third-dimensional consciousness were asked to volunteer to take on human forms on Earth and give birth to the Maldekians. Just over two thousand couples agreed to do so. With completion of this stage of planning, the Maldekians were ready for preparation for birth.

The cocooned beings who had been attended to by the dolphins were ready to emerge in the form of balls of consciousness and light. Their memories of the traumas of Maldek were removed first. Then these beings were treated with great care and respect as they were introduced to the animal species of Earth and taken through short-term blendings with specific animals. All of them, without exception, were blended first with the dolphins. They experienced the freedom and pure ecstasy and love of those beloved creatures. This experience imprinted their psyches with their own spiritual potentials, and restored their sense of purity and innocence. This was their initiation by water. Next, they were introduced to, and blended with, various bird species. Their initiation to adaptability by air and visual acuity was accomplished at this stage. Then these new Earthlings blended with flowers and trees and received a higher level of stabilization and purification. Blending with warm-blooded animals for brief experiences of the uses of animal instincts came next. These last two experiences with plants and warm-blooded animals were initiations into mammalian–dry land adaptability and the element of earth.

The final initiatory preparation took place when these en-souled beings were taken to the Sun for a blending and mutual encoding. The solar and galactic evolutionary plan was encoded into their souls, and their individual Divine Plans for growth and evolution were encoded in the Sun. The Sun would carry the encodings for these beings, as it does for all Earth inhabitants, as long as they lived. With this last initiation by fire and light, the beings entered into a deep sleep state during which they were assisted in dreaming their own births and lives. By then, the 4000-plus Pleiadian volunteers had long completed the down-stepping process into third-dimensional bodies, and had estab-lished their villages and colonies near what are known today as Bali, India, Samoa, and Hawaii.

The size and placement of land masses were different than today, especially in Samoa and Hawaii. In both those locations, what are now small islands were parts of two continents that no longer exist. In fact, there were twelve continents on Earth at that time instead of seven. (See map on pages 262-263.) Those who were born into the first Balinese families were from the Maldekian colony called Sogan. The Mars II colonists became the first children of India. The first Samoan newborns had for-merly inhabited Solaris on Maldek. The Hawaiian babies were those who had been the Free Orion colonists.

Approximately 2000 years into the cycle of what is now 26,000 years, babies began to be birthed to the Pleiadian-Earth couples. These young ones were well-nurtured, nourished, and loved by their parents. They were told mythological stories that captured the karmic and spiritual themes from their forgotten past, as well as new ones with morals pertinent to their next stages of evolution and spiritual awakening. They were, without exception, peaceful and loving groups of people with deep family and group loyalties and individualism in balance. The Pleiadian volunteers remained part of those cultures for nearly 2000 years, at which time they began to die out and not return. It was time for the Maldekian-Earthlings to be on their own again. Of course, the genetics they had inherited from their Pleiadian-Earth parents were perma-nently a part of their human experience, as they are still.

The timing of their departure was partially determined by an influx of new souls to Earth from another galaxy that had been taken over by dark forces. Over 40,000 of these displaced seekers of peace and Light arrived on Earth in the fourth dimension around 142,000 years ago. The Elohim assigned these beings to Earth because of the nature of your planet's function as a universal melting pot for damaged, displaced, and evolving spirits and souls. The Universal Federation of Galaxies had planned long before that Earth would be used as an experimental planet in the development of unity in diversity. The United States is today a microcosm on your planet of this function, just as the entire planet is a microcosm of the universe. To bring groups of beings from all over the galaxies and other solar rings within the Milky Way to Earth, and to find a way to facilitate individual and group enlightenment within and between diverse groups and spiritual paths was—and is—the goal. Therefore, as groups of beings such as these 40,000 needed a new home, Earth was it.

Fairies Arrive

By this time, the four colonies of former Maldekians numbered around 12,000, and the younger souls that were here before the arrival of the Maldekians numbered about 30,000. So the addition of 40,000 new Earthlings was quite significant. These latest arrivals were what you now know as fairies. They had lived as physical inhabitants of a planet about twice the size of Earth in their home galaxy. They had been about one-third of the population of the planet on which they lived along with physical beings similar to humans. So the fairies were accustomed to living among bigger races. Their role had always been that of peacekeepers and merrymakers. They teased and kept people happy and laughing at themselves and helped protect and preserve the magical child aspect of consciousness. They had taught the humans to sing, dance, and make harplike instruments. Therefore it was natural for them to take on the same roles on Earth.

The fairies were kept in the fourth dimension for over 5000 years when they first arrived on Earth. There they learned about plants and animals and the varied races of human beings. Their role as guardians of flowering plants was also a given, since their diets consisted of—and fibers for clothing were made from—

flowers. The fairies enjoyed the companionship of many devic beings, angels, and personal guides who were also fourth dimensional. Human dreamtime was a favorite time for the fairies as well, for they could interact with the humans in their astral bodies. The humans with whom they interacted were greatly impacted by these rendezvous, and began to create stories and legends about "the little people." Songs and simple music were slowly introduced into the cultures of the various human tribes and colonies, including those young souls who were just evolving from first- and second-dimensional consciousness.

After 5000 years in the fourth dimension, the fairies began to downstep into third-dimensional bodies. At first, they came into uninhabited regions of the continent that existed in the vicinity of the Hawaiian Islands. After acclimating to third-dimensional Earth, the fairies migrated to the regions in which humans lived, introducing themselves only to young children in the beginning. The love, acceptance, and delight of the children were so great that they told their parents, and soon the fairies lived among the big people as well. As the little ones taught the humans more sophisticated songs to sing, and instruments to make, they became more and more endeared to the people. Festivals were held to celebrate and share music among villages and colonies, and soon the entire continent was filled with nearly 20,000 fairies. The fairies taught the people lighthearted competitive games to play at these gatherings. These games were very much like today's sack races, bobbing for apples, blind man's bluff, and relay games. As a result, the humans learned to take themselves and competition less seriously, and to laugh at themselves more freely.

Fairies Meet the Merpeople

Fairies gradually infiltrated and broadened the cultures in Bali, Samoa, and India, as well as North and South America, Asia, Africa, and what later became known as Lemuria and Atlantis. In Lemuria, the fairies discovered the existence of merpeople. Around 4000 of the fairies moved into the coastal areas around Lemuria and began to interact regularly with the dolphins, whales, and merpeople, all of which existed in large populations in that area.

The merpeople were being prepared to be the first true

Lemurians and the heart of the Lemurian culture. They were ecstatic, tantric beings whose senses of personal freedom, self-worth, and unconditional love were highly developed. Merpeople were also quite spontaneous, childlike, and totally innocent, much like the dolphins and fairies. Their main distinguishing trait was a deep dedication to their roles as guardians of all lifeforms. These merpeople were adept at astral travel and interdimensional communications as well, and as a part of that function they, too, interacted with humans during dreamtime. They took the human spirits in their astral bodies and introduced them to the seas and the many lifeforms there. They swam through the cosmos hand-in-hand with humans' astral bodies and helped them understand their relationships to various stars and star systems. As the merpeople guided these humans back toward Earth and their bodies, they would show the humans the lines of energy and light shining from specific stars to designated spots on Earth. Subconsciously, the humans received much awareness and preparation for future spiritual awakening, enlightenment, and reunion with the higher collective consciousness.

The fairies and merpeople mutually delighted in one another's company. Their land and sea experiences were shared freely and generously, and all involved were greatly expanded by these sharings. As humans began to migrate onto the Lemurian continent, the merpeople remained hidden for a time while secretly observing them and communicating with the fairies about human activities, attitudes, and life styles. Again, the small children were the first to be introduced to the merpeople, and with these initial contacts, the human children were strangely altered. Their parents began to notice subtle changes in the childrens' eyes and speaking voices. Their eyes became very watery and yet more focused at the same time. The children were opening their third eyes and seeing auric fields of color around people and plants. Their voices acquired a slight echoing resonance that came from deep inside their chests, and the very sound of their voices was enough to stir the hearts of the adults and older children. You see, upon physical contact with the merpeople, the souls and the Ka bodies of the young ones were activated and anchored into their physical forms. As a result, the universal stream of unconditional love began to flow through them spontaneously and freely. Even those who had not directly contacted the merpeople opened their hearts and eyes more just by being around the children. When the adults asked the children what had happened to them, the children innocently replied, "The sea people gave us new stars inside." This child's interpretation was at first believed to be fantasy; but as a few of the adults experienced fleeting visions of light in their own third eyes, and feelings of light opening in their chests and bodies, they began to slowly realize that the stories from the children were perhaps more than fantasy.

After a few months of contact, the children were told which specific adults they could bring with them to meet the merpeople. The dozen adults who were chosen had already started experiencing heart and third-eye awakening, and with their first meeting and swim with the merpeople they were spiritually "cracked open." They swam and sat at the edge of the waters and sobbed as the depth of unconditional love moved through their dormant chakras and consciousnesses. Soon another twelve, and then another, were brought to meet the merpeople until, after a few weeks, the entire population of the southern coastal area was interacting with the merpeople and the fairies. It was a delightful and joyous time for all, and the people were extremely grateful to, and respectful of, their Lemurian friends.

Gradually, more and more people migrated onto the continent of Lemuria, with colonies located in each of the four directions. The colony on the East was comprised mostly of tribal groups of indigenous beings who were already living on Earth when the Maldekians arrived. They were younger souls who had been birthed into lower dimensions to evolve from "the bottom up," so to speak. The eastern coast extended just about to the present Cascade Mountain range, with most of what is now the United States and Canada submerged beneath the ocean. From part of Texas, down through Mexico and most of Central America, was another continent. This land mass extended considerably further west than it does today, however. The eastern Lemurians had come from that continent via small canoelike boats that held about twelve people each. There were originally four boats containing forty-eight people that arrived on Lemurian shores.

The new inhabitants on the South of Lemuria had come from a southern continent in the vicinity of what is now called the Hawaiian Islands. They had invented simple boats with sails in order to travel to the "big land," which was occasionally vaguely visible from high peaks on clear days. These people were members of the former Maldekian Free Orion Colony who had been born of Pleiadian parents. There were originally around 120 settlers from this group who landed in Lemuria. They were also the first to be introduced to the merpeople.

On the West of Lemuria, the young indigenous souls came from Asia. They, too, traveled by water in simple crafts they had invented. However, their water crafts were more like rafts than boats. One raft and its passengers had been toppled, and the people killed, on their first journey. When they arrived there were only about 100 people left.

The North was settled by migrators from the present-day Alaskan/Canadian continent who had crossed a marshy peninsula to explore the continent of Lemuria. These early Lemurians were also young indigenous souls whose urges toward exploration and discovery had awakened. There were around 200 of these people.

The new colonists on the South of Lemuria began to meet the merpeople and interact with them, and as a result, their lives and consciousnesses were awakening quickly. By the time the sailboats were sent back to the Hawaiian continent and returned to Lemuria with another 120 people, those who had stayed behind to begin colonization were very altered. As the new families arrived, they were at first confused about the strange behavioral and attitudinal changes in their old friends. Those who had spiritually awakened initially acted mysterious about what had brought about the changes, yet promised that the new arrivals would soon have their own firsthand experiences. For a few weeks the latter explored nearby areas, established dwellings and storage buildings, created cooking areas, gathered necessary raw materials, and settled in. When the time came for the latest arrivals to meet the merpeople, they had already been impacted greatly through their exposures and interactions with the first Lemurians. Therefore, they were ready and had much the same experiences as the first humans had upon meeting the merpeople. Joyful celebrations were held with feasting, music, and shared stories between the merpeople, fairies, and humans; and all were greatly enriched. Theirs was a happy and rapidly unfolding way of life and, for many years, they lived in a carefree manner, and with constantly renewed inspiration.

The merpeople, like the dolphins, are Light Beings from Sirius who came to Earth not only to experience third-dimensional reality, but to create a bridge between the stars, dolphins, and humans. They carry the DNA of humans and dolphins combined, just as they do on Sirius, in order to create a spiritual magnetism toward spontaneous right action founded in divine love. In other words, all of their doing springs forth from their naturally sacred way of being. Action comes from their beingness, not from willful egos. They are selfless, unconditionally loving and giving, and dedicated to Oneness of all things. And still their own lives are self-fulfilling, joyous, receptive, and overflowing. This may seem to be a contradiction.

How can you be totally selfless and yet be receptive and self-fulfilled? It is the way of Divinity and Oneness—the only way. The divine human must learn this seemingly paradoxical way of being and doing in order to find peace and completion. Why?

Because your own spirits require that it be so. The divine human being is one who has transcended all belief in separation and "win/lose" mentality. These outworn ways of thinking and being are replaced with awareness of, and dedication to, the Oneness of all things and beings and to a "win/win" way of interacting and cocreating with others. To do so, you must be willing to allow your heart to open fully, to relinquish all control and resistance, and to "be ye as little children" again. You must observe and participate in life as if all life is sacred and cherishable—because it is. You must relearn how to be enthusiastic, and how to live in awe and wonder. You must let go of all of your shallow ways and be fully present with life, as if each and every day is a precious gift you are given to experience to its fullest. When you live this way, you naturally begin to overflow. You become lovingly contagious, just as the merpeople were to these early Earth dwellers. And from that place of self-fulfillment, this overflowing love and exuberance for life spills onto others around you. *You give because you love. You love because you are grateful. And you are grateful because you love.* It is really simple. But you must risk letting a little sophistication slip away. You must chance being looked at strangely and not always being understood. And you must lose control. That is what the merpeople, dolphins, and fairies, each in their own way, have to teach.

The merpeople came to Earth because of their deep desire to give to and interact with other lifeforms—and because they were needed. The heart of what many of you fondly remember or sense as the Lemurian way is in truth the Sirian dolphin and merpeople way. And yet, that too became jaded over time.

About fifty years into the colonization of the Lemurian continent—approximately 136,000 years ago—the Pleiadian and Andromedan hierarchies had established a fourth- through sixth-dimensional City of Light inside a 14,000-foot mountain at the exact center of that continent. This peak was very similar in shape to Mt. Fuji, and was the first mystery school to be established on Earth since the long Ice Age. The top of the peak was glacier covered, which gave it a year-round, snow-capped-peak appearance. These tall white peaks were key to holding higher-dimensional frequencies due to the purity of the crystalline formation of the ice and snow. The Lemurian peak was called

Wabasi, which means "the soul's way home" or "the way to the stars." Its appearance was always a source of awe, and intriguing for the Lemurians of all the colonies, and yet traveling to it did not work. Somehow, explorers would find themselves lost in the jungles that surrounded Mt. Wabasi like a wide moat; or they would run into areas with so many snakes that they were afraid to attempt to move through. You see, Mt. Wabasi was heavily protected by the planetary guardians until the correct time came for it to be accessed, and then only for sincere spiritual purposes.

At the fifty-year point, however, the Pleiadian and Andromedan teachers and guardians telepathically began to communicate—first with the merpeople and then with selected individuals on the South—that it was time for a few initiates to come to the mountain. These messages were always confirmed for the people by the merpeople in the beginning, but later a person's receipt of this telepathic invitation was taken for granted as legitimate. When people were called to the center of the island, it was always considered a great honor, and the individuals who were chosen were supported and revered by their constituents.

Ma-Ra, the First Lemurian Initiate

The first to be called by the guardians, as the Lemurians called them, was a twenty-year-old woman who had been "baptized" with the merpeople, and christened by the fairies within hours of her birth. When she was born, a star was visibly seen emanating from the center of her chest by those with clear third-eye vision, and they knew she was blessed with special gifts. She was named Ma-Ra, which meant "the goddess who is mother of the Sun." Therefore, when she was called, her people were greatly moved, and yet considered it natural that she should be the first chosen initiate. She was told to prepare by fasting on only seawater for three days and nights, and on the fourth morning to eat only what the fairies brought her. The fairies were told telepathically to collect flower petals from specific species and to bring them to Ma-Ra in fresh spring water in a stone bowl. Ma-Ra was told to first drink only the flower water, and then to sit facing the rising Sun in a full lotus position with her arms raised, bent at the elbows and palms open facing the Sun. This position is one of deep surrender of the personality will and fusion with the light of divine will, purpose, and truth. As she sat in this position for several hours, she was taken on a visionary journey, during which she was shown her own past and future.

Ma-Ra saw herself as a priestess in the Temples of Melchizadek on Maldek, being initiated in the ceremony of divine sovereignty. This was a spiritual rite of passage given to those who had attained a level of spiritual purity and wisdom that enabled them to be responsible and accountable for living as spiritual authorities unto themselves and others. It was also a recognition that the initiate was in direct contact with his/her Higher Self. Ma-Ra saw herself being dressed in a white robe for her initiation and led to, and placed in, a shallow human-size stone bath. The bath was spring fed from below its rock-lined bottom and considered very sacred. As the water covered her body, she had felt a sharp bolt of electrical light pierce her third chakra. She had breathed deeply to release resistance to this piercing light, as her whole body began to shake violently and to become less and less solid, until all that was left was an etheric form made of billions of points of sparkling light. As she witnessed her complete surrender to this transfiguration in her past Maldekian life, she simultaneously reexperienced it in her twenty-year-old Earth body. Her Ka was completely activated, connecting her Higher Self with her human form during this experience. All self-doubts and blocks on all levels were cleared like smoky vapors rising from, and leaving, her body. When her body became physical again, she was more than she had been. Her inner knowing of limitlessness, life beyond form, memories of her Maldekian enlightenment, and her own soul's origins and purpose were completely restored.

As the Maldekian past-life initiation vision and reexperience were completed, Ma-Ra instantly became bigger than Mt. Wabasi and found herself flying above the precession of her future lives. She saw pain and struggle, great love and compassion, deep wounding and separation, and eventually a life in which she would be reinitiated as a sovereign queen in Egypt around 10,000 B.C. That lifetime would be the next one on Earth during which she would experience total enlightenment and spiritual freedom. Next, she saw herself as an enlightened priestess of the mystery schools of Isis (called the Temples of the Mara, in Hebrew countries), giving birth to a special child who was named Jesus Christ. She saw herself taking him to the river one moon cycle after his birth and giving him a baptismal initiation as a divine sovereign being. This was the meaning of baptism in its origins and truth: a releasing of the initiate from all illusions and past ties, and an honoring of the person's spiritual awakeness, alignment with Higher Self, and ability to serve and act as a spiritually sovereign being.

Ma-Ra's love for, dedication to, and honoring of this tiny one brought ancient future tears of remembrance to her eyes. [And to Amorah's eyes as she channeled this material and saw the visions.] Ma-Ra wept even more as she watched him mature and saw herself taking him to Egypt to be initiated and taught in the pyramids. She observed herself and her future eighteen-year-old son walking hand-in-hand on the backs of crocodiles, as if they were nothing more than stepping stones, into the death chambers of a mazelike temple. They dropped hands and entered individual chambers where they were immediately put into a deep sleep. For three days, while asleep in these chambers, they faced all of their worst fears and ego allurements. If either had succumbed to any of these experiences, she or he would immediately die. Both

emerged four days later and were quietly and secretly taken to the
Great Pyramid for a final initiation ceremony before returning to
their homeland.

The visions faded again and she saw herself in the Cities of
Light on Sirius being prepared for her final service as an Emissary
of Light on Earth. She saw even later visions of herself appearing
in radiant light form to many people on Earth, and sometimes
speaking to the people and sometimes simply opening their
hearts. She saw the fall of the Catholic Church and orthodox reli-
gions and wept again as she witnessed the return of sacredness to
Earth and sovereignty to her people. She saw mass awakenings
and the Second Coming of Christ en masse, during which she
and her Earth son and a host of other radiant ones held out their
hands to welcome many thousands of beings into the higher-
dimensional Cities of Light.

Once again the visions faded and she was simultaneously filled
with, and one with, a great huge Light that seemed to fill and
connect her with all of existence. As she let go into this Infinite
Sun, she was blended with the collective consciousness of All
That Is, and she knew total peace and surrender. After a few minutes of Earth time, she found herself walking down a golden aisle
of light toward two golden light thrones. Sitting on them were
the two most radiant beings she had ever seen, one male and one
female. As she approached them, she was filled with even more
love and radiant light than before. The Holy Father and the Holy
Mother each extended a hand to her as she knelt before them.
Then the Holy Father spoke to her, saying, "Daughter of darkness, you have returned to the Light from whence you were conceived. You may remain here with us if you choose to do so, for
you have no need to return to Earth for yourself. You are complete
now. But if you choose to do so, you may return to Earth and step
into the lives you saw flashing before you. If you choose this, you
will first go to the sacred mountain and be trained in the ways of
alchemy and transcendence of limitation. Then you will return to
your people briefly and bring the sacred laws to them. This is only
if you choose to go back. What would you have your own destiny
be, my child?"

As Ma-Ra looked deeply into the eyes of the Holy Mother
and Holy Father, tears of great love and completion flowed once

more. Softly, she responded, "I cannot stay here with you while they remain on Earth. My love for my own future on Earth, all of it, and for Earth's people and their lives, calls me to return and fulfill my purpose there."

The Holy Mother replied, "My beautiful daughter, Earth and her people will awaken with or without you. If it is your mother-ly pull and magnetism that pulls you to return, be honest about it." This last statement was intended to challenge Ma-Ra's sense of knowing versus her self-doubt about her own motivations. She sat in silence and contemplatively retreated inside for a few moments as she felt the truth of the words. Then she answered, "Holy Mother, I am that I am." As she released their hands, con-sciousness slowly returned to her body on Earth where she still sat in full lotus, palms facing east. The Sun was at about a sixty-degree angle in the sky, and the fairies all around her on the ground slept deeply. She saw the bowl of flower petals in front of her, reached down, and slowly ate each petal individually, thank-ing the fairies and the flowers for their gift.

As the fairies awoke, they were startled to see her. They excit-edly told her about the great beam of light that had surrounded her and filled the area. She had become a body of light within the beam at which time the fairies had fallen into a deep trancelike sleep and dreamed of the subterranean worlds they would inhab-it in future times. Two of the fairies had been told in their dreams to accompany Ma-Ra to the base of Mt. Wabasi where they would find a cave. They were to leave Ma-Ra at that point and go into the cave deep beneath Earth's surface and be prepared to be the first king and queen of the fairies. Their roles would be spiri-tually somewhat like that of a Holy Mother and Holy Father, as well as teachers and guardians, to the fairies. He was the being who later became known as Pan and she was named Pandora.

The three left for their journey the next morning just after a sunrise ceremony with their human, fairy, and merpeople friends. A fire was lit on the beach to be tended and kept burning until a signal was received that all three chosen ones were safely at their destination at Mt. Wabasi. It was a three-day journey before they arrived at the entrance to the cave where Pan and Pandora left Ma-Ra. Prior to entering the cave, they assisted Ma-Ra in build-ing a large fire and sending smoke signals back to the people on shore. Then the fairies and Ma-Ra parted. Ma-Ra intuitively found her way to an ancient-feeling grove, where she prepared to spend her first night alone. As she fell into a deep sleep, her astral body separated from her physical body and she discovered that her body was surrounded by about thirty beings dancing around a fire, playing panflutes, singing, and laughing. Some of the beings were fairylike, only larger. There were half-animal, half-human beings. Some were half-goat, others half-horse or unicorn, while still others appeared to be part-bird. She was intrigued by these unique and strange ones all around her, and as she rose from her sleeping body, she, too, was pulled into the dance. After a few minutes, the music and dancing ended abruptly as a metal trumpet was sounded. A dwarf-size male and female were carried into the grove on gold, fabric, and flower-decorated carriers and all of the other beings turned to welcome and honor them with a Namasté. Ma-Ra instinctively did the same. As she lifted her head afterward to look at the two beings, she was summoned tocome beforethem. The carriers were lowered to the ground, and the small male and female stepped out to greet her. She was startled when she recognized the faces of Pan and Pandora, and they all began to laugh heartily.

Next, Ma-Ra was led to a golden throne in the center of the grove. It was empty except for a gold and silver cape and a jeweled crown in the seat. The throne was surrounded by flowers and flower petals, which were also being strewn along the path in front of her as she approached the throne. Two young females in white, flowing gowns with garlands of flowers in their hair and around their necks, wrists, and ankles picked up the cape and extended it to Ma-Ra. As she walked forward, the cape was draped around her shoulders, after which the two young women placed the crown on her head. This last act was met with peals of laughter, applause, music, and general excitement and celebration. Ma-Ra felt confused and yet at home and familiar with her new surroundings and people. As the celebration continued, Ma-Ra sat on the throne patiently awaiting some message or offering from her hosts and followers. Instead, when she awakened on the ground inside the grove just before sunrise, all was quiet and seemingly undisturbed. She stood, slowly stretched and released the stiffness from having slept on the ground. As she did so, a small lark landed on her hand and offered her a flower in its beak. She took the flower, inhaled its essence and sweet fragrance, then ate the petals. Small animals were coming out from behind trees, or emerging from holes in the ground, and even a large deer stepped into the clearing. They seemed to be there to get a look at her, and yet there was a feeling of expectancy from them as well. She greeted them with gentle laughter and delight, squatted and extended her hand as a welcome. A squirrel cautiously walked over to her, sniffed her fingers, then scurried away. The others just stood staring.

Ma-Ra decided to try talking to the animals, and asked them what they wanted from her. In reply, the deer turned and looked in the opposite direction toward the peak of Mt. Wabasi. As Ma-Ra observed the deer, she felt as though she were being invited somewhere up the mountain. She asked the animals to lead her where she needed to go, and as she did so, the deer, the bird, and the squirrel began to turn and go toward the mountain. Ma-Ra followed. Occasionally, one of the creatures would turn and look at her, but otherwise, it was a straightforward trek for nearly two-and-a-half hours. At that time, the animals stopped and sat down, looking at Ma-Ra to indicate that she should sit as well. Within minutes, several fairies brought bowls of flower water, fruit, waferlike cookies, and honey. The animal guides and Ma-Ra ate the foods as the fairies told her how excited they were that she had finally come. They had been told for several years about her impending arrival, and had prepared food and shelter for her. Another hour-and-a-half walk brought Ma-Ra, the fairies, and her animal guides to a small cave whose opening had been extended into a room with a thatched roof and grass-and-twig walls. A sleeping pad had been created of straw covered in tightly woven linen. A fire pit had been built inside the cave with a hole in the thatched roof to let out the smoke. The fairies told Ma-Ra she would be staying with them for a while and learning about plants, animals, minerals, and their relationships with fairies and humans. She was being initiated into the world of fairies and nature.

Ma-Ra spent four months in her new mountain home, with fairies and animals as her guides and teachers. By day, she was taken on trips to different areas of the mountain and taught the ways of herbs and flowers. She learned to recognize the creation signatures of all plants and understand their uses in healing, nutrition, and spiritual awareness. She learned how to make flower essences and herbal remedies, and how to call on animal spirits for guidance and teaching. By night, she almost always found herself in the grove with the same host of humans and other creatures as on her first night there. At times, fairies or humans came to her there to ask her to settle disputes or give them advice. Even humans from her home on the South of Lemuria would show up at the grove in their astral bodies. Ma-Ra would give advice, teach, recommend herbs and flowers, and sometimes take them on spiritual journeys to the stars or inside the mountain. Upon awakening, she was always surprised by her dreams, and by the fact that she had so much more knowledge and ability while sleeping. She consistently seemed to know exactly what those who came to her needed, and she gave it freely.

One morning as she awoke, she heard voices outside her hut. As she came into the clearing outside, a very tall male stood with several of the fairies. The fairies were pleading with him that Ma-Ra should be left with them a little longer. They had grown very fond of her, and wanted a little more time with her before she was taken away. The man spoke very authoritatively, telling the fairies that she had completed what she had come to them for and must continue her initiations inside the mountain now. As Ma-Ra approached, the man turned toward her and greeted her with a

Namasté. He then identified himself by saying, "Hello, Ma-Ra, Queen of Heaven and Earth. Your next journey of remembering awaits you. My name is Ha-Ra and I live in the City of Light at the center of the mountain. I am your own male counterpart. I have never been physically embodied as you have, even though I appear to you to be physical now. I am, as you are, an Emissary of Light from the Ancestor Stars (their name for the Pleiades at that time). Soon you and I will be together again, but first you must complete your initiations in the City of Light. There you will learn to transcend the seemingly limited physical world, reunite with your galactic consciousness, and remember what you are here to teach the people.

"We are forerunners of what humans are becoming, regardless of their origins. Many of the humans on Earth, as well as Earth herself, have been imprisoned in the past by dark beings who would control instead of empower others. Even whole worlds have succumbed to these controlling ones, and yet they too must eventually return to the Light—for Light is Truth and Truth is Light. All of existence will know this soon. The people of Earth must learn to trust themselves and God/Goddess again. They are afraid to become mature, responsible, and sovereign beings, and believe themselves to be only the products of creation and not the creators. They will learn to be cocreators with God/Goddess as they remember the divinity of their own souls and spirits. We must prepare for that time now, as well as for the times in between. You are a radiantly beautiful goddess whose role on Earth is to nurture your children, all children, back into their own remembrance of Truth. And I am your male link to other worlds, left behind that we might bridge the many worlds as One. Let us go now."

As Ha-Ra became silent, the two looked into one another's eyes for what seemed like eternity in an instant. Their light bodies magnetically reached out to each other and they became transfixed as a single point of light and consciousness. Ma-Ra was able to see his visions and experience his thoughts as her own. Ha-Ra felt her feelings and her deep surrender and compassion. For those moments, only one flame burned brightly, as their two flames united, completely blended and whole again. As Ma-Ra let go completely, she lost all sense of time and space, thoughts, feelings, and sensations and yielded to the Oneness with All That Is. When she returned to individuated consciousness once more, she opened her eyes to find herself inside a crystalline City of Light inside Mt. Wabasi. Through her complete surrender, she had teleported to the inside of the mountain within Ha-Ra's consciousness and then rematerialized as Ma-Ra. This was her first lesson; and from that point on, when she wanted to go from one place to another, all she had to do was teleport herself there.

She remained inside the City of Light for many months. She learned and remembered very quickly in these sacred surroundings. Her teachers were Sirian, Pleiadian, and Andromedan Light Beings who quickened her frequencies with higher-dimensional energies and encodings. It was more a return to who she truly was than it was a process of learning and changing. And yet it all had to be done with third-dimensional methods in order to ground it into her life on Earth. She became one with, and read the crystal records of, Earth. She astral-traveled to Sirius, Alcyone, and Orion to be initiated and reeducated as to the role of each star system in the unfolding Divine Plan for Earth and your solar ring. She astral-projected in order to swim with whales, dolphins, and merpeople, and rediscover their roles as time and record keepers, teachers and
holders of Christ
consciousness,

and guardians of life, respectively. She journeyed in the bodies of animals, and in her Pleiadian and galactic light bodies, and blended her physical instincts with her multidimensional consciousness, creating a grounding for her Higher Self on Earth. She fully reunited with Ha-Ra as her mantle of light was activated, giving her access to all her memories as needed to fulfill her service to the Divine Plan.

When her trainings were completed, Ma-Ra teleported herself back to her home village on the Lemurian shores. Though she had been gone for over a year by Mt. Wabasi time, she soon discovered that her people perceived her to have been absent from them for only one moon cycle. Yet, in order to share the appropriate small portion of her experiences with her people, many months were required. It was not Ma-Ra's role to teach them how to teleport, or any of the other initiatic trainings. She was only to share her learnings from her four months with the fairies studying plants, minerals, and animals with those who showed natural interest and aptitude. Other than that, she could share with the people the general nature of the teachings from the City of Light, but not the details. Those who were called would learn as she had learned. Otherwise, it was simply inappropriate to try and teach those who were not ready.

For the next few years, Ma-Ra traveled back and forth between Mt. Wabasi and the shore. She often accompanied new initiates to the mountain and through their first initiation of teleportation to the inside of the mountain. Pan and Pandora held similar roles within the fairy kingdom, and yet the teachings were quite different. The fairies were taught about their galactic origins and relationship and service to the Goddess specifically. They were the most cherished children of the Goddess because their creation was specific to third- and fourth-dimensional joy of creation itself. The fairies were literally created to delight in creation, and to feel their emotions deeply. The Goddess loved and cherished the fairies and impulsed them with celestial music and light. The fairies personified this music, love, and delight, and impulsed the Goddess through the feelings that accompanied their experiences. Their role was and is to embody and protect the essence of what you know as "the magical child self." Without the existence of the fairies, the magical child consciousness of humans would be all but lost. The fairies help keep human innocence, playfulness, joy, wonder, sexual spontaneity, and humor alive.

Pan, Pandora, and Ma-Ra brought these teachings about the interrelatedness of all living things back to their respective people. The fairies were to help keep the magical child selves alive in the humans, and the humans were to love and protect the fairies and cherish them as the Goddess does. This is still intended to be their appropriate roles, although it has not been honored by most humans for a very long time.

During Ma-Ra's lifetime on Lemuria, around fifty people were called to Mt. Wabasi and initiated. The Lemurian mystery schools and spiritual culture were begun and continued to expand beyond that time. When she was eighty years old, Ma-Ra completed her purpose on Lemuria and ascended. She became the first Ascended Master on Earth, setting a precedent for many millennia to come. Following her ascension, the people of Lemuria gradually became more widespread as their population increased. The people in the four directions of the continent began to meet one another about twenty years following Ma-Ra's ascension, or about 130 years into inhabitance of the Lemurian continent. These meetings were peaceful and exciting for the people from all groups. The younger-souled beings from the West, North, and East had by that time met and associated with both fairies and merpeople and were quite open-hearted and pure in their intent. Therefore, their meeting with more evolved humans was a natural next step in their own evolution.

Further Development of Lemurian Culture

For around 500 years these early Lemurians wove together a culture whose spiritual foundation was in the interrelatedness with the fairies, merpeople, and nature. Those who were called to Mt. Wabasi were only about two percent of the overall population of the continent. The Lemurians supported and celebrated those who were called, but the continent's population as a whole was not directly involved in the mystery school initiatic training. The majority of the Lemurians were learning about love, sexual freedom, balance with nature, and unity-in-diversity among species—as well as among the humans of different origins. All of the Lemurians were primarily lighthearted, and filled with childlike innocence, purity, and curiosity.

A shared language was gradually created that enabled these diverse groups to communicate with one another. Methods of tool making, architecture, boat building, food preparation, weaving, singing, and instrument making were shared among the groups. The people as a whole seemed almost obsessed with finding new and better ways of performing everyday activities. Stone masonry was one of the Lemurians' early discoveries that had the greatest impact on their society. Beginning with simple rock and mortar structures, they quickly branched out to include artistic touches such as stone and wood carving, pottery and clay sculpting, and drawings in stone. All of these were begun within the first 630 years of human colonization of Lemuria.

The First Incans

During the following 500 years, many more people from varying locations found their way to Lemuria. One group of 120 male explorers arrived on the southeast coast of Lemuria near the end of this 500-year period. They were the newest Earth inhabitants at that time. Four thousand Pleiadians from a planet in the Maya system had come to Earth to give birth to a group of 10,000 souls from a planet called Raman in the Orion system. Though these Plei-adian Maya were more spiritually evolved than the Ramanians, they too were still moving toward their own enlightenment and spiritual mastery. Most of the Pleiades was in a transition to being a galactic mystery school; those who were not quite at that stage of growth yet were being sent to Earth for their further evolution. The Pleiadians who established the first Incan colonies were those who gave birth to the Ramanians. Their fourth-dimensional light bodies were simply downstepped over a few weeks time until they were fully in third-dimensional bodies. They were in a deep sleep state for the last few days of this shift into Earth bodies, after which they awakened in their new homes.

The Ramanians' home planet in the Orion system had been imprisoned and its people enslaved for nearly 100,000 years when a nuclear explosion caused the entire planet to spontaneously combust. It had been left lifeless and devoid of surface water. The Ramanian souls whose bodies were killed in the fire had been cocooned by the Galactic and Pleiadian Emissaries of Light and brought to the oceans and dolphins on Earth about 1300 years prior to the arrival of humans on Lemuria. About 500 years into the Lemurian colonization, these Ramanians began to be born in the areas that are now called Central America and northern South America. Their home planet had been very technologically advanced. After they experienced two or three early lifetimes on Earth as Pleiadian offspring, they strengthened quickly and began to focus on inventions that would take them beyond being survivalists.

The Pleiadians had developed a more sophisticated culture for the Ramanians to come into than had previously been established on Earth. Adobe and stone buildings already existed when the Ramanians were born. Cultivation practices using primitive plows had begun. Musical instruments somewhat like the recorder, lyre, drum, and guitar of today's world were already part of the early Incan lifestyle. Even simple jewelry making and gem polishing were part of their way of life. After about three generations, the new Earth dwellers invented wheeled carts and began domesticating wild donkeys to pull them. Weapons were also a part of their early inventive focus, important to their psyches for protection as well as means for killing animals for food. Bows and arrows, slings, and spears were naturally the first to be created. But more brutal weapons such as spiked mallets soon followed.

Their Pleiadian/Incan parents created a loving and safe environment for the Ramanian refugees, yet the children were deeply ingrained with distrust and defensive behavioral patterns. It was not uncommon for children to attack and accuse one another of misdeeds. At times, they would even become hysterical and begin hitting their parents and screaming. Though their parents were by nature a loving and peaceful people, they were not yet master beings themselves. And some of the parents lost their tempers and found themselves angrily spanking and punishing these difficult children. Of course, distrust increased, and yet the Ramanians understood control through punishment. They even had a victim's type of respect for those using force. Therefore, the parents who used rash means to control their children did get more results than the more compassionate parents.

Their social structure quickly became patriarchal, even though it did not begin that way. The Ramanian men had a strong drive for control and power. The women had been considered fair game by their oppressors on Raman. Even the married men had vented their frustrations on the women and children. Therefore women and children had been, and quickly became again, the lower-class citizens. The Pleiadians were not a patriarchal people, so this created some conflicts within the Incan colonies.

About three generations into life on Earth, these colonies began to be divided into those that were primarily souls of Ramanian origins and those of Pleiadian origins. Though the colonies were always somewhat mixed and all had shared genetics, the souls of those of likemindedness tended to be drawn toward one another as they died and were reincarnated.

One such group of mostly Ramanian/Incan men, while on a hunting expedition, came upon a tribe of about 100 people. These tribespeople were part of the young-soul group birthed on Earth. These Incans immediately knew that they had nothing to fear from these innocent, and still quite primitive, people. Therefore, they befriended them thinking that good relations might prove beneficial later on. As they learned to communicate with one another over time, the tribespeople told the newcomers about a "big land" to the northwest and across a strip of ocean only a few miles wide. Stories were told about creatures that were half-human and half-fish, and little people called fairies. The mysterious Mt. Wabasi was also mentioned in the intriguing tales. The Incan interest was sparked. The men were so magnetized to explore this land that they quickly set about improving on the simple boats of the tribespeople. They made larger boats, adding sails and oars that were held in place easily. Around 1000 years into life on Lemuria, 120 Ramanian men embarked upon their first journey to its shores.

Because there were villages spread out around the coastline no more than five miles apart, the Incans quickly met their first Lemurian people. The fairies and merpeople had been warned about these newcomers in advance, and therefore warned the Lemurians that these people were different. The Lemurians were told that these men had come from very difficult past circumstances and tended to be rough and controlling as a result. Extension of hospitality with clear boundaries for the women was the best approach.

Meanwhile, on their way to Lemuria, extremely high winds had arisen, and the men had worked very hard to keep control of the boats in the choppy waters. While attempting to lower the sails, two men had fallen overboard. They were both rescued by mermaids and brought back to their boats, heaving and gasping for breath. Though the mermaids disappeared quickly afterward, the men had been astonished by the appearance of such creatures—especially ones who were so obviously female. There were mermen in the seas as well, but it had been planned that the mermaids would meet the men first in order to humble them somewhat. So when they arrived on shore, the men were still shaken by the storm that had come and gone so quickly—and by their brief glimpses of the female rescuers who had saved two of them.

With a combination of hand gestures and drawing in the sand, the men managed to communicate enough to find out that the merpeople were well known to the Lemurians and much loved and respected. The Ramanians were awed by this fact and it made them less guarded and controlling. Thus the relations between the two groups began harmoniously and with minimal conflict. About two days into their visit, some of the men began to make lewd advances toward a few of the women. Their husbands, fathers, and other males in the group simply and nonthreateningly stepped between the visitors and the women, gesturing that the women were off limits. The Incans took these gestures to mean that the women were the property of the men who intervened, and they backed off from their advances.

The Incans were amazed by the happiness and lightheartedness of their hosts. At first, they mistook the Lemurians to be simpleminded, but soon realized that they were quite intelligent and somehow familiar. Of course, Lemurians of the South were still primarily of Free Orion and Earth/Pleiadian origins. They had somewhat common backgrounds with the Ramanian/ Incans, though much further removed from those old ties. The Incans remained with the people only a few days before going inland. The fairies kept out of sight, as did the merpeople. They knew these newcomers were still too unpredictable to make themselves vulnerable. When the men returned to the shore before going back to their own homes across the water, they told their new friends that they would return soon. After receiving gifts of flower leis, fruits, and delicate foods for their trip home, they departed. The Incan men were definitely altered by their new acquaintances, though they would have been hard pressed to explain it in words.

When the Incan men arrived back at their city, they were already anxious to return to Lemuria. They told stories and tried to share their experiences with the people at home. Yet, speaking in terms of feelings was not common to their people and there was really no other way to adequately describe what had happened to them. Within two weeks another expedition began, this time with 200 men. This second trip was very similar to the first except that there was no accident at sea. The merpeople did send three mermen and two mermaids to swim about 100 yards from the boats and make themselves seen by the men. The first reaction of the new men was to want to have sex with the mermaids, but since they were not swimmers that seemed impossible. It did serve as the source of jokes and suppositions, however. Once on shore, the men were met by the Lemurian acquaintances of the first Incan men, who again presented them with leis of flowers, fruit and honey water, and an array of foods. They visited and ate, as the new men watched them, astonished by the openness, generosity, trust, and apparent naiveté of the people.

When the men wanted to know if the Lemurians had ever had sex with the mermaids, the Lemurians were so astonished by the question that they could scarcely answer. Merpeople were sacred; they were from the stars like the dolphins. The people learned from them and honored and revered them so highly they could not even imagine such a thing. As the visitors watched the reactions of the Lemurian men to their questions, the new men thought these Lemurians to be somehow less masculine than themselves. In the backs of their minds, the Incans registered the Lemurians as easy marks if they ever needed them for any reason. However, in the meantime, they simply enjoyed the hospitality, explored the land and its resources, shared stories as best they could, and became very comfortable with these strangely joyful people. Some of the Incan men were becoming much more relaxed. They were even learning manners, and how to be considerate of others—although at times it still surprised them and they attempted to shift back to their old macho attitudes. The Lemurians felt deeply compassionate toward these men who were, to their way of thinking, so obviously unhappy and insecure. They attempted to be even kinder and more gracious and understanding with their guests than they would normally be. And it worked.

The Incan men felt at times captivated by these gentle Lemurians. They found themselves laughing with their hosts and hostesses, learning to swim, enjoying vegetarian foods, and bridging language barriers. After a few weeks of exploration on Lemuria, the Incans were enjoying an evening of music and conversation with the Lemurians when a woman asked one of the visitors about their women. The guest seemed puzzled by her question until she finally made him understand that her people wanted to meet the Incan women. The men looked at one another with puzzled expressions. They could not imagine why anyone would care one way or another about meeting their women. They were just women and did not matter beyond how they served the men and cared for the children. Yet it was difficult to answer the question. The Lemurian women were such an intrinsic part of Lemurian culture—certainly not as important as the men, in their eyes, but more important than women in their own culture. The Incan men were actually embarrassed by the question and awkwardly tried to reply that they could not see the purpose of bringing women with them. A Lemurian man entered the conversation at that point and asked directly, "Do you not consider your women important enough to bring them here to meet us? We would make them very welcome and comfortable." The visitor replied, "Our women are different. They don't want to travel. They belong at home with the children and their work. They would not want to come here." The Lemurian man boldly asked, "Did you ask them?" The Incan man got up and walked away without answering. Such an idea had never occurred to him or any of the others for that matter; and he was too embarrassed to say so.

The Incans returned home soon after that night, but the evening's conversation had stuck in their minds. During the journey home, they discussed it in length. They realized they were afraid for the women to feel important and valued because they would have no one to control. And yet, these new friends were more joyful and satisfied than they had ever even hoped to be, and the women were respected and treated as equals. Prior to arriving home, the issue was dropped; they decided that they were different from these strange Lemurians, and that it was best not to test the strength of their system.

A few months passed without anymore trips, though the men secretly longed to go back. Those who had been to Lemuria were noticeably changed when they returned home. They argued less, often walking away instead of yelling and fighting as they had formerly done. These men ceased using so much intimidation to control their wives and children, and were more silent than before. Their wives and children often found them gazing off into the distance as if their minds were far away. The men's hearts had just begun to open and feel traces of joy and innocence, and they could not forget. At times these men felt lonely, tired, and uninspired. A few of them even tried to explain it to their wives, but they did not know how to be vulnerable and open with their own families. This made them even lonelier. Finally, one of the men decided to move

to Lemuria with his family. As he began to announce his decision
to the others, he was met with mixed responses. For a few of the
men, it was the only impetus they had needed to make the same
choice. Others were angry about their decision and tried to talk
them out of going. But the men were determined to leave; they
could not go on living the old way anymore without withering
away. And so, shortly afterward, ten men along with their wives
and children left their homes for Lemuria. A few other men went
with them to explore the possibility as well.

When their boat arrived on shore, the Lemurians were there
to greet them with the usual leis of flowers, drinks, and food. The
women and children were greeted and acknowledged equally with
the men, and the men were relieved to finally let go of their controlling and dominant image and simply be one of those arriving
to live on Lemuria. Feasting and celebrations were held to welcome the newcomers. They were even invited to share the homes
of their hosts until their own were constructed. All of the men
who had come to consider the same alternative life style as their
friends soon departed for their homeland to bring their families
to Lemuria as well.

Within 100 years of the first Incan explorative trip to
Lemurian shores, over 5000 Incans of both Pleiadian and Ramanian origins, including women and children, became part of
the Lemurian culture. They mixed mostly with the southside
dwellers, although a few began their own village slightly inland.
Meeting the fairies and merpeople happened in gradual stages, as
it had with the early Lemurians. But all of the people, new and
old, were eventually friendly with, and in awe of, their diverse
friends. Deep healing took place within the people of Ramanian
origins as trust, innocence, emotional opening, and love were
refound. They were finally safe to come home to their true selves,
and they discovered themselves to be really good people. Self-
respect and self-worth were restored in these people, men and
women alike. Couples began to heal the male/female pain and
separation and to love one another deeply. As the fairies told stories of the Goddess and the merpeople shared stories about the
stars and the Dolphin Starpeople (the Sirians), the Incans were
humbled and opened even more. They began to develop a new
sense of spiritual connectedness and a value system based on hon-

oring the sacredness of all things and all people. Their hearts were filled with gratitude and love for the original Lemurians, the mer-people, fairies, and dolphins. They even learned to understand the roles of animals as guides and teachers about instinctual nature, and the full use of their senses.

When the first Incan/Lemurian was called to Mt. Wabasi about 100 years after their people came to the continent, a great celebration was held. The woman who was called was named Glory. That was not the way it was pronounced, but it is the meaning of her name and what I will call her. Glory was twenty-three and the new mother of twins: a boy and a girl. She had been named because of the feeling she brought about in people at her birth. Her eyes were very clear and bright. Her parents felt she was the glory of their lives, since she was the first child born to them after fifteen years of marriage. Glory had seemed to be a normal child but with an inordinately empathetic and caring nature. She was never a self-centered child even in the normal sense. It was as if she had been born to be aware of, and sensitive to, the needs and feelings of others. When she was called to the center of the island, Glory's babies were only nine weeks old. She was told to leave them with a woman who had just lost her new-born baby. This was a heartrending challenge for Glory. And yet, she reasoned that after becoming an initiate she would bring so much more to her children than she could otherwise. Therefore she knew she must go. After six months, Glory returned and shared care of her two children with the surrogate mother. She was again called to Mt. Wabasi when the children were two years old to take her next initiation. There were four such trips to Mt. Wabasi by the time the children were ten years old, after which Glory was a fully enlightened, initiate priestess.

By the end of her third trip to the mountain, temples had been built in which the Mt. Wabasi initiates did healing work and spiritual teachings for the Lemurians. The priests and priestesses did not initiate people or teach the advanced mystery school trainings. But they did teach basic morality, ego transcendence, harmony with nature and the Goddess, herbal and flower essence healing, and ceremonial and ritualistic practices. For instance, the Lemurians were taught to honor the seasons on the equinoxes and solstices. They were taught to recognize specific stars and constellations and their higher purposes. The Lemurians sent prayers and offerings to the stars and the starpeople. They danced and celebrated the full moons. Marriages and sex were sacred beyond measure and sources of great love and joy to the people.

Glory's son, Matthew as I will call him, was the next Incan to be called to Mt. Wabasi. He was only sixteen at the time, and one of the youngest ever called. Soon afterward, two other Incans were called and the people of all group origins were very supportive and delighted by these initiations. When Matthew returned a year after going to the mountain, he announced that he was to marry a young Incan woman who was currently inside the mountain. She was named Mara—after the original Ma-Ra—as were a few other females. Matthew and Mara would move to an Incan village and take the Lemurian sacred ways to their people.

Development of Incan Spirituality

When Matthew and Mara arrived in the land of the Incas, they were met with much curiosity and skepticism by most of the people. There were, however, a few villages where Incans of mostly Pleiadian roots lived; and in these villages spiritual practices indigenous to the Pleiades had been established. Matthew and Mara were pleased to find these villages and discover that there were several areas in which the aspects of spiritual traditions were similar to and, in some cases, identical to those of Lemuria. It was, therefore, easy for them to stay in these villages first, sharing and comparing the two spiritualities and blending them together. The primarily Ramanian-based Incan villages were still basically patriarchal and nonspiritual. Matthew and Mara established small temples and ceremonial stone circles where they conducted equinox, solstice, and full-moon gatherings. All of the Incans were always invited to every gathering. A few of the Ramanian-based villagers came to these ceremonies from time to time, but they were by far a small minority.

It was around 150 years after Matthew and Mara joined the Incan villages and began teaching there that the Incans finally united for a common purpose—to protect their villages from invasion and destruction by a group of still-primitive hostiles. These hostiles were from an area to the north of the Incan territory and had left their home on an explorative journey looking for more food sources. When they stumbled upon their first Incan village and saw the comparatively rich life style of its people, the invaders raided the village and stole as much food, tools, and pottery as they could carry. The Incans were caught completely off guard, and, therefore, the hostiles were able to steal freely. The thieves returned to their own tribe at the northeastern shore of the continent, told stories about the Incan life style, and displayed loot from the Incan villages. These people, who were the first Aztecs, were eager to go back to the Incan villages to learn more about the people and steal more goods. After a half dozen raids, the Incans sent messages among the villages about the Aztec thievery. As a result, a group comprised of people from every village posted guards around the northern end of their territory and soon stifled the Aztec efforts. When the Aztecs planned a new strategy that included attacking the guards, they were met with more sophisticated Incan means of self-defense. The Incans, however, had agreed to try and take prisoners and find out who these people were and why they were raiding their villages. When six Aztec men were captured, the Incans realized communication would be much more difficult than with other groups. These raiders were still speaking with hand signals and grunts and were extremely superstitious about drawing images. Only the simplest messages about basic survival needs were successful in the beginning. Eventually the Aztec prisoners numbered around thirty people, and communications broadened somewhat. The Incans were able to let the Aztec prisoners know that they could go if they would lead the Incans to their people. They also assured the prisoners that no violence would be used if they were cooperative.

By the time the Incans led their prisoners out into the jungles toward the Aztec camp, all of the Incan villages had united for protection. Trust bonds were forming between the diverse groups, and evening conversations among the Incan people included sharing stories about similarities and differences. It was the first time the people of the many villages had truly been open to, or had seen a need for, more intimate communication with one another. Their shared vulnerability served to help them open to each other in a whole new way. And as the problems with the Aztecs were resolved, at least temporarily, the Incans became a closer knit group. The spiritual ceremonial practices were more widely shared, as were basic teachings about reincarnation, inter-relatedness with nature and the stars, and simple moral laws. Finally an Incan way of life and spirituality was forming with influences from the Pleiadian and Lemurian cultures, as well as some of their own that were derived from life experience.

For over 1000 years, the Incan culture took on more and more of a spiritual focus, though remaining pre-initiatic in its structure and consciousness. The Aztecs presented some problems to the Incans from time to time, but these conflicts were generally short-lived and easily resolved. Resolution came chiefly through sharing of culture, development of communication, and teaching the Aztecs to construct dwellings, make simple tools, store food, and other basic skills. Therefore, the Aztec nation, which at that time contained only around 1000 people, evolved more quickly as well.

In the meantime, Lemuria continued to grow as the spiritual center for the planet with more and more people becoming initiates, enlightened teachers, healers, and priests and priestesses. The crystal cities at the center of Mt. Wabasi had initiated and brought more than 1000 people to enlightenment and ascension by about 2500 years of Lemurian colonization. At that point in time, there was an influx of over 10,000 new souls to the planet from the Pleiades. Most were born on Lemuria, though around 2000 were taken to Machu Picchu to establish a spiritual colony there. These Pleiadians were at about the same evolutionary level as those who had begun the Incan civilization in the northern part of the same continent. They came with full memories intact and with instructions about the development of a sacred society there.

Earth's Divine Plan Prepared for and Implemented

The Pleiadians who became Lemurians were to be the roots of Egyptian spirituality in the distant future. Because of this long-term plan, most did not come to Earth in downstepped higher-dimensional light bodies, but were born as humans are today. These future Egyptians needed to experience the Lemurian initiations in order to fully align with the Divine Plan for Earth. For 20,000 years, the Pleiadians and other Lemurians continued to expand Lemurian spirituality. The culmination of every initiate's training concluded with a choice to ascend and become higher-dimensional guides and masters, or to commit to serving Earth in human form. Though the agendas for future human lives varied greatly, there were common themes. For instance, teleportation to the crystal Cities of Light inside the mountain was a standard first initiation. At the end of the initiates' trainings, it was also standard for the people to be shown visions of their own future lives. It was like being shown a map of everywhere you will ever go all at once. Then you would step onto the map—or into your next life—and begin to put one foot in front of the other. Your own Higher Self, as well as the Higher Council of Twelve, would present you with your options and you would choose. After each life, you would review your life individually and then in relationship to your overall plan to determine what step to take next.

Those who were initiated in this way fell into three main categories. One group consisted of those who would ascend and become higher-dimensional guides and master teachers for evolving humans; these beings might, rarely, choose to precipitate a physical body for a specific purpose in their service, but they need not take on karmic patternings. A second group would complete the initiatic path and become enlightened three more times prior to completion on Earth between 1995 and 2013 A.D.; two of these enlightenments would take place in female bodies, and two in male bodies. During the precession of their lives, they would take on a primary karmic pattern and myth and transcend it in two different spiritual paths, once as a male and once as a female in each one; ascension or conscious death would be their final step. Many of these beings would experience physical death or ascension during Earth changes in order to assist others into the Light.

A third group was comprised of those who would take on seven, specific, solar ring karmic themes and transform and transmute them through numerous lifetimes. Each karmic series of lives would end in one of seven different spiritual paths and culminate in ascension. During each lifetime in which the person would ascend, he or she would be of the same gender—either seven ascension experiences as male, or seven as female (twin flames can ascend together in two bodies as well, as long as one of the bodies is the same gender as those of other ascension experiences)—up until the final ascension between A.D. 1995 and

2013, these beings would experience many lives as male and female, often simultaneously as what you call twin flames. At the time of the final ascension, these bodhisattvas must have fully integrated all of their male and female lives and both twin flames into one body. That is one reason the emphasis on the *unio con-juncto,* or sacred marriage, is so important at this time on Earth. The balance between male and female energies internally and externally must be attained now in order for Earth and her people to take their next evolutionary steps.

You see, although there was a sacredness and equanimity between both genders in Lemuria, it was a primarily Goddess-based spiritual civilization. Atlantis was primarily God-based. Now it is time for a spirituality based on God/Goddess/All That Is that acknowledges and practices equanimity, sovereignty, and transcendence of duality. In order to ascend, a being must have balanced his or her inner male and female energies and surrendered into Divine Oneness with All That Is. Those who chose, and were chosen for, the third Lemurian path of seven ascensions prior to leaving Earth, would do so in seven of the following cultures and spiritual paths: Lemuria, Atlantis, Egypt, Maya, Inca, Aztec, Machu Picchu, aboriginal Australia, India, Goddess/druid groups in Europe and England, Buddhism, Christ consciousness, Bali, and other smaller indigenous spiritual communities around your world such as the Hopi, other Native American, African, and South and Central American tribes. Prior to the seventh ascension, a blending and remembering of all of the previous six ascension experiences occurs. The final ascension takes place when the other six spiritual paths have become fully integrated into the body consciousness. And the body consciousness must be fully aligned in the Pillar of Light with all nine-dimensional aspects of the person's higher consciousness.

Many of you who are reading this book were most likely enlightened and/or ascended in Lemuria and chose either the second path of four enlightenments or the third path of seven ascensions. Some of you may have been in Lemuria but did not complete your initiations at that time. If this is the case, you are here to complete them now. For all of you, the time for remembering is at hand. You must define your own myth, your ego allurements, and your solar ring karmic patterns in need of transformation and transcendence. Only sincere dedication to impeccability will work for the initiates on Earth now. The time for fence-straddling is long past. If you are here to be enlightened and/or ascend in this life, you can no longer afford the luxury of hit-and-miss, or fascination-based, spirituality. Your spirituality can no longer be an aspect of your life. It must be the focus and foundation of your life. All aspects of life are sacred and joyful and are experienced as such before anyone can complete the evolutionary journey home to Oneness.

[Author's Note: The following is an excerpt from a channeling by Ra *in* The Pleiadian Workbook: Awakening Your Divine Ka:

> *By the year 2013, everyone who remains on the Earth must have an understanding of the following four evolutionary principles: 1) Our purpose here is to evolve physically, emotionally, mentally, and spiritually. 2) Every human being is a Divine Essence made of Light and love whose nature is goodness. 3) Free will is an absolute universal right; impeccability calls on the self to surrender its free will to Divine Will in faith and trust. 4) All of natural existence is sacred beyond how it serves or meets the needs of the individual self. At this time every human alive is being presented with these four spiritual premises in subtle or direct ways. It is a planetary law that before the end of a major time cycle such as you are in at this time, every single living person must be reminded of the four evolutionary principles they are expected to embrace. . .*

> *The seven solar ring karmic patterns, which are currently being exaggerated in order to be brought into awareness and transformed, are: arrogance, addiction, prejudice, hatred, violence, victimhood, and shame. These seven sources of pain, illusion, and separation are given in the order in which they developed in your solar ring beginning on Venus and expanding on Mars and Maldek.]*

Ra continues:

Though there is obviously much more Earth history, what has been given here is the basic information needed to stir your memories. In appendices B and C in this book, you will further be gently reminded of your own past and present genetic and star roots.

There you will find maps of Earth from 145,500 B.C., when the Maldekians arrived; and from 102,000 B.C., when the Divine Plan for Earth was begun. These maps are accompanied by charts that outline the chronological order in which the major soul groups on your planet arrived and from whence they came. It further tells what current races were genetically seeded by these beings.

Remember! It is your wake-up call. The alarm has gone off and the "Snooze button" is inoperable. This is not a command or a threat. It is simply how it is! Your solar ring and planet are submerging themselves deeper and deeper into the Photon Band every moment of every day. Time is bending and stretching and changing. You might notice time lapses or accelerated time periods in which you accomplish half of or twice what you formerly did. The next day you might find yourself at the end of what should take many hours done in only an hour. You are in a time warp. As you become completely submerged in the Photon Band between 1998 and 2001, this time warp will be even more pronounced. It will expand to include more dimensional warps as well. Some of you have already experienced a few of these. You are sitting in your chair reading a book. As you move from one line to the next, you suddenly realize you were in a City of Light temple, or inside the Sphinx or a Mayan ruin. You had a complete conversation with a higher-dimensional being there or a psychic opening. Or perhaps you relived a past life. And all of this was literally during the movement from one line of your book to the next. You shrug it off, you get full-body confirmation chills, or you drop your book and close your eyes quickly so you can remember. You will become more and more lucid during your waking hours of the dream in which you live. These dimensional warps, or lucidity bleedthroughs, will become more frequent as the photon energies increase. You will begin to hear your own past and future voices calling out to you in those moments in between breaths and thoughts, and between waking and sleeping. You will suddenly experience cellular awareness of being in a different body and in your current one at the same time.

Those who resist their own spiritual awakening and deepening will find themselves devolving quickly. Fatal illnesses will accelerate from early stages to final stages so quickly that your doctors will be at a loss with how to deal with them. Everything is accelerating, and those who try to keep their foot on the brakes all the time will wear them out and come to a crashing halt. Your options are still many and diverse, and yet, if you have made it all the way through this book, you are more than likely to "make it" this time. Therefore, the messages that I, Ra, bring you are not a threat—and possibly no surprise either.

In Part V, I have asked Amorah to present a few techniques or practices to assist you in making it through this critical transition time from self-exploration to self-mastery. As you do these processes, be innovative, contemplative, and open to discovering more than what you have already known. If you are not open to newness, you limit your own possibilities. Expand your world, let go of your paradigms; become a true rememberer, and therefore a world bridger, dimensional traveler, and anchor of the Pillar of Light through nine dimensions here on Earth. And most of all, remember it is a dream, and the outcome is up to you!

"So-la-re-en-lo"
(with great love and devotion)
Ra, spokesperson for the Pleiadian Archangelic Tribes
of the Light,
members of the Pleiadian Emissaries of Light, guardians
of your solar ring,
members of the Galactic Federation of the Light of the
Central Sun,
member of the Universal Federation of Galaxies

Part V

PART V
PROCESSES FOR CLEARING
AND SPIRITUAL ALIGNMENT

Commitment and Invocation to Remember

When you send out a prayer or invocation to your own Higher Self, guides, or any Light Beings, saying that you need help, desire to take a spiritual step, or wish to make a specific commitment, you are always heard. For instance, when you get stuck and cannot find your way through a problem or attitude, you can call out for help. When doing so, you must sincerely commit to doing whatever is necessary and in your highest good to aid in your own process. Whether you need to understand, forgive, heal, or transcend, life rearranges itself to place what you need in your path. You might have a revealing dream, or meet a new healer to whom you feel magnetically drawn. You might receive a message during meditation, or suddenly remember a deeply buried trauma just as you are falling asleep. Whatever you need will come.

In this process, you are being guided to call upon the Higher Council of Twelve, who serve the Light as well as the Supreme Being of Light for Earth. These beings comprise the main spiritual hierarchy for Earth at this time. They are responsible for all guides, angels, devas, and the execution of universal law. When you call on them, you need to be very clear and sincere about what you ask them for or commit to. What is being suggested here is to tell them that you are ready to remember your own spiritual myth and divine purpose fully; then ask them for the help you desire. (For those of you who prefer to do the exercises in this section with guided processes on cassette tapes, information for ordering tapes is in the back of this book. You will turn tapes on when you see the tape icon $\boxed{\circ = \circ}$ after reading each exercise.)

To make it simpler, follow the step-by-step process below:

1. Close your eyes.

2. Take a few deep breaths. Inhale down to the base of your tailbone while pulling your consciousness into your body more fully. Then extend your inhalations to your feet while continuing to pull your consciousness into your body.

3. Visualize a four- to six-inch in diameter, grounding cord of light that connects your lower body to the center of the Earth.

4. Invoke your own Higher Self to come and be with you and blend with you in your aura at this time. Wait until you feel or sense this divine presence before proceeding.

5. Invoke the Pleiadian Emissaries of Light to come and be with you at this time. They will remain near, but outside, your aura.

6. Invoke three times each: the Supreme Being of Light, also known as the Spirit of Oneness; and the Higher Council of Twelve who hold and serve the Light.

6. Tell these Light Beings anything you wish to tell them about your spiritual path and help that you need at this time.

7. Tell these Light Beings the following (or in your own words): "I am fully committed to my own enlightenment and/or ascension in this life. I am also ready to remember my own past, my spiritual myth, and my divine purpose. I ask that the manner and speed in which I remember be that which would serve my highest and greatest good at this time and in the future. Help me have the courage to always act on what I know is needed quickly, graciously, and impeccably. So be it."

8. Be receptive and listen in case you are given any immediate messages or insights at this time.

9. When complete—or after about two minutes if no messages are given—open your eyes and proceed with your day.

Clearing the Memory Virus

As mentioned in Part IV, when the Maldekians were brought to Earth, it was determined that their memories of the explosion of Maldek be removed. It was believed at that time that these beings could retain most of their evolutionary growth without the specific memories of Maldek. And so this was done. Prior to their births, a "memory virus" was introduced to their fetal brains that would block their souls from connecting with the part of their brains that translates soul memories. This part of the brain is located at the top of the brain stem and extends into the brain stem about one-half inch downward toward the neck. This memory virus was implanted in all those who came to Earth from Maldek, Orion, and other star systems and galaxies as well.

Now it is time for these memory viruses to be removed from Earth's people. The memory virus appears clairvoyantly like a mushroom that is rooted in the upper brain stem and whose top spreads out above and to either side of the brain stem. Even if you are not sure whether or not you have this virus, the process will not be detrimental in any way, and can improve your ability to translate soul memories through your brain. You will use the Quantum Transfiguration Grid to clear this virus.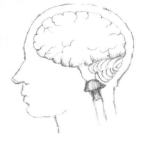

In this grid, an etheric infusion of billions of microscopic lasers of ultraviolet light from several directions enters the cells. (See illustration on following page.) In a sense, this confuses the cells, causing them to release whatever is out of affinity and then resume a clockwise rotation. Since the memory virus is out of affinity with your cells, brain function, and etheric health, the lasers push this foreign matter out of your energy field and body.

The process used for accomplishing this laser light show requires your involvement in an active way. Since this process tends to seem a little complicated when you first try it, it helps if you first go through the steps mentally and visually in increments. Therefore, practice the following steps prior to actually using the grid on your brain stem area.

1. Imagine a cube-shaped container made of clear glass floating in front of you.

2. Now imagine placing your hands above and below the cube and sending billions of tiny lasers of ultraviolet light through the cube from both hands at the same time.

3. Next, move your hands to the right and left sides of the cube and fill it full of ultraviolet lasers from those directions.

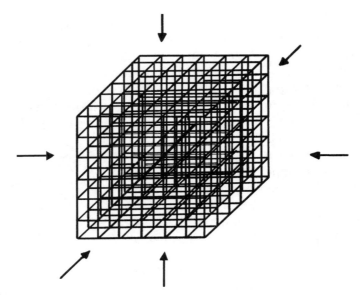

4. After that, place your hands behind and in front of the cube and once again infuse it with ultraviolet lasers.

5. Now that you have experienced the component parts of the light matrix generated in the chamber, visualize sending ultraviolet lasers from all six directions at the same time. In other words, imagine having three sets of hands, with one hand on each of the six sides of the cube and send billions of lasers through the cube from all six directions at the same time. See illustration above. You will see that the intersecting laser lines create many minuscule, linked cubes of light inside the original larger cube, like a three-dimensional tapestry of finely woven threads of light.

If these steps feel confusing to you, practice them until the process feels more comfortable and natural. Then you will be ready to actually do the clearing session.

When working with the Quantum Transfiguration grid, it is necessary for you to hold the intention and vision of this interlaced grid of laser lights in order to help the Pleiadians anchor the frequencies and light patterns as well. In fact, the easiest way to do this clearing session is lying down. After calling in the Pleiadian Emissaries of Light, you will ask specifically for the

Pleiadian laser surgeons. Then you will place both of your hands on the lower part of the back of your head while visualizing millions of lasers of ultraviolet light streaming through the entire area of your brain stem and lower middle brain. The Pleiadian laser surgeons will assist you in dissolving the memory virus.

The following is the process for clearing your memory virus:

1. Lie down in a comfortable position and close your eyes.

2. Call on your Higher Self to be with you.

3. Call on the Pleiadian Emissaries of Light. When you feel they are with you, ask specifically that the Pleiadian laser surgeons come forth.

4. *Optional:* Invite any other guides or Ascended Masters you enjoy working with to be with you and oversee the process as well.

5. Tell your guides and the Pleiadians that you are ready to have the memory virus removed completely and permanently. Ask the laser surgeons to assist you in accomplishing this.

6. Place both hands behind your head in the area shown in the above illustration.

7. Visualize or intend that millions of ultraviolet lasers penetrate every cell. Focus on the dissolution of the mushroom. The laser surgeons will be working on it as well.

8. When the intensity of the energy suddenly dies down and you feel as if the lasers are no longer meeting any resistance, the process is done. This will take between ten and twenty-five minutes.

9. Take at least a twenty-to-thirty-minute epsom salt bath. If you have access to a hot mineral spring, it would be even better. You need to keep the back of your head submerged in the water throughout the soak.

Transforming and Transcending Ego Allurements and Karmic Patterns

In Part IV, seven solar system karmic patterns were given. They are: arrogance, addiction, prejudice, hatred, violence, victimhood, and shame. These are the primary subconscious—and conscious—karmic vices that were developed on Venus, Mars, Maldek, and Earth. There are also seven ego allurements that are specific to Earth: lust, laziness, gluttony, pride, anger, envy, and greed. These last seven are specifically the traps of the negative ego. This negative ego is the aspect of your personality that refuses to surrender to spirit, wants to be in control, keeps you feeling separate, and wants you to feel special. It does not matter whether you feel better than or less than, as long as you feel special.

The ego allurements specific to Earth are part of the Incan mystery school teachings. Once you have awakened to the realization that you are not your body and your personality, that you are a sacred immortal spirit, the next step is to transcend ego and become spiritually responsible and pure. Transformation and eventual transcendence of the seven ego allurements are the way to do so.

Recognition and acknowledgment of the karmic patterns and ego allurements that you still get trapped by are essential first steps. This requires being impeccably honest with yourself. To help you with the transformation and transcendence of these karmas and vices, use the following process as often as you feel the need. You will need to use this process for each of the karmas and ego allurements that you still get trapped by. However, you may wish to address only one issue each time you do the process. Take time to really feel and fully experience each part of the guided process. Otherwise it will not be very effective.

The process for transforming and transcending karmic patterns and ego allurements is as follows:

1. Find your comfortable position. Then ground yourself with a grounding cord, or by using the breathing process for pulling your consciousness into your body as given in step 2 of the previous section.

2. Call in your Higher Self to be with you.

3. Call in the Pleiadian Emissaries of Light to assist you in this process, if you would like. Call in any other guides, angels, or Ascended Masters with whom you feel spiritually connected.

4. Choose either a karmic pattern or ego allurement that you wish to begin transforming and transcending. Affirm your readiness to transcend it and ask for help.

5. Think about the most recent experience in which you succumbed to the karma or ego allurement. Remember it in detail. See clearly the place in which it occurred.

6. Observe yourself in the situation and notice how you were breathing. Observe where your body contracted. Notice what emotions were present. Notice your body posture. What did you say, think, and imagine? Be thorough, but as nonjudgmental as possible.

7. Recall the attitudes and responses of the person or persons with whom you had the experience.

8. Now let the scene go. Affirm silently or out loud: "I am sincerely ready to give up _____(fill in the blank with your issue such as pride or victimhood). I ask my Higher Self, my guides of the Light, and the Pleiadian Emissaries of Light to assist me in transcending this issue. My true divine self is already pure and transcendent. All else is illusion." Use your own words or add to these if you would like.

9. Next imagine yourself in the identical situation as the one in steps 5 through 8. See the place in which this new version of the original experience takes place.

10. See and feel yourself responding transcendently to the situation and people involved. In other words, imagine what it would be like to be in the purity of your divine essence behaving impeccably. Notice how you would breathe in this remake or reframing. Observe how the contractions in your body are gone. Notice what you say, think, and imagine. Observe your heart

remaining open.

11. Now watch the other person or persons involved to see how they respond to you differently this time.

12. When you have fully imagined, seen, and felt the newly reframed situation as it will be when you have transcended your particular issue, then let it go.

13. Affirm: "I am the divine and pure essence that I am. I completely forgive myself and all others in my past who were involved in the illusion of _____(fill in the blank) in which I have participated. I am free of this illusion now and forevermore."

14. Open your eyes and go on with your day. 🖸

Male and Female Energy Balancing

The process for balancing your internal male and female energies is very simple. In a meditative space, you will visualize an infinity symbol above and below you. You will affirm your desire to balance your male and female energies internally and in your life. Then you will use a gold infinity symbol horizontally at each chakra location beginning at the crown and working your way down. The energy running through the infinity symbol will help you to redistribute the energies in your chakras and body between your right and left, or male and female sides, respectively. (See illustration on next page.)

The male and female energy balancing process is as follows:

1. Sit or lie down in a comfortable position.

2. Ground yourself and bring yourself to a centered and present focus.

3. Call on your Higher Self to be with you throughout the meditation to assist you in balancing your male and female energies.

4. Visualize Yin/Yang symbols floating in the air above your head and below your feet. Feel your body suspended in the energy field between these two symbols. Relax and notice any feelings, thoughts, or energy shifts for about one to two minutes. Intend that these symbols remain there throughout the meditation.

5. Next, visualize a gold infinity symbol located on your crown, or seventh, chakra. See the gold energy running through the symbol continually. Ask that the infinity symbol redistribute and balance your male and female energies in your seventh chakra.

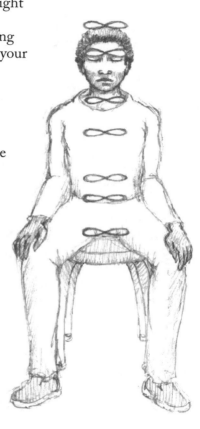

6. After about two minutes, or when you feel complete, move the infinity symbol in front of your third eye, or sixth, chakra. Again, imagine the gold light running continually through the symbol balancing and redistributing your male and female energies in your sixth chakra.

7. After two minutes, or when you feel complete, move the infinity symbol to your throat, or fifth, chakra. Intend that the gold light running through the symbol balances and redistributes your male and female energies in your fifth chakra.

8. After two minutes or so, repeat the same process as before with the infinity symbol at your heart, or fourth, chakra.

9. Repeat the process for your third, or solar plexus, chakra.

10. Repeat the process for your second, or sacral, chakra.

11. Repeat the process for your root, or first, chakra.

12. Open your eyes and continue with your day.

You may do this meditation as often as you feel a need for it. It is also recommended that you work with the Masculine, Feminine, and Yin/Yang Love Configuration Chambers of Light as shown in *The Pleiadian Workbook*.

Aligning with the Higher Collective Consciousness

Coming into alignment with the higher collective consciousness of Earth's people is an important aspect of spiritual growth for all of us and for Earth at this time. Much competitive and "may the best person win" types of thinking and behaving have prevailed on Earth for a long time, especially in more modern cultures. There is, however, in the atmosphere surrounding Earth, a collective that consists of the higher consciousnesses of all of Earth's people. These beings work together for the highest good of all and to facilitate the actualization of the Divine Plan. The following is an excerpt from *The Pleiadian Workbook* about this group:

> Once, in a hypnosis session, I was taken to a place outside Earth's atmosphere where the higher collective consciousness of all of Earth's people exists. In this place I saw billions of smiling, loving faces without bodies, encircling the planet from just outside a clear bubble surrounding Earth. This higher collective consciousness was exclusively made up of loving, sweet, intelligent, innocent Light Beings: all of us living on Earth. These beautiful ones were observing and sending love and encouragement through the bubble to their counterparts on the planet's surface.

Mind-linking and aligning your purpose with this collective can be more than just your general intent. I was once told by Ra that humans can ask the higher collective consciousness for what we want. These requests are always looked at, and considered, relative to the overall highest good. Ra went on to say that when a minimum of four people ask at the same time for something that will impact every person on Earth, the collective can impulse everyone on the planet, if it is appropriate. For instance, I was awakened one morning with a vision of World War III breaking out in Bosnia. Ra told me to gather together between four and twelve people on that day and do the process for petitioning and mind-linking with the higher collective consciousness. We were to ask the collective consciousness to give everyone on Earth a one-minute reference point in peace and to ask the people on Earth to choose not to allow this war to begin. Those of us who requested this were to then remain together in a receptive and meditative state for ten minutes, holding the energy of peaceful choices. All of us experienced an ever-deepening inner peace accompanied by a sweet, innocent, childlike feeling.

In the following process you will be guided into a mind-linking and alignment with the higher collective consciousness:

1. Sit comfortably and close your eyes.

2. Ground yourself.

3. Take a few deep breaths and center yourself.

4. Call in your own Higher Self to be with you for the meditation.

5. Visualize a very large bubble with Earth floating inside it. Around the outside of this bubble are the angelic faces of all of the humans on Earth.

6. From where you are sitting, send out a golden infinity symbol, or figure 8, to these beings outside this bubble. While doing so, repeatedly say, silently or out loud: "I wish to connect with the higher collective consciousness." Imagine that your energy and message are being carried through the infinity symbol to the collective and that their love, energy, and/or messages are being carried back to you through the infinity symbol as well.

7. When you feel the connection is made, tell them whatever you wish to about your wishes for Earth, all people, and yourself. Ask them to help manifest these wishes in the way that would serve the highest good for all concerned. Tell these beings that you want to align all of your actions, thoughts, and desires with that of the higher collective consciousness and the Divine Plan.

8. Relax in a receptive manner for at least ten minutes and feel the communion with the collective.

9. When you are through, open your eyes and go on with your day.

When doing this in a group, the more the merrier! The process will be identical except that everyone will petition for the same thing from the collective at step 7. Examples of suggested group petitions are: protection of the rain forest; for every human to have a one-minute experience of being unconditionally loved or loving (choose one specific thing at a time); for every human to have a reference point in the sacredness of Earth as a whole, or of individual elementals, other humans, animals, or whatever you feel drawn to invoke; for everyone on Earth to have an experience of equality and connectedness with all races. If your group wants to do a longer process, I have been told that three petitions within a meditation period are all that can be accepted. The process would then be for the group to align with the higher collective consciousness via infinity symbols. Then take one specific request at a time and petition for it together. Hold the energy and focus for ten minutes. Together, petition the next request. Again hold that focus for ten minutes. Then petition together your last request, holding the focus for another ten minutes. It will be easier if you have a spokesperson guiding the process for everyone.

You may connect with the higher collective consciousness as often as you would like personally. Group petitions are to be done a maximum of once daily.

I would like to close this book with the words to a song I wrote in early 1990. It is my gift and hope for the healing and spiritual awakening of Earth and all her people.

ASK GREAT SPIRIT

I wander through this Earthly
walk
just looking for my
home.
Sometimes I've thought I'm
destined
to be lonely and alone.
Which way's the right way?
Which way do I go?
How am I to under-
stand?
How am I to know?
I look upon polluted
lands
and I can find no peace.
I walk upon Mother
Earth;
I'm searching for release.
I look up to the
heavens
but gray skies appear.
I'm listening for the
answers
but I have yet to hear.

And I ask, "Great Spirit,
show me the way."
And I ask, "Great Spirit,
teach me today."
And I ask, "Great Spirit,
guide all I say,
that I may share with others
the Light along the way."

And Great Spirit answers,
"I am everywhere.
I'm the spirit of the rivers

and the spirit of the air.
I'm the spirit of the eagle,
the buffalo, the deer.
I'm in everything you see
and everything you hear.
And when you look into the
eyes
of anyone you see
the eyes that are looking back

are all a part of me.
And you can learn from everyone
and everything you see;
for everything that's anything
is another part of me."

The spirit of the stars
is calling me home.
The spirit of the mountain
says I am not alone.

The spirit of the water
is telling me to flow.
The spirit of the spotted owl
is telling me to know.
The spirit of the land
is crying out for peace.
The spirit of the Mother
is calling for release.
The spirit of the sky
is asking to be clear.
The spirit of the Father
is asking me to hear.

And I ask, "Great Spirit,
show me the way."
And I ask, "Great Spirit,
teach me today."
And I ask, "Great Spirit,
guide all I say
that I may share with others
the Light along the way."

And Great Spirit answers,
"Make this your home.
Take care of the mountains
and you'll never feel alone.
Clean up the waters
and they will help you flow.
Be a friend to Brother Owl
and he will help you know.
These lands are in danger
and you must work for peace.
Stop raping Mother Earth
and you will find release.
When the skies are not
polluted
you will then be clear
to listen to the Father,
to see and feel and hear."

And I thank you, Great Spirit,
for showing me the way.
And I thank you, Great Spirit,
for teaching me today.
And I thank you, Great Spirit,
for guiding all I say
that I may share with others
the Light along the way.
And I will share with others
the Light along the way.
Ho!

Appendices

APPENDIX A

Chronology for Venus, Mars, and Maldek

The outline of historic events in this appendix is given in chronological order for each of the above named planets. Year "0" in each case is used to represent the beginning of human life on the named planet. As the numbers increase, they refer to how many years humans have inhabited the particular planet when the event occurred.

VENUS

Year	Historical Significance
prehuman	Signature plants introduced
	Armada of Andromeda: A group of angelic beings from Andromeda requested the opportunity to experience self-motivation and sovereignty in humanoid third-dimensional bodies. When this request was approved by the hierarchies for this galaxy—the androgynous Supreme Being named An and the Elohim Higher Council of Twelve—a plan was set into motion. This plan, which is referred to as the Armada of Andromeda, laid out planetary laws for those who would be born into physical forms and was agreed upon by An, the Higher Council, and the angels, or future humanoids.
0	Arrival of Andromedan angels whose light bodies were downstepped to third-dimensional: birth of the first Venusians
500	Beginning development of musical instruments
1200	Class division becomes apparent
	Inbreeding has resulted in a mutant group of Venusians who were considered "ugly" and unintelligent
1500	"Ugly ones" leave the original colony and begin their own
2000	Beginning of physical art forms
3000	Currency system created
3500	Crime began that was incited by prejudice and extreme class division

Year	Historical Significance
3800	Criminal rebels leave the original colony, discover the "Ugly Ones" colony, and become part of the colony
3801	Rebels control the "Ugly Ones" and declare war on them
	By consensus, "Ugly Ones" agree they want the rebels removed from their colony; hierarchies remove rebels and take them to the fourth dimension of Mars
3800–5200	Government formed to protect wealthy and establish control over lower classes in original colony; class division strengthens
	Original colony flourishes in art and music
	Colony of "Ugly Ones" slowly recovers from violence against them and begins to develop spiritual values
5200	New Andromedan angels born in both colonies
5250	Emissaries of Light arrive and reunite the two colonies; spiritual values are taught to the Venusians
5700	Emissaries of Light leave Venus
5700–10,400	Andromedan angels born every 500 years to remind people of spiritual purpose and past learning
	Steady artistic and agricultural growth
	Fear of self-trust deepens in Venusians
	Prejudice and arrogance deepen
10,400	Large flood creates more unity
10,450–15,600	Venusians discover the higher collective consciousness and deepen spiritually
	New angels born every 500 years
	Slow, gradual material evolution with focus on spiritual evolution
15,600	Seraphimlike race of linear beings introduced
	Original Venusians and seraphim-Venusians adjust to one another
16,600	Mating begins between the two Venusian races
16,800	Offspring from crossbreeding inspire study of biological science and human genetics
16,800–20,800	Predominance of science and decline of spirituality
20,800	Large quake kills one-fourth of population and destroys most large buildings
20,800–25,925	Emphasis on "man against nature," science, and technology

Year	Historical Significance
	Majority of Venusians decide they do not want more new angels to be born and bring spiritual teachings; it is done
	Class division and prejudices strengthen again
	Spiritualists become dogmatic, similar to modern-day orthodoxy
	Dark net grows between Venusians and higher collective consciousness
25,925–25,980	20 percent of population begins a spiritual revolution
	New angels and seraphim born to warn the people about darkness they are creating
25,980	Chemical-triggered explosions cause quakes, atmospheric fires, water pollution, and deaths of two-thirds of population
25,980–26,000	Higher Council of Twelve, Pleiadian Emissaries of Light, Andromedan Emissaries of Light, and seraphim hierarchy intervene, introducing spiritual principles, healing modalities, meditation techniques, and reconnection to higher collective consciousness
26,000	Hurricanes and tidal waves create minor damage
	Government dissolved
26,000–31,200	Sovereignty with cooperation and cocreation become focus
	Unity in diversity consciousness is born
	Population gradually increases to previous size
31,200	Comet lands in ocean
	Animals are introduced
31,400–31,420	Ancient mutant colony site of the "Ugly Ones" is rediscovered and rebuilt to house one-third of the growing population
31,420	Trade and travel begin between the two colonies
31,900	Quake destroys much of the new city; residents ask original colony for help, and their request is declined due to crop failure in original colony; alienation and estrangement result
31,925	Animals begin to attack humans and humans begin to kill and eat animals
32,300	Colonies reunite and restore harmony between groups
	Vegetarianism renewed

Year	Historical Significance
32,300–36,400	Human psychology birthed All Venusians desire and work toward unity in diversity and peace Animals and humans become friendly and harmonious again
36,400	"Leave well enough alone" policy enacted at cyclical change
37,200	Lethargy sets in; citywide meetings in both colonies held to brainstorm, meditate, and solve problems
37,200–38,200	New angels and seraphims sent to restore spiritual practices and healing modalities As they die, one-third of Venusian souls leave Venus and go to fourth dimension of Mars to reunite with former criminal Venusian outcasts Avatars sent to both cities to inspire and enlighten people
38,200–41,600	Age of Enlightenment: initiatic trainings introduced; many are enlightened, ascend, and form higher-dimensional hierarchy Art and music peak
41,600–46,800	Venus becomes a home to spiritual and initiatic mystery schools Ascended Masters form an order similar to the Great White Brotherhood of present-day Earth
46,800	Great flood; original colonists flee to mountains to the newer city—karmic abandonment issues between the colonies healed Reconstruction begun on the original colony
46,900	Higher Council and An send message to Venusians: 1) Do you want to ascend as a group? 2) Would you prefer to go to a new planet? 3) Do you wish to remain and accept new evolutionary challenges? Venusians choose to remain and invite new souls to be born among them who are in need of the abundance of love, spirituality, and beauty they have created A group of damaged beings from Virgo is sent
47,000	Original Venusians take on karmic patterns of the new damaged ones from Virgo Year "0" on Mars as human life begins there

Year	*Historical Significance*
47,000–52,000	Spiritual decline: male/female distrust, violence, and separation begin; anger, self-doubt, perfectionism, sense of failure to heal the damaged ones, resentment, hostility, and prejudice prevail
	Police state: crime and insanity rampant
	Dark astral planes formed
52,000	End of Venusian human life by lower group mind consensus: they believed their failures made them unworthy to live
	Pole shifts and other major planetary changes destroy all life

MARS

0	Life begins with the former Venusian criminal outcasts
250	one-third of Venusian population who left Venus in Venusian year 38,200 incarnate
250–5100	Patriarchal culture develops
	Extreme violence and oppression of women is common though improves slightly when the newer Venusians are born
	Gay and lesbian "closet" counterculture develops
5100	Pleiadians born to Martian families
	Pleiadian children begin to teach and heal the Martians
5125	Gays and lesbians come out of the closet
	Gay male and lesbian couple mutilated and hung in public area
	Law of instant karma imposed
	Patriarchs leave to organize a new colony
5175	Martians and Pleiadian Emissaries of Light hold meeting to determine guidelines for next 5200-year cycle
5200	Pole shift, quakes, changes in length of days and nights
5200–5700	Law of instant karma continues
5700–10,400	Little recurrence of violence
	Focus on rehabilitation takes precedence over punishment
	Spiritual temples built and become centers of social and spiritual activities

Year	*Historical Significance*
	Peace and steady progress and evolution on all levels
10,400	Pleiadian Emissaries of Light return and share karmic stories
	Purification ceremonies held
	Martians request opportunity to practice nonprejudice
10,400–10,600	Spirituality and healing abound
10,600	Last Venusians begin to reincarnate
10,680	Suicide among new Venusian reincarnates results in past-life memory patterns being removed from the rest of the new Venusian reincarnates
10,875	Partial memories restored as newest Venusians die and reincarnate
13,000	Segregation occurs when newest Venusian reincarnates migrate to the former patriarchal colony and establish their homes there
13,050	Weapons invented in both colonies
	Walls and moat built around the original city
13,100	New colonists declare war on and attack original city
	Water pollution
	Entire population of original city massacred
	Migrators return to and reclaim the original city
	Army establishes governing rule over people
13,100–13,200	Gunpowder invented
	Culture focused around army and war preparations
	Mining and forging of metals begun
13,200	Lyran warriors from Orion invade, conquer, and enslave Martians
13,210–13,400	Construction of pyramid for destructive purposes
	Lower astral planes become quite predominate
13,400	First nuclear blast from the top of the pyramid
13,500	Lakes and springs are noticeably drying
13,500–15,500	Water tables so low that water rationing is necessary
	Holes in ozone develop from nuclear blasts resulting in intensification of solar rays
	Skin cancer develops
	Daily violence increases
	Too little oxygen
	Police state
	Prison and work camps created
15,500	Pleiadian Emissaries of Light arrive and impose law of instant karma

Year	Historical Significance
15,500–15,600	Spiritual teachings and healing modalities reintroduced
	Group meditations held; eventually attended by a mix of Martians and Lyrans
15,600	Pleiadian delegation meets with all people, offering new guidelines
	Violent Lyrans leave Mars
	Two colonies established: one with a spiritual focus, one with a technological focus
15,600–16,100	Instant karma law continues
	Pleiadian priests, both named Ra, live in each colony
	Steady spiritual growth in new city; temple built for Ra
	Old city experiences boredom and very little growth
	Small contingent of psychic explorers in old city begin to investigate the pyramid and question Ra about psychic power; Ra teaches them meditation techniques
16,100–16,600	Solar power and greenhousing discovered
	Steady, slow growth of technology, spirituality, and in general
16,600–17,100	Parasitic plague damages food, building materials, and fibers used for clothing and paper
	Martians learn about ecological balance in order to eliminate plague
	Violence reemerges in old city
	Old city divides into violent and nonviolent segments
17,100	Ra leaves old city because of fifty-fifty vote and non-violent ones go with him to the newer, more spiritual city
17,100–18,500	Two cities remain estranged
	Old city—patriarchy reigns; devolves to original state of male competitive games, brutality, and female oppression; misuse of psychic power
18,500	Lyran-Orion invaders return, killing many, enslaving the rest in both cities
18,550	Nuclear atmospheric explosions resume via pyramid; quakes result, killing many people and destroying many buildings
18,600	All life destroyed by nuclear blast that creates sponta-neous combustion of atmosphere around and on the planet

MALDEK

Year	Historical Significance
0	5000 souls brought into the third dimension by solar angels and Lucifer
	Four separate colonies formed: 1) 750 Martians, 750 former Andromedan slaves; 2) 1500 former Orion slaves; 3) 1000 black hole survivors; 4) 1000 young souls from another part of the Milky Way
0–2000	Acclimation, genetic healing, establishment of life styles, and early development of simple social structures
2000	Pilgrimages begin; Martian/Andromedan colonists meet Young Soul colonists
2003	Invention of simple wheel and cart; trade begins
	Beginning development of small trade village between the two colonies
2004	Martian/Andromedan colonists travel with Young Soul Colonists and discover Orion colonists camped across a river; camps established on both sides of river; within six months a raft invented and Martian/Andromedan and Young Soul colonists take it across the river to meet Orion colonists
2006	Trade village established by the river between Martian/Andromedan Colony and Orion Colony
2012	Another river is crossed near an ocean; leads to members of the formerly united colonies meeting the Black Hole colonists
2012–2600	Music and primitive art develop
	Trade broadens
	Gradual improvements in previous inventions
	Steady cultural growth
2600	Maldekians' pineal glands and crown chakras receive initial activation
2700-2800	Primitive houseboat, floating bridge, and swinging bridge invented
	Ornamental buildings and hieroglyphics developed
2800	Solid bridge constructed
	Mixed marriages create offspring from mixes of all colonies except the Black Hole Colony
2800–3200	Writing tablets, then papyrus invented
	60-character written language created

Year	Historical Significance
	First schools opened
3200	Second trip to Black Hole Colony; travelers take gifts and help rebuild the Black Hole Colony after floods and mud slides
	Members of Black Hole Colony travel back with the visitors to see the other three colonies
3202	Black Hole colonists segregate from other colonies again
3202–5125	Inventions and cultural growth continue
	Population increases
	Mining and metallurgy begin
	Jewelry making invented
5125–5200	Pleiadians born in all colonies and villages to bring spiritual teachings, stories of the Maldekians karmic histories prior to coming to Maldek, and introduce people to Pleiadian Emissaries of Light and their function
	Colonies renamed: Martian/Andromedan Colony becomes Mars II; Young Soul Colony becomes Solaris; Orion Colony becomes Free Orion; Black Hole Colony becomes Sogan; trade village between Mars II and Free Orion becomes the Town of Miracles; trade village between Mars II and Solaris becomes Freedom Town
	Temples of Melchizadek constructed in all four major colonies
5200–10,400	Spiritual growth; Melchizadek Temples flourish
	Secondary focus on art, music, and architecture
10,400–10,800	Reintroduction of karmic patterns: Mars II—violence and patriarchy; Free Orion—distrust, paranoia, competition, power struggles, and fear of domination; Solaris—shame, low self-esteem, and neglect; Sogan—addiction, denial of pain and problems, obsession with happy facade, venereal disease, loveless sex
	Trade is strained
	Steam-powered land vehicles invented
	Jails and imprisonment created for violent ones
10,800	Life sentences and capital punishment begun for third-time violent offenders
10,800–11,400	Gangs develop

Year	Historical Significance
	Police force that carried weapons developed
	Guns and ammunition invented
	Civil wars between gangs and others in all colonies
	Maldek colonies become police states
11,600–15,525	Crime under control again
	Preventative measures taken through education
	Police state maintained
	Population increases to 7000
	About one tenth of population involved in spiritual temples
	Several Maldekians become enlightened
15,525–15,600	Pleiadians born into all colonies and villages to bring spiritual teachings and karmic healing and transformation
15,600–16,600	1000 years of grace
	Law of instant karma in effect
	Police forces disbanded and jails destroyed or converted to other uses
	Spiritual and psychological practices renewed and become strong
	Healing ceremonies held
	Several more Maldekians enlightened
	(16,100) Giant flood destroys Sogan; Soganites evacuate to Solaris and gradually to other colonies
	New Sogan Colony with only 300 residents built closer to other colonies
16,600–20,800	Lucifer's gradual fall from grace: his negativity impacts all Maldekians, changes weather, blocks solar encodings Maldek is thrown out of orbit and explodes, creating asteroid belt
	Cocooned souls and damaged higher-dimensional beings taken to the oceans of Earth to the dolphins
	Lucifer goes to Orion War Colony still held by the Lyrans

APPENDIX B

145,500 B.C.

(Based on world map on pages 262-263.)

When the cocooned Maldekians arrived on Earth around 145,500 B.C. they were taken to the ocean area marked "Cocoon Site" on the map. At that time there were 25,000 new human souls living on Earth in multiple locations. There were twelve main locations where these new soul beings became third-dimensional. They are listed on the chart below as numbers 1 through 12. The merpeople lived third-dimensionally in four primary locations, which are listed as numbers 13 through 16. The Maldekians were born to Pleiadian parents in four locations, which are listed as numbers 17 through 20.

The fairies were next and were dispersed near all of the other locations where humans lived. The fairies will not be listed since they did not crossbreed with humans. Later in Earth's his/her-story, there was a time when fairy and human souls united in the fourth dimension. Certain humans at that time had chosen to be guardians and preservers of the fairy heritage.

Five thousand Pleiadians came to the planet to parent 10,000 Orion refugees from the planet Raman. This group is listed as number 21. Eight thousand more Pleiadians were born on Lemuria to parents of mixed origins. They are group number 22. Group 23 is comprised of 2000 Pleiadians who precipated bodies at Machu Picchu.

The chart below consists of all of the above-mentioned beings who make up the entire human population of Earth between 145,500 B.C. and 102,000 B.C. The new souls who arrived on the planet after 102,000 B.C. are listed in Appendix C.

SOUL GROUP	ORIGINAL POPULATION	COSMIC ORIGIN	CURRENT EARTH RACE SEEDED
1	800	new Earth souls	Russian, Polish
2	2500	new Earth souls	Iranian, Pakistani
3	2500	new Earth souls	Chinese, Mongolian, Korean

World Map of 145,500 B.C.

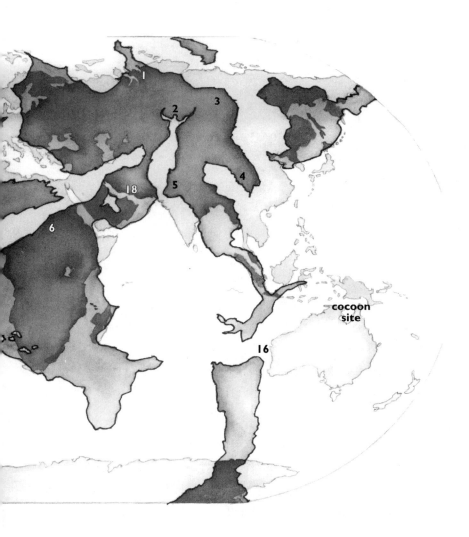

SOUL GROUP	ORIGINAL POPULATION	COSMIC ORIGIN	CURRENT EARTH RACE SEEDED
4	2000	new Earth souls	Japanese (later mixed with Lyran/Orion invaders)
5	2500	new Earth souls	Cambodian, Laotian, Vietnamese, Chinese
6	2500	new Earth souls	East African
7	2500	new Earth souls	South and West African, Arabian
8	2000	new Earth souls	North African
9	2500	new Earth souls	Norwegian, Swedish, Finnish
10	2000	new Earth souls	various Native American
11	2500	new Earth souls	Maya
12	2500	new Earth souls	Aztec, various Native American
13	1800	Sirian merpeople	Hawaiian
14	2000	Sirian merpeople	indigenous Alaskan and Canadian
15	5000	Sirian merpeople	Polynesian
16	3000	Sirian merpeople	not applicable
17	800	Pleiades (Merope)	Balinese
	1700	Maldek (Sogan)	Balinese
18	1200	Pleiades (Maya)	East Indian
	2000	Maldek (Mars II)	Indian

SOUL GROUP	ORIGINAL POPULATION	COSMIC ORIGIN	CURRENT EARTH RACE SEEDED
19	1000	Pleiades (Merope)	Samoan
	3000	Maldek (Solaris)	Samoan
20	1000	Pleiades (Electra)	Hawaiian
	3000	Maldek (Free Orion)	Hawaiian
21	4000	Pleiades (Maya)	Incan
	10,000	Orion (Raman)	Incan
22	8000	Pleiades (Merope, Maya, Alcyone)	various Native American
23	2000	Pleiades (Alcyone)	South American, especially those of Machu Picchu

As you review the stories of the various groups from Maldek, you will be able to trace the origins of specific karmic patterns and tendencies to their origins on Earth. When a race is seeded by specific souls with unique stellar and karmic encodings, that race always genetically carries those traits and their evolutionary patternings. At this point on Earth, most humans have experienced lifetimes in many or all of the existing races. This means that each of our souls has been impulsed with the encodings from all of the star systems and all of the evolutionary experiences of these races. Though the race to which you are born strongly affects your lifetime, the soul memories and evolutionary imprints are just as strong an influence.

APPENDIX C

102,000 B.C. to A.D. 1995

(Based on world map illustration on pages 268-269.)

102,000 B.C. was the beginning of what you might call the Divine Plan for Earth. Up until that time, seeding for the Divine Plan and a hierarchical order in the fourth through ninth dimensions had been established. The subconscious patternings for the future races and their own enlightenment triggers had developed as well. The new soul root races for the most part were still fairly primitive, but some were connecting with Pleiadian-based groups on Earth and the fairies and merpeople. These interactions were accelerating their growth in the areas of language development and quality of life, though they remained intellectually quite simple. Merpeople began to go through a metamorphosis and intermarry with the more evolved humans on Lemuria between 102,000 B.C. and 96,000 B.C. This created the roots of a mixed Pleiadian/Maldekian/Sirian prototype for genetic encoding and soul evolution.

At the onset the implementation of Earth's Divine Plan, the orbital cycles around the central sun of the Pleiades, Alcyone, had stabilized to 26,000 years. Major Earth changes and a pole shift took place just prior to the changeover at 102,000 B.C., leaving the face of the planet dramatically changed. Some of the land masses that broke away from major continents literally became free floating, as a few were previously. (The map on the following pages shows the world at that time.) Though there have been many other planetary changes since that time, the maps for 145,500 B.C. and 102,000 B.C. are the ones Ra has channeled to me and asked me to present at this time. The soul groups and current races listed in the following chart will be shown in their approximate origin locations on the map. These will cover all major soul groups who arrived on Earth between 102,000 B.C. and modern times. Also included will be the surviving groups of people from pre-Divine Plan days shown in Appendix A. These latter surviving groups number 1 through 14. Under the column labeled "Earth or Cosmic Origin," the Soul Group number from Appendix B will be given. A few of the original groups had no physical survivors at the time of the pole shift, but were reincarnated again in their original regions at a later time.

All others will be shown with the year the beings arrived on Earth. You will notice that the numbers do not add up to the current popula-

World Map of 102,000 B.C.

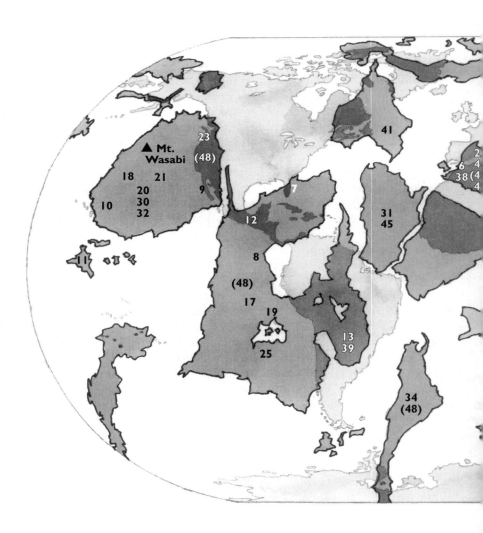

tion of Earth. This is because our current population includes soul fragments, soul split-aparts, twin flames, parallel lives, and even nonsouled
beings. In addition, many of the souls on Earth at this time were created by humans on Earth and by higher dimensional beings in other star
systems and galaxies. These souls tend to arrive one at a time, or at the
most in very small groups of a dozen or less. The information given
below refers only to souled beings upon arrival in human form on the
planet in larger groups. All dates given are B.C.

There is one other group that has held a key role on the planet since
the 102,000 B.C. turning point. This group is comprised of 144,000
Light Beings from the seventh through thirteenth dimensions. The
number 144,000 is a key creation number and is the number of compo-
nents of original consciousness. In other words, when the first conscious
experience of God/Goddess/All That Is took place, it was as if that sin-
gular consciousness had been in "no mind" or dreamless sleep. Upon
awaking, the first thought of this One consciousness was "I am" or "I
exist," and this was a great revelation. In a deep hypnosis state, I experienced this original self-consciousness revelation. When the One went
to sleep again, it dreamed of itself and through dreaming created a second consciousness, which was the first experience of male and female.
Within each consciousness lay 144,000 aspects, each aspect containing
144,000 smaller aspects. Therefore, the number 144,000 is the key to
unlocking the human consciousness creation formula as well as eternal
memory.

104,000 years ago, in order to ground the Divine Plan on Earth,
144,000 Light Beings from the seventh through thirteenth dimensions
throughout several galaxies volunteered to create souls through which to
embody. Each agreed to first precipitate third-dimensional bodies in
Lemuria and teach the mystery schools there. These beings had the
ability to accelerate and decelerate their vibrational frequencies at will,
thus becoming physical and nonphysical as required. Later, these beings
served similarly in Machu Picchu, Maya, and Egypt. Working with the
sacred principle of the four directions, four elementals, and planetary
balance, the higher-dimensional intervention in four cultures seeded the
secrets of enlightenment and ascension for all humans. These 144,000
beings also took on lifetimes of human karma in much the way Mother
Mary, or Ma-Ra, did in Lemuria. After attaining enlightenment, each
one dreamed, or visioned, his or her future lives, including the karmic
patterns, traumas, diseases, and transcendent experiences, as well as
their own timing of future enlightenments and ascensions. Each one
entered the path of either four or seven cycles of evolution and enlightenment, as described by Ra in Part IV. Within those cycles their souls

split into male and female halves in order to experience separation, and eventual resolution of duality. And in each one's final lifetime on Earth and in their final enlightenment or ascension, both soul parts, or twin flames, would be reborn into one body. Male/female balance and the initiation of *unio conjunctio,* inner sacred marriage, must be attained.

When the Ascended Master Jesus Christ came to Earth almost 2000 years ago, he embodied the 144,000 within One. This seemingly miraculous event was preplanned before the beginning of the Divine Plan for Earth. The second coming of Christ en masse is when 144,000 individuals are all awakened to their own Christ consciousness at the same time. They are the collective bride of Christ: the divine counterpart with whom he mates and births transcendence and enlightenment for the entire human race, planet Earth, and beyond. Through the orgasmic merging of Christ and the 144,000, a great cycle is completed. And that orgasm will be one for all of us to remember.

Woven within the tapestries of Venus, Mars, Maldek, and Earth histories are all the threads of hope, understanding, forgiveness, love, grace, wisdom, and transcendence needed to weave the new tapestry of the Age of Light. However, this tapestry will be woven collectively. As I interweave the threads of my own nine-dimensional remembrance, and you interweave yours, and all the other awakening ones interweave theirs, we will have a glorious cocreation that is rich in all our colors, experiences, sounds, flavors, textures, and patterns. We are each whole and vital within ourselves and simultaneously interdependent. That is the beauty of the Divine Plan. It is an "all or nothing" plan. And we cocreated it. We are finally nearing the completion point. Only total integrity, honoring of the sacredness and free will of all life, impeccability in daily living, and clearing of karmic patterns will work.

The chart below outlines the major origins of all of the weavers of this tapestry. As you look through the chart, avoid the temptation to judge others, whether they be the Anunnaki or Pleiadian Light Beings. Realize that all are weavers of the grand tapestry. Impulse them with your love. Send them messages of your faith in their ability to be responsible as sacred cocreators. Release your judgments and send them forgiveness. Ask them to forgive you for ever judging in the first place. Choose to send positive thought and emotions into the world, free yourself from all destructive influences, and notice how the tapestry of the Age of Light takes form. So let us celebrate one another's successes, free of competition and jealousy. Let us marvel at the beauty of one another's souls and spirits without reserve. And let us enjoy the remaining steps from "here to there" in confidence and joy, allowing these ancient records to set us free.

SOUL GROUP	B.C. DATE	ORIGINAL POP.	EARTH or COSMIC ORIGIN	CURRENT EARTH RACE SEEDED	COMMENTS
1		370	1		
2		2100	3		
3		270	4		
4		1800	6		
5		1000	8		
6		900	9		
7		625	10		
8		700	11		
9		3000	12, 20, 22		
10		1000	20		
11		800	19		
12		6000	21		
13		640	23		
14		1300	17		
15	98,000	30,000	new souls	Fijian	Pleiadian starseeds
16	98,000	20,000	new souls	Australian	Pleiadian starseeds
17	98,000	20,000	new souls	South American	Pleiadian starseeds
18	98,000	30,000	new souls	Lemurian	Pleiadian starseeds
19	95,000	7200	Orion	South American	Born into existing tribes of group 17; arrival on Earth was an evolutionary choice
20	72,000	7000	Earth fairies	fairies in many areas	Had been fourth dimensional for 31,000 years; their physical lives prior to that were on Lemuria

NOTE: At 59,000 B.C., a breach was created in the fifth dimension by a group of beings from Orion under Lucifer's leadership. Though these beings remained in the dark regions of the fifth dimension for many years, using the astral planes to psychically control those on Earth who were spiritually weak, the fifth-dimensional breach opened a gateway through which beings from other galaxies and star systems could easily enter.

SOUL GROUP	B.C. DATE	ORIGINAL POP.	EARTH or COSMIC ORIGIN	CURRENT EARTH RACE SEEDED	COMMENTS
21	59,000	6000	Andromeda Galaxy	Lemurian–reborn	Home planet (spontaneously combusted due to galaxy) intense solar radiation
22	59,000	8800	distant galaxy	Atlantean–later mixed with group 6, spreading into many European and Russian areas	Invaders brought here by fifth-dimensional dark lords to begin a new civilization
23	59,000	9000	distant galaxy	Lemurian-Alaskan and Canadian Eskimo	Born into other coastal groups of Lemuria
24	59,000	17,000	new souls	African	Born into group 16 and later migrated and rein-carnated into groups in the southern half of Africa
25	59,000	18,500	new souls from another arm of the Milky Way	South American indigenous	Starseeds created by higher-dimensional Light Beings
26	59,000	7500	new souls from another arm of the Milky Way	African	Starseeds created by higher-dimensional Light Beings; born to group 4 Earth dwellers

SOUL GROUP	B.C. DATE	ORIGINAL POP.	EARTH or COSMIC ORIGIN	CURRENT EARTH RACE SEEDED	COMMENTS
27	51,000	12,000	Pleiades– Electra	Samoan, Melanesian	Beings who had reached sixth-dimensional consciousness who chose to downstep to the third dimension
28	51,000	5000	Pleiades– Maya	Fijian–many reincarnated into indigenous tribes around the globe	Fifth-dimensional beings who chose to be born to group 15 parents
29	51,000	19,000	Pleiades– Merope	African	Fifth-dimensional beings who chose to be born to group 4 and group 26 parents who had migrated to this island

NOTE: At 50,000 B.C., the thirteenth dimension, which is also called the Infinite Sun, Great Spirit, or God/Goddess/All That Is, sent a wave of love and divine grace through all of existence. This wave was encoded with the ability for every consciousness in existence to receive its greatest desire, as long as it harmed no one. At that time, many beings who had been enslaved and controlled by others were released to find freedom. The third dimension was the most common choice, since it represented the opportunity for these beings to ground their higher-dimensional consciousnesses and experience free will. This occurred exactly at the beginning of a 26,000-year cycle and set a precedence for evolution out of victimhood by reinstating faith in divine love and grace. A very high and beautiful period ensued which lasted for 22,000 years. Though certain regions were still exploring dominance/submission roles and, in general, evolving, this time was infused with love, hope, renewed faith, and determination.

SOUL GROUP	B.C. DATE	ORIGINAL POP.	EARTH or COSMIC ORIGIN	CURRENT EARTH RACE SEEDED	COMMENTS
30	50,000	28,000	Andromeda Galaxy	Lemurian–Polynesian	Fourth-dimensional beings who escaped enslavement by dark fifth-dimensional overlords; down-stepped into third-dimensional bodies as opposed to entering by means of physical birth
31	50,000	6300	distant galaxy	South American	Fifth-dimensional beings who escaped enslavement by dark overlords; down-stepped in order to be born to human parents from groups 17 and 19 who had migrated to this region
32	50,000	100,000	Orion	Lemurian and Atlantean by migration–later seeded the Native American Comanche tribe	Fifth-dimensional beings who escaped enslavement by dark overlords; down-stepped into physical bodies, bypassing human birth
33	50,000	19,500	distant galaxy	Samoan, Melanesian	Fourth-dimensional beings enslaved by fifth-dimensional overlords; physically birthed to group 27 parents

SOUL GROUP	B.C. DATE	ORIGINAL POP.	EARTH or COSMIC ORIGIN	CURRENT EARTH RACE SEEDED	COMMENTS
34	50,000	7000	Arcturus	South American	Fifth-dimensional beings who escaped enslavement by dark overlords; down-stepped into third-dimensional birth; crossbred with members of group 13 who migrated to this region
35	50,000	20,000	unnamed star in the Milky Way	Russian, Polish, Czech, Ukrainian	Fourth-dimensional beings who escaped enslavement by dark overlords; born to group 1 parents; due to reincarnation of original group 1 and 2 souls, there were about 2500 humans in this region when the new arrivals began to be born
36	50,000	7700	distant galaxy	African	Born to humans from groups 4 and 26 after escaping enslavement by dark overlords on the fifth dimension
37	50,000	50,000	Scorpio	African	Fifth-dimensional beings who escaped enslavement; physically born to human parents from groups 5, 17, and 19 whose population in this region was about 5000

SOUL GROUP	B.C. DATE	ORIGINAL POP.	EARTH or COSMIC ORIGIN	CURRENT EARTH RACE SEEDED	COMMENTS
38	50,000	23,000	far side of the Milky Way	Atlantean–European and Russian	Fifth-dimensional beings who escaped slavery; physically born to human parents from groups 6 and 22
39	50,000	38,000	far side of the Milky Way	South American	Fourth-dimensional beings who escaped enslavement to be born to human parents from groups 13 and 25 who had crossbred
40	28,000	7300	Lyra	Atlantean–European	Fifth-dimensional dark control lords who had conquered an Orion solar ring several thousand years prior to their invasion of Mars; precipitated third-dimensional bodies rather than experiencing physical birth; began to infiltrate Atlantean culture with black magic and competition for power
41	28,000	7,000	Pleiades–Merope	Canadian and Native American indigenous; later migrations became early Hopi and Mayan tribes	Ffth-dimensional beings who precipitated bodies; later crossbred with migrating members from groups 6, 22, and 38 who had previously crossbred

SOUL GROUP	B.C. DATE	ORIGINAL POP.	EARTH or COSMIC ORIGIN	CURRENT EARTH RACE SEEDED	COMMENTS
42	24,000	20,000	Arcturus	Atlantean–Azores	Fifth-dimensional dark-control war riors who precipitated physical bodies; enslaved and/or killed members of groups 5, 31, and 37 who occupied the northeast continent; soon migrated to Atlantis to vie for control there
43	24,000	23,000	Pleiades–Maya, Taygeta	Fijian–reincarnated en masse in Egypt and Greece around 10,000–12,000 B.C.	Fifth-dimensional beings who precipitated bodies in order to counter dark influences and assist the humans who had asked for help
44	24,000	4000	new souls: Andromeda Galaxy	Russian, Polish, Czech,	Starseeds born to parents from groups 1 and 35
45	24,000	100,000	new souls: Pegasus Galaxy	South and West Indies	Starseeds born to parents from groups 31, 37, and 5 who had crossbred
46	17,000	75,000	distant galaxy	African	Damaged fourth-dimensional beings whose planet had been thrown out of orbit by a huge comet shower; born to crossbred parents from groups 4, 26, 36, and 46

SOUL GROUP	B.C. DATE	ORIGINAL POP.	EARTH or COSMIC ORIGIN	CURRENT EARTH RACE SEEDED	COMMENTS
47	9500	300,000	new souls: this solar ring	many regions of the globe	Created by a fusion wave of collective human consciousness brought on by a higher-dimensional power struggle between Sirian Light Beings who guard and protect human evolution, and combined efforts of the Anunnaki from Nibiru, the Lyran warriors, Lucifer, and the Satanic collective unconscious
48	9500	43,000	Pleiades– Alcyone, Maya, Electra	several areas of the globe –a few of the primary areas are shown as (48) on map	Fifth-dimensional beings who precipitated human bodies to assist in grounding the nine dimensions of Light in order to counter dark control efforts

SOUL GROUP	B.C. DATE	ORIGINAL POP.	EARTH or COSMIC ORIGIN	CURRENT EARTH RACE SEEDED	COMMENTS
49	9500	800	Nibiru	Atlantis–England, Egypt	Fifth-dimensional control lords who precipitated physical bodies in order to bring radiation and fear implants to control human evolution and take control of the rich mineral kingdom on Earth; the extraterrestrial group known as the Grays, who serve the Nibiruans, were also introduced at this time by the Anunnaki of Nibiru

NOTE: Throughout the time periods covered on this chart, other smaller groups of both higher-dimensional Light Beings and dark beings have come onto Earth.

However, the major influences on our world today are given. Allow this information to trigger your own genetic memories and patterns from other lives, so that as a species we can finally clear our past of all karmas and physical miasms and come into present time. *For present time is where all creative potential exists.*

ORDERING INFORMATION

For brochures and information on upcoming workshops, private healing work with Amorah's graduate students, and sacred site tours , write
or call:

Pleiadian Lightwork Associates
P. O. Box 1581
Mt. Shasta, CA. 96067
Phone: 916-926-1122
Fax: 916-926-1112

For the guided exercise tape to accompany Part V, send a check or
money order in the amount of $14.50 ($11.95 for the tape plus $2.25
shipping) to:

John Schultz
P.O. Box 661
Mt. Shasta, CA. 96067

ABOUT THE AUTHOR

Amorah Quan Yin, born November 30, 1950 in a small town in Kentucky, has been a natural healer and psychic since birth. As a child, she saw fairies and miniature spaceships made of blue light in the flowers and bushes around her home. She communicated with the fairies, Christ, Mother Mary, angels, and other Light Beings. These relationships were very innocent, intimate, and visibly real to her from an early age. When she closed her eyes in a darkened room, she saw swirling mandalas of multiple bright colors, images, and scenes. Upon awaking or falling into sleep, past-life movies played before her. These gifts gradually shut down when she entered public school and succumbed to peer pressure.

At age sixteen, upon the death of her grandmother, once again her full sensory perception, as she prefers to call it, partially reopened. Sporadic psychic experiences, which she prefers to call Full Sensory Perception, finally led to her spiritual awakening in early 1979. Though "haunted" by past-life memories, Amorah considered herself an atheist by then, disillusioned with organized religion. However, in her first past-life healing session with a regressionist, she found herself on a mountainside meadow with thousands of others as Jesus delivered a sermon. As Jesus spoke, there suddenly appeared a gigantic spaceship made of stellar blue light just above the woods to his right. Then another spaceship appeared, and another—until six of the huge crafts had come and gone. She describes the scene as follows: "All around me people fell to the ground covering their heads and whimpering. But I stood, hands above my head in ecstasy, silently repeating, 'Home, home,' and weeping tears of joy. I felt a magnetic pull at my third eye and found myself eye to eye with Christ. He lasered my third eye with a beam of intense light, followed by a cellular flood of light and energy. I burst into tears of spiritual awakening and joy. I had reexperienced a cellular awakening, my soul's remembrance of itself, and enlightenment all at once."

At that time, Amorah had no reference points as to the meaning of enlightenment. She had never heard of spaceships having any connection with spiritual or religious phenomena. She had never even heard of auras or oversouls or *shaktiput*—all of which she had experienced vividly during the regression. Upon opening her eyes at the end of the session, she saw her own aura reflected in the window across the room, as well as the aura of the regressionist.

It was years before she fully understood the connections between the Christ, Sirius, enlightenment, the Pleiades, and the spaceships of light. She eventually learned that the extraterrestrial Light Beings who taught and healed her while she slept were from the Pleiades, and that their work was to help bring about the Second Coming of Christ en masse: when many of us here on Earth become actualized, Christed Beings. She later identified the blue spaceships as being from Sirius and learned that the Sirians and Pleiadians shared a common purpose.

With her spiritual awakening came a natural healing ability and a reactivation of her Full Sensory Perceptions. Through books, classes, spiritual work, time with a spiritual teacher, and her own increasing awareness, Amorah broke away from traditional jobs in 1985 and began teaching about—and making jewelry with—crystals and gemstones for healing and awakening. Private healing sessions and teaching were erratically intermingled with her other work until 1988, when she sold her jewelry company, moved to Mt. Shasta, California, and began building a full-time teaching and spiritual healing practice.

It was in Mt. Shasta that she more fully developed her communications with the Pleiadian Emissaries of Light, the Sirian Archangels, Christ, Quan Yin, Saint Germaine, other Ascended Masters, angels, and archangels. These communications and relationships have become as natural to Amorah as they were when she was a child. She has worked to develop clear and strong discernment in her choices about those beings with whom she is in communication. She experienced some terrifying invasions and abductions with what she calls the "dark E. T.'s" that have made her very careful.

Amorah is well respected and known as a very capable and gifted seer and teacher in the Mt. Shasta area. The majority of the material she teaches writes about is self-learned through her own spiritual practice and past-life recall, or channeled from her Higher Self, the Pleiadian Emissaries of Light, or other guides and Ascended Masters.

BOOKS OF RELATED INTEREST
BY BEAR & COMPANY

BRINGERS OF THE DAWN
Teachings from the Pleiadians
by Barbara Marciniak

CONTACT CARDS
An Extraterrestrial Divination System
by Kim Carlsberg and Darryl Anka

EARTH
Pleiadian Keys to the Living Library
by Barbara Marciniak

HEART OF THE CHRISTOS
Starseeding from the Pleiades
by Barbara Hand Clow

THE MAYAN ORACLE
Return Path to the Stars
by Ariel Spilsbury and Michael Bryner

THE PLEIADIAN AGENDA
A New Cosmology for the Age of Light
by Barbara Hand Clow

THE PLEIADIAN WORKBOOK
Awakening Your Divine Ka
by Amorah Quan Yin

Contact your local bookseller

~ or ~

BEAR & COMPANY
P.O. Box 2860
Santa Fe, NM 87504
1-800-WE-BEARS